NUTCASES

FAMILY LAW

AUSTRALIA
Law Book Company
Sydney

CANADA and USA
Carswell
Toronto

HONG KONG
Sweet & Maxwell Asia

NEW ZEALAND
Brookers
Wellington

SINGAPORE and MALAYSIA
Sweet & Maxwell Asia
Singapore and Kuala Lumpur

NUTCASES

FAMILY LAW

FIRST EDITION

by

REBECCA PROBERT, BA (Hons), LLM.
Senior Lecturer, School of Law
Warwick University

London ● Sweet & Maxwell ● 2007

Published in 2007 by Sweet & Maxwell Limited of
100 Avenue Road, London NW3 3PF
www.sweetandmaxwell.co.uk
Typeset by LBJ Typesetting of Kingsclere
Printed in the Netherlands by Krips of Meppel
Reprinted 2006

No natural forests were destroyed to make this product.
Only farmed timber was used and replanted.

A CIP catalogue record for this book is available
from the British Library.

ISBN 978–0–421–95850–0

CONTENTS

TABLE OF CASES

1. INTRODUCTION

Defining the Family

The following cases illustrate the way in which the definition of "family" has evolved over the years. All were cases under the Rent Acts in which the applicant's entitlement to succeed to the tenancy depended on whether he or she was a member of the deceased tenant's family.

Key Principle: **The term "family" requires that there should be "a broadly recognisable de facto familial nexus" between the parties**

Ross v Collins 1964

Miss Collins had lived in the same house as the tenant for 22 years, and had acted as his unpaid housekeeper since the death of his wife. In return for this the tenant provided her with free accommodation. She cared for him when he was ill and wrote affectionate letters to him when she was absent from him. The parties never addressed each other by their Christian names and did not pass themselves off as members of the same family.

Held: (CA) Miss Collins was not a member of the tenant's family and therefore not entitled to the tenancy. Even though the concept of "family" was not limited to those linked by blood or formal legal ties such as marriage or adoption, it still required, in the words of Russell L.J., "at least a broadly recognisable de facto familial nexus" (p.432).

Commentary

The case illustrates that whether or not one individual is regarded as a member of another's family depends on the nature of that relationship. It is not necessary that there should be any legal relationship—such as marriage or adoption—between the parties: a *de facto* family relationship (i.e. one that exists as a matter of fact) will suffice. At the same time, it is not sufficient that the parties behaved in a way that family members might behave. In this case Miss Collins cared for the tenant as a devoted daughter might have done, but this did not make her a member of his family. As the principle set out by Russell L.J. makes clear, it is necessary for the relationship to bear some resemblance to what the majority of society would regard as a family. This means that the legal test established in this case is somewhat circular—it is a family if it looks like a family—but, as the following cases show, it also means that it has the capacity to evolve with changing social attitudes.

Key Principle: **"Family" is not a technical term but bears its ordinary meaning**

As the following three cases show, the ordinary meaning of "family" may change over time.

Gammans v Ekins 1950

Mr Ekins had lived with the tenant for over 20 years. He had taken her name and passed as her husband, but they had never married and had no children. After her death he remained in the property. When the landlord sought possession he claimed the protection of the statutory provisions on the basis that he was a member of the tenant's family.

Held: (CA) Mr Ekins was not entitled to succeed to the tenancy, as he was not a member of her family.

Commentary

Gammans v Ekins is often cited as evidence that in the 1950s cohabiting couples were not regarded as a "family". The truth is a little more complex. True, the language of the Court of Appeal was moralistic in tone, with one of the judges suggesting that that those who were "living in sin" should not necessarily be entitled to rights that were conferred on married couples or were denied to those who lived together platonically. Yet it should be noted that the county court judge had initially decided that Mr Ekins *was* a member of his cohabitant's family, which indicates that there was not a consensus on the familial status of cohabiting couples at this time. In other contemporary cases, cohabitants with children had been held to be members of each other's family (see e.g. *Hawes v Evenden* [1953] 1 W.L.R. 1169), and all of the judges in *Gammans* noted that their conclusion might have been different if children had been involved. A final complicating factor in *Gammans* was that the person seeking the protection of the legislation was the male partner of the tenant. Lord Evershed opined that it would not be natural to refer to a childless *husband* as a member of the wife's family. This reflects a society where wives and children were the dependants of the man: they were his family, while he was an individual in his own right. The defendant had contravened not one social norm but two: the norm of marriage and the norm of male dominance.

Dyson Holdings Ltd v Fox 1976

Ms Fox had been living with the tenant for 21 years. The parties had no children. After the tenant's death she continued to reside in the property for over ten years, paying rent, until Dyson Holdings Ltd learned that she had not been married to the tenant and brought proceedings for possession.

Held: (CA) Ms Fox was a member of the tenant's family and as such entitled to succeed to the tenancy.

Commentary

The three members of the Court of Appeal expressed different opinions regarding the earlier decision in *Gammans v Ekins*: Lord Denning M.R. thought that the case had been wrongly decided, while James and Bridge L.JJ. were content to accept that it reflected the meaning of "family" in 1949 but not the meaning that should be attached to it in 1975. The case thus illustrates how the meaning of the term "family" may evolve over time: as Bridge L.J. put it, "it is, I think, not putting it too high to say that between 1950 and 1975 there has been a complete revolution in society's attitude to unmarried partnerships of the kind under consideration. Such unions are far commoner than they used to be. The social stigma that once attached to them has almost, if not entirely, disappeared." (p.512). Yet it is interesting to note that the shift of opinion suggested by the judges in this case was far from absolute, and that *Dyson* was distinguished in a number of later cases (see e.g. *Helby v Rafferty* [1979] 1 W.L.R. 13). In 1988 the issue was resolved by Parliament, which enacted legislation providing that a "person who was living with the original tenant as his or her wife or husband shall be treated as the spouse of the original tenant" (Rent Act 1977, Sch.1, as amended by the Housing Act 1988). Of course, this raised a further question: how should same-sex couples be regarded for these purposes?

Fitzpatrick v Sterling HA 1999

Mr Fitzpatrick had lived with the tenant for seventeen years in a loving and stable same-sex relationship. For the last eight years of the relationship Mr Fitzpatrick had nursed the tenant, who had suffered a stroke. After the tenant's death he sought a declaration that he was entitled to succeed to the tenancy, either on the basis that he was living with the tenant as if he were the tenant's husband or wife, or on the basis that he was a member of the tenant's family.

Held: (HL) Mr Fitzpatrick was a member of the tenant's family and as such entitled to succeed to the tenancy.

Commentary

Fitzpatrick is one of those cases of huge symbolic import but little practical significance. It was the first case in which the English courts recognised that a same-sex couple were a "family". Yet family law—perhaps ironically—does not tend to confer rights on "family" members generally, but rather on spouses, cohabitants, parents and other specified categories. The Rent Acts were virtually the only pieces of legislation to use this term, and by this time they were of diminishing application. So in practical terms the case did little to improve the legal rights of same-sex couples. The case did, however, pave the way for further changes (see below). Indeed, it is a measure of *Fitzpatrick's* influence that the case has already been superseded as a precedent after a relatively brief period: matters have moved on. Looking back, it is the conservatism of the judgments that is most striking. The House of Lords refused to recognise that a same-sex couple could be said to be living together as husband and wife, while simultaneously holding that the parallels between their relationship and that of a married couple justified them being recognised as members of each other's family. But then, law reform has to proceed by small steps.

Key Principle: **A same-sex couple may be deemed to be living together as if they were husband and wife**

Ghaidan v Godin-Mendoza 2004

Mr Godin-Mendoza and Mr Wallwyn-Jones began to live together in 1972. In 1983 they moved into the flat that was to be their joint home until Mr Wallwyn-Jones' death in 2001. Mr

Godin-Mendoza claimed that he was entitled to succeed to the tenancy, which had been in the sole name of Mr Wallwyn-Jones. As a result of the decision in *Fitzpatrick v Sterling HA* (above), he was entitled to succeed on the basis that he was a member of Mr Wallwyn-Jones's family. This, however, entitled him to lesser rights than those that he would have received had he been living with a partner of the opposite sex. Mr Godin-Mendoza therefore claimed that this constituted discrimination on the ground of sexual orientation under art.14 of the European Convention on Human Rights.

Held: (HL) The fact that Mr Godin-Mendoza had fewer rights than he would have had if he had been in a heterosexual relationship with the tenant constituted discrimination under art.14 of the ECHR in combination with art.8 (respect for private and family life). The relevant legislation would be construed in a way that included same-sex couples.

Commentary
As with *Fitzpatrick* before it, the precise legal point established by *Ghaidan v Godin-Mendoza* has been overtaken by events, in this case by the passage of the Civil Partnership Act 2004. This legislation not only allowed same-sex couples to register a partnership and thereby acquire virtually all of the same rights as married couples, but also conferred on same-sex cohabitants the same rights that opposite-sex cohabitants already enjoyed, such as they were. In practical terms, the willingness of the court to interpret a statute conferring rights on heterosexual couples as including same-sex couples was an evolutionary dead end.

The case was, however, a legal landmark in the recognition of same-sex couples and an important contribution to the growing jurisprudence on human rights. Only Lord Millett dissented from the view that the legislation could be read in such a way as to include same-sex couples. By contrast, in a vigorous judgment Baroness Hale pointed out that marriage is now largely gender-neutral—no particular roles are dictated for husbands and wives beyond the obvious biological constraints—and committed same-sex relationships can be described as "marriage-like" just as stable opposite-sex relationships can be. With regard to the scope of the Human Rights Act, Lord Nicholls noted that s.3 might "require the court to depart . . . from the intention of the Parliament which enacted the legislation" although he also acknowledged that "[t]he meaning imported by the application of section 3 must be compatible with the underlying thrust of the legislation being construed."

(para.33). The line between the "intention" of Parliament that may be disregarded, and the "general thrust" of the legislation that may not, will perhaps not always be easy to draw.

Is it likely that this approach to s.3 will lead to further change in the field of family law? While the judges accepted that protecting the traditional family or marriage is a justifiable aim, it is clear that the link between a particular rule and the role it plays in protecting the "traditional" family will now be examined rather than assumed.

Human Rights and Family Life

As the following cases show, there are parallels between the UK courts' concept of "family" and the idea of "family life" as developed by the European Court of Human Rights in the context of art.8. In both contexts certain relationships (those based on marriage or adoption) will automatically be regarded as falling within the scope of the category, while in other cases the nature of the particular relationship will need to be considered.

Key Principle: **The relationship created by a valid and genuine marriage will automatically be regarded as family life**

Abdulaziz, Cabales and Balkandali v UK 1985
Mr Abdulaziz, Mr Cabales and Mr Balkandali were refused permission to join their wives, who were all lawfully and permanently settled in the United Kingdom. Their wives claimed that there had been violations of (*inter alia*) art.8. One issue was whether the relationship between each couple amounted to "family life".

Held: (ECHR) Each couple had entered upon "family" life to a degree sufficient for the purposes of art.8. As the court noted, "[w]hatever else the word 'family' may mean, it must at any rate include the relationship that arises from a lawful and genuine marriage." (para.62).

Commentary
The case illustrates the importance of a formal legal tie in creating "family life". In the case of a married couple, family life may exist

even before the parties have begun to live together. At the same time, however, it is important to note that a sham marriage—for example, one entered into solely for the purpose of improving the immigration status of one of the parties—would not be regarded as automatically giving rise to family life. Similarly, a marriage that is not legally valid might not give rise to family life. In the instant case, some doubt was expressed as to the validity of the marriage between Mr and Mrs Cabales. However, given the evidence that they believed themselves to be married and wished to live together as husband and wife, their relationship was also sufficient to constitute "family life".

Key Principle: **"Family life" exists between married parents and their child from the moment of the child's birth**

Berrehab v The Netherlands 1988

The issue in the case was whether Abdellah Berrehab, a Moroccan citizen, had the right to remain in The Netherlands after his divorce from his Dutch wife. Mr Berrehab challenged the refusal of a residence permit on the basis that this constituted an infringement of art.8 of the ECHR, since it would prevent him from remaining in contact with his daughter. One question for the Court was whether there was "family life" between Mr Berrehab and his daughter, given that the parties were not residing in the same household.

Held: (ECHR) A child born to a married couple is *ipso jure* part of that relationship and so "family life" exists between the parents and their child from the moment of the child's birth, even if the parents are not then living together.

Commentary

The case confirms the importance of a formal legal tie between the parties: such a tie creates "family life" automatically. It does not, however, always create it forever: the court did acknowledge that subsequent events might break the family ties between the parties. That had not happened in this case, as Mr Berrehab had remained in regular contact with his daughter, seeing her four times a week (which would, in the light of *Lebbink v The Netherlands* (below), be sufficient to create ties amounting to "family life" in any case).

---

le: **"Family life" exists between a mother and her the moment of birth**

elgium 1979
, Belgian law required the unmarried mother of a child to take certain steps to regularise her position regarding the child in the eyes of the law and rendered it necessary for her to adopt her own child in order to confer certain rights. It was claimed that this amounted to a violation of art.8.

Held: (ECHR) There had been a violation of art.8, as the legal requirements were based on a refusal to recognise the nature of the relationship between mother and child from the moment of the birth.

Commentary
Marckx was one of the first cases in which the Court was required to determine the meaning of the phrase "respect for . . . private and family life." The Court confirmed that the protection afforded by art.8 extended to all families, not just those founded on marriage, thus paving the way for a functional approach to family definition.

Key Principle: **"Family life" exists between a child and her biological parents from the moment of the child's birth if the parents are in a cohabiting relationship**

Johnston v Ireland 1986
Mr Johnston, who was separated from his wife but unable to obtain a divorce under Irish law, began to cohabit with another woman in 1971 and their daughter was born in 1978. They complained that the impossibility of regularising their family situation constituted a violation of, inter alia, art.8.

Held: (ECHR) The fact that Mr Johnston was unable to obtain a divorce from his wife and marry his cohabitant did not violate their rights under the Convention, which did not guarantee the right to divorce. Nor had there been any interference with the family life of the adult parties: art.8 did not impose any obligation to provide unmarried couples with the same rights that were afforded to spouses. However, the fact that Irish law did not adequately reflect their daughter's natural family ties with her parents did amount to a failure to respect her family life and was a violation of art.8.

Commentary

Since the decision in *Johnston* any legal distinctions between children based on the marital status of their parents have largely been eliminated. It remains the case, however, that preferential treatment of formalised relationships is regarded as justified. Of particular relevance for present purposes is the way in which the court recognised the relationship between cohabiting parents and their child as amounting to "family life." As the following case illustrates, if the parents are not cohabiting at the time of the birth the court will consider whether "family life" has been established as a matter of fact.

Key Principle: **Whether or not "family life" exists for the purpose of art.8 is a question of fact, depending upon the real existence in practice of close personal ties**

Lebbink v The Netherlands 2004

The issue in the case was whether there was "family life" between a father and his daughter. The relationship between the father and the mother had begun two years before the birth and ended when the child was 16 months old. During this time the parties had never cohabited, but the father was present at the birth, visited mother and child on a regular basis, and occasionally baby-sat. After the relationship between the parents broke down the father's request for access was refused.

Held: (ECHR) In the circumstances the relationship between father and child was sufficient to attract the protection of art.8 and the merits of his request for access should have been considered.

Commentary

The case involved an issue that has become increasingly familiar in recent years, namely that of contact between a father and his child after the relationship between the parents has broken down (see further chapter 8). For present purposes its significance lies in the fact that "family life" was found to exist in the context of a relatively short-term relationship that involved neither marriage nor cohabitation, illustrating the broad scope of the concept.

Key Principle: **"Family life" may be established even if there is no biological tie between the parties**

X, Y and Z v UK 1997

X, a female-to-male transsexual, had lived with a woman, Y, for a number of years. A child, Z, was born to Y as the result of artificial insemination by an anonymous donor. Under s.28(3) of the Human Fertilisation and Embryology Act 1990, the male partner of an unmarried woman who gives birth as a result of artificial insemination by donor is deemed to be the legal father, as long as he was involved in the process that led to the birth (see further chapter 7). X sought to be registered as Z's father but this was refused. This refusal was challenged by X, Y and Z, who claimed that there had been a violation of arts 8 and 14 of the Convention.

Held: (ECHR) While there was "family life" between the three applicants, there had been no violation of art.8 in this case. Given the lack of any common European standard on this issue, states should be afforded a wide margin of appreciation in deciding on the parental status of transsexuals.

Commentary

The basis of the complaint in this case has now been largely addressed by the passage of the Gender Recognition Act 2004, which allows for legal recognition of the reassigned sex of a transsexual. A transsexual who had not gone through the process of obtaining a gender recognition certificate would, however, still be in the same legal position as X in this case (see further chapter 2). The key point for present purposes is the recognition that X enjoyed family life with Y and Z, based on his long-standing relationship with the mother and the fact that he had acted as the child's father.

So far the focus has been on the generous scope of the concept of "family life." As the next case demonstrates, however, the concept of "family life" is subject to certain limitations.

Key Principle: **Under current Strasbourg jurisprudence, same-sex couples do not enjoy "family life" for the purposes of art.8**

Secretary of State for Work and Pensions v M 2006
The mother was living with a partner of the same sex, and her children spent the majority of their time with their father. The amount that the mother was required to pay by way of child support was higher than if she had been cohabiting with a man, as under the child support legislation the existence of a same-sex partner was not taken into account in calculating an individual's liability, whereas heterosexual cohabitants were treated as a unit for these purposes. The mother therefore appealed against the assessment on the basis that it was discriminatory and violated art.14 of the ECHR.

Held: (HL) The scheme had not infringed the Convention. "Family life" is an autonomous Convention concept, and must be interpreted in line with the Strasbourg jurisprudence. Since this had not, to date, recognised same-sex couples as enjoying "family life", art.8 was not applicable (and neither was art.1 of Protocol 1). Thus the requirement of establishing a link between art.14 and another Convention right had not been met.

Commentary
By the time the case reached the House of Lords, the issue was no longer one of practical import. On the first day of the hearing before the House of Lords, December 5, 2005, the Civil Partnership Act 2004 came into force and amended the relevant provisions, equating same- and opposite-sex cohabitants for all purposes. Despite this, important points of principle remained to be determined. For the human rights lawyer, the main interest of the case lies in the tightening of the requirements necessary to establish a breach of art.14: it is clear that a tenuous link with another Convention right will not suffice, although the exact nature of the link required will vary according to the article in question and the seriousness of the infringement. For the family lawyer, the key point is that "family life" within art.8 does not include same-sex couples. It was noted that "family life" is an autonomous Convention concept that should bear the same meaning in all states, and that the European Court of Human Rights had explicitly rejected the idea that same-sex couples were entitled to the respect for family life guaranteed by art.8. This leads to the slightly odd result that same-sex couples are deemed to be

"family" for certain purposes but do not enjoy "family life" in the context of art.8—although it has also been questioned whether there is as yet any decision of the European Court confirming that opposite-sex cohabitants enjoy "family life" either (note that in *X, Y and Z v UK* the court decided that the three applicants together enjoyed family life, not that each enjoyed "family life" with each of the others).

2. FORMAL RELATIONSHIPS: MARRIAGE AND CIVIL PARTNERSHIP

The Legal Concept of Marriage

Key Principle: **Marriage is defined as "the voluntary union for life of one man and one woman to the exclusion of all others."**

Hyde v Hyde and Woodmansee 1866

Mr and Mrs Hyde had married in the Mormon community in Utah, which at the time practised polygamy. He then left the community, renouncing (and indeed denouncing) the Mormon faith. The authorities in Utah passed a sentence of excommunication against him and declared that his wife was free to marry again. She subsequently contracted a marriage with Mr Woodmansee in Utah. Mr Hyde sought a divorce in the English courts.

Held: The marriage between Mr and Mrs Hyde would not be recognised by the English courts, even for the purpose of granting a divorce. Marriage, "as understood in Christendom, may . . . be defined as the voluntary union for life of one man and one woman, to the exclusion of all others." (p.133).

Commentary

Lord Penzance noted that in order for Mr Hyde to be granted a divorce in the English courts, he would first have to establish that the marriage that he had entered into in Utah was valid according to the law of the place where it was celebrated and then that what amounted to a divorce in Utah was in fact void. The judge preferred to take a different approach, adopting the view that a marriage celebrated according to Mormon rites was not a marriage at all and therefore that the English court had no jurisdiction over it.

While the actual point decided in *Hyde* on the recognition (or rather non-recognition) of a potentially polygamous marriage is no longer of relevance, the definition of marriage formulated by Lord Penzance—the "voluntary union for life of one man and one woman to the exclusion of all others"—continues to exert a considerable influence. It is still quoted at the start of civil marriage ceremonies (shorn of the preceding words "as understood in Christendom", in deference to the exclusively secular nature of such ceremonies).

It is important to recognise the deficiencies of Lord Penzance's dictum as a *legal* definition of marriage. First, it does not identify how marriage is different from cohabitation: no mention is made of the formalities required by the law to mark the married from the cohabiting. Secondly, it has the quality of an aspiration rather than a definition: not all marriages will last for life and a lack of sexual exclusivity does not affect the marital status of the parties (although adultery may lead one party to petition for divorce on the basis that the marriage has irretrievably broken down).

Lord Penzance's definition is still accurate in that marriage remains—in this jurisdiction at least—a specifically heterosexual institution, and in that an individual is not entitled to be a party to more than one formal relationship at a time. Civil partnerships may be marriage-like in form and function, but the official view is that such partnerships are not marriages. Perhaps the most interesting question raised by Lord Penzance's definition of marriage is why it continues to exert such an influence. The fact that a nineteenth-century judge formulated marriage in a particular way does not mean that the definition of marriage is thereby set in stone. The continued invocation of this definition to deny the status of marriage to certain unions tells us as much about current concerns as it does about legal history.

Key Principle: **A marriage contracted overseas between two persons of the same sex has the status of a civil partnership in English law**

Wilkinson v Kitzinger 2006
A lesbian couple from the UK married in British Columbia, which permits same-sex marriages. Ms Wilkinson then sought a declaration that her marriage was valid for the purposes of English law.

Held: Section 215 of the Civil Partnership Act 2004 provided that a same-sex marriage contracted overseas would be treated as a civil partnership for the purposes of English law. This carried essentially the same legal rights and responsibilities as a marriage. The law did not breach arts 8 or 12 of the European

Convention and, in so far as it did discriminate against same-sex couples, any discrimination had a legitimate aim, was reasonable and proportionate, and fell within the margin of appreciation accorded to Convention States.

Commentary
The case was the first legal challenge to the "equal but different" policy of the Civil Partnership Act: if a couple had married in one country, why should their relationship bear a different label in another? The problems for the parties were threefold. First, under private international law, capacity to marry is governed by a person's domicile: thus a person cannot evade domestic restrictions by marrying abroad. Secondly, the statutory provisions of the 2004 Act were clear. Thirdly, the jurisprudence of the European Court of Human Rights offered little assistance. The Court has not yet held that art.12 encompasses a right to marry a person of the same sex, nor even that childless same-sex couples can be said to enjoy "family life" to be protected under art.8. As Sir Mark Potter P pointed out in *Wilkinson*, this is an area "of considerable social, political and religious controversy, in respect of which there is no consensus across Europe." (para.44). However, the very vigour of the arguments mounted in defence of the traditional heterosexual concept of marriage in fact could be said to explain the importance placed by same-sex couples on such legal recognition: the term "marriage" is much more than a convenient label for describing a form of legal regulation precisely because of the historical, social and religious baggage that it bears.

Formalities

The formalities required for a valid marriage are set out in the Marriage Act 1949, while those required for a civil partnership are set out in the Civil Partnership Act 2004, as amended by the Civil Partnership (Amendments to Registration Provisions) Order 2005.

Key Principle: **The parties are married once they have exchanged their vows**

Quick v Quick 1953
The bride changed her mind about marrying her husband during the course of the ceremony. Vows had been exchanged

and a ring placed on her finger, but the vicar had yet to pronounce them husband and wife when she declared that she would not go ahead with the marriage, took the ring off her finger and left the church.

Held: The parties were already married and it was too late for her to change her mind.

Commentary
Perhaps understandably, there is little case-law on the precise moment of the ceremony at which the parties become married. The Australian case of *Quick* does provide a useful reminder that the consent of the parties lies at the heart of marriage. The minister's declaration—and indeed the signing of the register— comes after that consent is expressed, and thus a failure to make such declaration or to register the marriage cannot affect the validity of what has already taken place. By contrast, the Civil Partnership Act 2004 provides that "two people are to be regarded as having registered as civil partners of each other once each of them has signed the civil partnership document." (s.2). The act of signing brings the civil partnership into being. This follows from the fact that no specific vows are required of those registering a civil partnership.

Key Principle: A marriage is only void for failure to comply with the stipulated formalities if such failure is "knowing and wilful" on the part of both parties

Greaves v Greaves 1872
The husband claimed that the marriage was void on the basis that the licence had not been issued until the day after the wedding had taken place. The wife had been aware that an application had been made for the licence the day before the wedding, and had been reassured by the husband that the vicar had told him that the marriage could proceed.

Held: The marriage was valid.

Commentary
The case illustrates that both parties must know of any failure to comply with the necessary formalities before the marriage can be

annulled on this basis. The interesting point left open by the judge is whether it is sufficient to show that the parties were aware that a licence had not been obtained, or whether it would also be necessary to establish that they realised that a licence was a necessary formality. More recent cases suggest—if only by implication—that the former is the appropriate test, since otherwise any ceremony entered into in good faith would create a valid marriage (see e.g. *Gandhi v Patel* below).

Key Principle: **A celebrant who knowingly and wilfully solemnizes a marriage contrary to the provisions of the Marriage Act 1949 is guilty of an offence, but only if the ceremony performed was one which, if properly performed, was capable of creating a valid marriage**

R v Bham 1966

The defendant had performed a ceremony of *nichan* (an Islamic marriage ceremony) in a private house. He was charged with solemnising a marriage contrary to the provisions of the Marriage Act 1949.

Held: (CA) The conviction would be quashed. The ceremony in question did not purport to be a marriage of the kind allowed by English domestic law. The offence of solemnizing a marriage contrary to the provisions of the Marriage Act 1949 was not committed where the ceremony performed was not one that was recognised as capable of creating a valid marriage.

Commentary

The decision in this case means that a person does not commit any offence by conducting a ceremony that is altogether outside the provisions of the Marriage Act (for example the ceremonies that took place in *A-M v A-M* and *Gandhi v Patel*, considered below). By contrast, a person who solemnizes a marriage of the type envisaged by the Marriage Act but knowingly and wilfully fails to observe certain formalities will be guilty of an offence. The justification for the distinction is not immediately obvious, especially since the parties to a non-marriage may be unaware that the ceremony that they have gone through has no status in English law.

Key Principle: **A wedding ceremony that is too far from the form prescribed by the Marriage Act 1949 creates a "non-marriage"**

Gereis v Yagoub 1997

A couple went through a marriage ceremony in a Greek Orthodox church. They were fully aware that the church had not been licensed for the celebration of marriage, and that the priest who conducted the ceremony was not authorised to marry them. They had been advised to go through a civil ceremony of marriage but failed to do so.

Held: They had "knowingly and wilfully" failed to comply with the legal requirements and their marriage was therefore void. However, the ceremony was sufficiently close to the prescribed form to avoid being categorised as a "non-marriage."

Commentary

The significance of this case lies not in the (uncontestable) decision that the marriage was void (under s.49 of the Marriage Act 1949), but in the suggestion by counsel that a marriage that was too far from the form prescribed by the Marriage Act was merely a non-marriage. This suggestion was rejected by the judge on the basis that the ceremony was sufficiently close to the prescribed forms: it "bore the hallmarks of an ordinary Christian wedding and . . . both parties treated it as such." (p.858). However, this left open the possibility that in a future case a marriage might be relegated to the non-status of a non-marriage if it was too far from the prescribed forms, as the next case illustrates.

Gandhi v Patel 2001

A man who was separated but not divorced from his wife went through a ceremony of marriage with another woman. The ceremony took place according to Hindu rites in a restaurant.

Held: The ceremony was too far from the forms prescribed by the Marriage Act 1949 and the result was a "non-marriage".

Commentary

To date, this is the only example of the courts holding that a ceremony of marriage gave rise to a "non-marriage" on account of the parties' failure to observe the necessary formalities. While the Marriage Act 1949 does not include a category of "non-marriage", the court's creation of such a category is justifiable. Under s.49 of the Act, a marriage is only void if the parties "knowingly and wilfully" fail to comply with certain formalities. This raises two questions: what is the result if the parties "knowingly and wilfully" fail to comply with other formalities laid down in the Act, or if they unwittingly fail to comply with those core formalities set out in s.49? The answer to the first is that the marriage is still valid: the stipulation that the parties should marry within certain hours, for example, is directory rather than mandatory. The answer to the second is that it will depend on exactly how far the ceremony departed from the required form. In this case the parties did not comply with either the required preliminaries or the legislative stipulations as to where a marriage may take place and by whom it should be conducted. By contrast, if the parties make some attempt to comply with the law, an unwitting omission will not invalidate the marriage.

The difference between a void marriage—which, in the eyes of the law, never existed—and a "non-marriage" may appear to be illusory. It is, however, of considerable practical significance for the parties themselves. Even a void marriage carries certain legal rights—if a court decides that a marriage is void it has the same power to make orders dealing with the assets of the parties as it does upon divorce. A non-marriage has no legal consequences whatsoever.

The Presumptions in Favour of Marriage

Key Principle: **There is a presumption that a couple who are cohabiting and are reputed to be married have in fact gone through a valid ceremony of marriage**

Chief Adjudication Officer v Bath 2000
Mr and Mrs Bath had gone through a ceremony of marriage in a Sikh temple that was not registered for marriage. At the time both were recent immigrants and spoke little English. They lived together until the husband's death thirty-seven years later. Mrs Bath was then refused a widow's pension on the ground that her marriage had not been valid.

Held: Mrs Bath was entitled to a widow's pension, either on the basis that the evidence that the temple was not registered was insufficient to rebut the presumption that the ceremony had been properly performed, or on the basis that they had been living together for a long period of time and had been presumed to be married.

Commentary

While it is difficult to disagree with the result in *Bath* as a matter of justice, the reasoning of the three judges is far from clear. The parties had been presumed to be married because they had gone through a ceremony of marriage that was believed to be valid. Once that ceremony had been proved to be invalid, it ought to have been inappropriate for the court to extend the benefit of the presumption to the parties.

A-M v A-M 2001

In 1980 a couple went through a Muslim ceremony of marriage in their flat. The husband was already married, but under Islamic law he was entitled to take more than one wife. The ceremony was conducted by an Islamic mufti from a London mosque and was attended by the friends of both parties. The couple signed a document entitled "certificate of marriage" and it was clear that the event was intended to be a formal marriage by Islamic processes. The parties continued to live together after the ceremony and were believed to be husband and wife. Doubts later arose as to whether English law would recognise the validity of the ceremony that had taken place, and a number of unsuccessful attempts were made to regularise the position. The relationship subsequently broke down.

Held: The 1980 ceremony was not within the scope of the Marriage Act 1949 and was neither valid nor one in relation to which a declaration of nullity could be granted. However, given that the parties had lived together and had been reputed to be married, and in the light of the fact that they were aware that the 1980 ceremony had not created a valid marriage and had taken active steps to rectify the situation, it would be presumed that a marriage had been celebrated overseas in a country that permitted polygamy while both parties were domiciled in a country that permitted polygamy. The court thus held that the parties had entered into a valid marriage.

Commentary

The operation of the presumption in this case was more logical, if more artificial, than in *CAO v Bath*, since in this case the parties had at least realised that the original ceremony was invalid and had some incentive to go through a second ceremony. However, the precise chain of events suggested by the judge seemed to be an imaginative leap rather than a presumption based on the evidence before the court.

Martin v Myers 2004

Edward and Amy Myers had lived together for many years and had seven children. Upon Edward's death, Amy continued to reside in the home they had shared, which had been in Edward's name, and her will purported to leave the property to one of her sons. After her death her daughters claimed that their parents had never been married and that their mother had therefore no title to property to pass. The evidence was that their mother had always been very vague on the question of her marriage, and had once told one of her daughters that in fact she had never married.

Held: Although the parties had lived together for forty years and had passed as husband and wife during that time, there was clear and convincing evidence establishing that they were not married.

Commentary

The reasoning in this case is far preferable to that in *CAO v Bath* or *A-M v A-M*, and illustrates that the presumption should have only a limited role to play in modern times. The presumption was developed at a time when the registration of marriages was less efficient (and the survival of the registers a matter of chance), with the result that there might be no evidence that a ceremony had taken place. It was therefore appropriate for the courts to presume that a couple who were living together and regarded by the community as married had in fact gone through a ceremony of marriage. By contrast, today, as the judge pointed out, "the absence of a certificate is strong evidence, unless marriage abroad is a real possibility." (para.23)

Key Principle: **There is a presumption that a ceremony of marriage was properly performed if the parties afterwards cohabit and are reputed to be husband and wife**

Piers v Piers 1849

John Piers became acquainted with an actress, and began to live with her. They had seven children. After his death the two youngest claimed that a marriage had taken place between their parents before they were born. There was second-hand evidence that a ceremony had been performed on the Isle of Man, and that the couple had been accepted as married by respectable members of the community. However, there was no evidence of any licence having been granted, or any register of the marriage, and not everyone believed the parties to be married.

Held: (HL) The presumption that the ceremony had been properly performed could only be rebutted by very strong evidence to the contrary. In the circumstances the marriage was presumed to have been validly celebrated.

Commentary

The case demonstrates the weight that was attached to the presumption in favour of marriage, although the judges differed as to exactly how strong the evidence against the marriage must be. Later cases have confirmed that there must be evidence "which satisfies beyond reasonable doubt that there was no valid marriage" in order to rebut the presumption (*Mahadervan v Mahadervan* [1964] P.233 at p.246).

The Right to Marry

Key Principle: **Restrictions on the right to marry must not infringe the very essence of that right**

B and L v UK 2006

A relationship developed between B and L, the latter being B's former daughter-in-law. At this point the marriage between L and B's son, C, had already been ended by divorce, as had that between B and C's other parent, A. B and L wanted to marry, but were informed that they would be unable to do so until both C and A were dead.

Held: (ECHR) In placing such restrictions on the right to marry, UK law was in violation of Art.12 of the European Convention on Human Rights.

Commentary

The government has now taken steps to bring the law into conformity with the European Convention. Once the relevant order takes place, it will be possible for a man to marry his former daughter-in-law (or a woman her former son-in-law) without the necessity of the parties waiting for the deaths of their former spouses (and the same rule will apply to civil partnerships). The somewhat arbitrary nature of the restrictions imposed by the previous law was one of the factors that led the ECHR to hold that UK law violated art.12: in particular, it was felt that the possibility of the restriction being waived by a private Act of Parliament undermined any possible rationale for the rule.

***

Key Principle: **There must be a rational connection between the restrictions imposed on the right to marry and the objectives of the policy**

R (Baiai and others) v Secretary of State for the Home Department 2006

Under the Asylum and Immigration (Treatment of Claimants, etc) Act 2004 and the Immigration (Procedure for Marriage) Regulations 2005, persons who were subject to immigration control and wished to marry (other than according to the rites of the Church of England) had to give notice at specified registration centres. Such notice would not be accepted unless the person subject to immigration control either had entry clearance for the purpose of marriage or a certificate of approval to marry granted by the Secretary of State. Such approval would only be given in limited circumstances. Each of the three applicants in this case had applied for certificates of approval, which had been refused. Each then claimed that the scheme was incompatible with the ECHR.

Held: The scheme infringed arts 12 and 14 of the ECHR. It was not denied that the legislature had the power to impose restrictions on the right to marry in the interests of an effective immigration policy. The objective of preventing sham marriages was sufficiently important to justify limiting rights under art.12. The judge also held that the area was one in which considerable deference should be accorded to the legislature, given that the issue required consideration of social and political issues, that the court had no special expertise in the area of immigration policy, and that the right claimed was not one that required a high degree of constitutional protection. However, the measures adopted were not rationally connected to the legislative objective. The scheme was inflexible and arbitrary. It was also discriminatory because it only applied to those marrying according to non-Anglican rites.

Commentary

The decision is to be welcomed for the way in which Silber J. investigated whether there was any connection between the scheme and its claimed objectives. Undoubtedly one of the key influences underlying Silber J.'s decision that the scheme infringed art.12 was the government's failure to provide any reason for the distinction between Anglican ceremonies and those conducted according to other religious rites. While the Home Office did provide reasons for the exemption of Anglican ceremonies, it did not address the question as to why other religious ceremonies should have been included, given that the evidence of sham marriages related to civil ceremonies. Another influential consideration was that the scheme did not take into account those factors that might be relevant to determining whether a proposed marriage was a sham, for example whether the parties had been together for a period of years, had had children or purchased a home together. At the time of writing the future of the system is unclear: the government has appealed against the decision and the application process has been suspended while the Home Office decides what to do next.

Annulments

The grounds on which a marriage may be held to be either void or voidable are now set out in ss.11 and 12 of the Matrimonial Causes Act 1973 (MCA 1973), and the equivalent (but not identical) grounds on which a civil partnership may be annulled are set out in ss.49 and 50 of the Civil Partnership Act 2004. The following cases discuss various points that have arisen over the years under both common law and statute.

Transsexuals and Intersexuals

In 2004 the Gender Recognition Act was passed, providing transsexuals with a means by which their change of gender could be legally recognised. The earlier case law on the status of transsexuals and intersexuals for the purposes of marriage remains of interest: first, because there may be occasions when the common law applies (for example in relation to those who do not choose to take advantage of the statutory procedure), and second, because it provides a case-study of the scope of human rights arguments.

Key Principle: **At common law, a person's sex is defined at birth, by biological criteria**

Corbett v Corbett 1971

A male-to-female transsexual went through a ceremony of marriage with a man. The marriage was not a success, and the husband petitioned for a decree of nullity after only a few months.

Held: A person's sex was to be determined at birth, rather than at the time of the marriage. The criteria for determining a person's sex were primarily biological. If the chromosomal, gonadal and genital factors were congruent, this would be decisive. Only if they were not congruent could other criteria, such as psychological factors, be taken into account. Applying these tests, the respondent was, in the eyes of the law, a man. Therefore the marriage was void, since marriage is a relationship between a man and a woman. In addition, the respondent was incapable of consummating the marriage.

Commentary

For a first-instance decision heard in 1970—and decided before the legislation was rephrased in 1971—*Corbett* has proved remarkably enduring. Until recently, it was followed in other jurisdictions and by higher courts within this country. Only in the past few years have things begun to change, and in this country legislation was necessary to bring about a change of policy.

The fact that *Corbett* remained unchallenged for so long should not obscure the deficiencies in the reasoning of Ormrod J. His reason for excluding consideration of the psychological factors was that "having regard to the essentially hetero-sexual character of the relationship which is called marriage, the criteria must, in my judgement, be biological, for even the most extreme degree of transsexualism in a male or the most severe hormonal imbalance which can exist in a person with male chromosomes, male gonads and male genitalia, cannot reproduce a person who is naturally capable of performing the essential role of a woman in marriage." (p.106). Yet what is the essential role of a woman in marriage?

Ormrod J. did not spell this out, but his earlier description of marriage as "the institution on which the family is built, and in which the capacity for natural hetero-sexual intercourse is an essential element" would seem to suggest that the ability to have sex and to procreate are both essential elements. Yet the barrenness or sterility of the parties has never been a ground for nullity, and the issue of capacity or willingness to consummate the marriage is only relevant to whether or not the marriage is voidable (rather than automatically void) which is a decision for the parties themselves. The reasoning amounts to little more than an assertion that marriage is a heterosexual institution.

Yet even the passage of the Gender Recognition Act 2004 does not render the decision in *Corbett* redundant. While it is now possible for a transsexual to obtain a Gender Recognition Certificate from a Gender Recognition Panel recognising his or her reassigned sex, the courts may still be called upon to determine the sex of those who have not undergone this process. It should also be noted that the 2004 Act does not alter the law relating to consummation, and a future petition for nullity for incapacity to consummate might therefore seek to rely on Ormrod J.'s decision that a male-to-female transsexual (or vice-versa) is incapable of consummating a marriage.

Key Principle: **If the biological factors are not congruent, psychological factors, hormonal factors and secondary sexual characteristics may be taken into account to determine a person's sex**

W v W (Nullity: Gender) 2001

The respondent's sex had not been clear at birth and she had been classified as a boy because her father had wanted a son. She subsequently underwent gender reassignment surgery and went through a ceremony of marriage with a man. When the marriage broke down he petitioned for a decree of nullity on the basis that the parties were not respectively male and female.

Held: The petition would be dismissed. *Corbett* was distinguished on the basis that the biological factors were held not to be congruent in this case, and therefore other factors could be taken into account. Taking into account the psychological factors (the fact that the respondent had chosen to live life as a woman and had surgery to achieve this), hormonal factors and the respondent's secondary sexual characteristics, it was appropriate to classify the respondent as a woman.

Commentary
The case was distinguishable from *Corbett* on the basis that there was genuine uncertainty about the respondent's sex at birth. However, it was at least arguable that the biological criteria were congruent: the respondent had male chromosomes, testes rather than ovaries, and genitals that were male rather than female. Despite this, the judge held that it would be an incorrect application of Ormrod J.'s test to apply it regardless of how close to the line between male and female each factor fell. Accordingly, a broader range of factors had to be taken into account in determining the respondent's sex. The case is significant for a number of reasons. Charles J. not only distinguished the decision in *Corbett*, but also argued for a different conception of marriage—one that placed greater emphasis on the financial, civil, contractual and general living arrangements of the parties, rather than emphasizing the sexual dimension of the relationship. Moreover, as the judge pointed out, for the purposes of marriage—and now civil partnerships—a person must be either male or female. The facts of *W v W* indicate that not every person can be easily categorised as one or the other, and brings into question the law's requirement of such categorisation.

Key Principle: **A failure to recognise the reassigned sex of a transsexual infringes the ECHR**

Goodwin v UK, I v UK 2003
In both cases the applicants were post-operative male-to-female transsexuals, whose treatment had been provided by the National Health Service. They argued that their rights under both art.8 and art.12 of the ECHR had been infringed by English law, which continued to treat them as male.

Held: (ECHR) There was a breach of both art.8 (right to respect for private and family life) and of art.12 (right to marry and found a family). It was artificial to insist that post-operative transsexuals were not deprived of the right to marry on the basis that they remained able to marry a person of their former opposite sex. The court should maintain a dynamic and evolutive approach.

Commentary

The decision in *Goodwin* was handed down only four years after the Court had concluded in *Sheffield and Horsham v UK* [1988] 2 F.L.R. 928 that the law did not violate the Convention. It was difficult to identify any legal or medical changes between the two decisions. In 1998 only four of the signatories to the Convention refused to recognise the reassigned sex of a post-operative transsexual (the UK, Ireland, Andorra and Albania), and the same was true in 2002. The Court acknowledged that while it was not formally bound to follow its previous judgements, "it is in the interests of legal certainty, foreseeability and equality before the law that it should not depart, without good reason, from precedents laid down in previous cases." (para.74). Yet in the absence of any external reason for departing from the decision in *Sheffield*, the Court was forced to argue that the factors upon which it had relied in that case were no longer of decisive significance. The decision does the court credit; the reasoning does not. The decision did, however, provide the impetus for Parliament to pass the Gender Recognition Act 2004.

Bellinger v Bellinger 2003

A male-to-female transsexual who had undergone gender reassignment surgery went through a ceremony of marriage with a man. She then sought a declaration that the marriage was valid.

Held: (HL) The House of Lords noted that it was conscious of the humanitarian case for recognising transsexuals and of the international trend towards such recognition. It felt, however, that to recognise a post-operative male-to-female transsexual as being female for the purposes of marriage would be a change in the law with far-reaching ramifications and was a point unsuitable for judicial determination. As the legislation could not be construed so as to achieve compliance with the ECHR, a declaration of incompatibility would be made. The marriage was void.

Commentary

The fact that legislation had been proposed obviously provided reassurance to the House of Lords that the matter would be speedily resolved without the need for judicial innovation. The main significance of *Bellinger* lies in their Lordships' approach to the Human Rights Act, and their identification of the limits of "interpretation." The decision has been contrasted with that of *Ghaidan v Godin-Mendoza* (see chapter 1), but the task facing the House of Lords in *Bellinger* was arguably more difficult than that in the later case because of the degrees of transsexuality that may exist (what if the individual in question has not undergone surgery, or has only undergone partial surgery?). It was held that there "must be some objective, publicly available criteria by which gender reassignment is to be assessed." (para.42). Such criteria are now provided by the Gender Reassignment Act 2004.

Finally, it should be noted that at common law, the criteria set out in *Corbett* remain the only criteria by which the sex of a child can be determined at birth.

Capacity to Marry

The test of capacity has been formulated in the context of marriage but would be equally applicable to civil partnerships.

Key Principle: **The test of a person's capacity to marry is whether he or she is mentally capable of understanding that it involves the responsibilities normally attaching to marriage**

In re Park 1954
The deceased had made a will a few hours after entering into a marriage. That will was subsequently set aside on the basis that the deceased was not of sound mind at the time he made the will. The validity of the marriage was then challenged.

Held: (CA) The marriage was valid. The correct test to apply was whether the deceased had understood the nature of the contract into which he was entering, and the responsibilities normally involved in that contract.

Commentary
The case illustrates that the law may require different levels of understanding for different actions. The deceased had had a sufficient understanding of the contract of marriage, even if he had not been able to make a valid will. The test laid down in the case was relied upon in the following case, which expanded on the responsibilities normally involved in the marriage contract.

Sheffield County Council v E and S 2004

E, a 21-year-old with the mental functions of a 13-year-old, was in a relationship with S, a Sch.1 offender with a history of sexually violent crimes. Sheffield County Council sought an injunction to prevent a marriage between them. The preliminary issue for the court was the test of capacity to be applied.

Held: The appropriate test was whether the person in question had the ability to understand the nature of marriage and the duties and responsibilities it creates, not whether he or she is able to appreciate the consequences of marriage to a specific person.

Commentary

In this case the desirability of protecting a young mentally disabled woman vied with the right of an individual to marry the person of his or her choice, however misguided that choice might be. As Munby J. emphasised, the test is whether a person has capacity to marry, not whether they are wise to marry. In any case, it was the relationship, rather than the marriage, that the council was keen to prevent.

Of particular interest is Munby J.'s definition of marriage as "a contract, formally entered into. It confers on the parties the status of husband and wife, the essence of the contract being an agreement between a man and a woman to live together, and to love one another as husband and wife, to the exclusion of all others. It creates a relationship of mutual and reciprocal obligations, typically involving the sharing of a common home and a common domestic life and the right to enjoy each other's society, comfort and assistance." (para.132). It is possible to criticise this as a *legal* definition—any agreement to "love one another as husband and wife" is hardly capable of enforcement by the courts—but as a broad definition of what marriage entails, which would be comprehensible to the average lay person, it does capture the essence of marriage. And it should be borne in mind that the legal rights and responsibilities that flow from marriage—as opposed to divorce or the death of a spouse—are somewhat limited. For most married couples, it is the day-to-day interactions summarised by Munby J. that are more important.

Key Principle: **The inherent jurisdiction of the court may be invoked to prevent the marriage of a person who lacks capacity to consent to the marriage**

M v B, A and S (By the Official Solicitor) 2005

The local authority was concerned that the parents were planning a marriage for their 23-year-old daughter, who suffered from a severe learning difficulty. It sought a declaration that the daughter lacked capacity to marry and that it was not in her best interests to leave the jurisdiction.

Held: The daughter lacked the capacity to consent to a marriage, and the court had the power to make an order restraining those responsible for her from entering into a contract of marriage on her behalf.

Commentary

It is now clear that the inherent jurisdiction of the court may be invoked in this context even if the person lacking capacity is an adult. (If the person lacking capacity is under the age of 18, then the wardship jurisdiction may be invoked instead).

Key Principle: **The inherent jurisdiction of the court may be invoked to protect vulnerable adults who may otherwise be prevented from exercising a free and informed choice whether or not to marry**

Re SA (Vulnerable Adult with Capacity: Marriage) 2005

The local authority was concerned that a profoundly deaf 17-year-old girl might be married against her wishes, and applied to the court to invoke the inherent jurisdiction.

Held: An order was made requiring that the girl should be properly informed about any proposed marriage, to ensure that she could exercise a free and informed choice whether or not to give her consent.

Commentary

The case is a further illustration of the scope of the court's inherent jurisdiction, envisaged in this case as extending to protect not only adults who lack capacity but also those who are vulnerable because of a disability (or indeed because they are subject to duress or undue influence or other constraints). The girl in question was happy for her parents to arrange a marriage for her, but wanted to be able to exercise some control over it, and the orders of the court were designed to ensure that she would have all of the necessary information.

Consent

The test of consent has been formulated in the context of marriage but would be equally applicable to civil partnerships.

Key Principle: **A marriage may be annulled on the basis of duress if the petitioner's will was overborne by pressure from another**

Hirani v Hirani 1983
The petitioner was a 19-year-old Hindu girl. When her parents discovered that she was having a relationship with a Muslim man, they ordered her to break it off and to marry a person of their choosing—or else leave home. The girl went through with the marriage but then petitioned for nullity on the basis that she had not consented to it.

Held: The parents' threats had destroyed the reality of the petitioner's consent to the marriage, which would therefore be annulled.

Commentary
An earlier line of cases had required that there should have been a "genuine and reasonably held fear caused by threat of immediate danger (for which the party is not himself responsible) to life, limb of liberty" (see *Szechter v Szechter* [1971] P 286 at 297). By contrast, the test established by *Hirani* is subjective in nature: the petitioner only has to show that his or her will was overborne, rather than being required to prove that a reasonable person would have been overborne by the pressure. It is also easier to satisfy in that it does not require the petitioner to show that there was any particular *type* of pressure: it is sufficient to show that there were threats or pressure which destroyed the reality of consent to marriage.

Key Principle: **Cultural expectations short of direct pressure do not amount to duress**

Singh v Singh 1971

A Sikh girl agreed to have an arranged marriage and did not meet her proposed husband before the wedding. When she finally met him, she decided that he was neither as handsome nor as well-educated as had been represented to her. She went through the ceremony but refused to have anything to do with him afterwards and petitioned for a decree of nullity.

Held: The marriage was valid. While the girl had obeyed the wishes of her parents there was nothing to indicate that she had not consented to the marriage.

Commentary

While *Singh* was decided at a time when the test of duress was more stringent, it is doubtful whether it would have been annulled even if the more liberal test adopted in *Hirani* had been applied. Although it is impossible not to feel sympathy for the petitioner, the problem for the court was that no threats had been made and she had given no indication that she did not want to go through with the ceremony. The law in this area has to strike a balance between ensuring that marriages are based on the full and free consent of the parties, and not allowing marriages to be challenged at a later date on the basis of the subjective reservations of the parties.

Key Principle: **Persuasion and arguments invoking cultural expectations may amount to duress**

NS v MI 2006

The petitioner was taken to Pakistan by her parents at the age of sixteen. She was under the impression that she was going on holiday, but once there she was told that she must marry the respondent. Her parents told her that they would kill themselves if she did not comply, and that she would not be allowed to return to the UK until she had gone through with the marriage. She accordingly married the respondent, and on her return to the UK sought a nullity decree.

Held: The marriage would be annulled on the basis that she had not consented to it, as her will had been overborne by the pressure brought to bear by her parents.

Commentary
In this case, there had been continued threats and emotional
blackmail over a period of some months. Munby J. also noted that
duress may take many forms: "where the influence is that of a
parent or other close and dominating relative, and where the
arguments and persuasion are based upon personal affection or
duty, religious beliefs, powerful social or cultural conventions, or
asserted social, familial or domestic obligations, the influence may
be subtle, insidious, pervasive and powerful." (para.34). It is clear,
therefore, that if an individual's will is overborne by arguments
based on cultural expectations with the result that he or she is
persuaded into a marriage, the court will grant a decree of nullity.
It remains doubtful, however, whether this would assist an individual in the position of the petitioner in *Singh v Singh*, or those for
whom cultural expectations are so deeply embedded that further
persuasion is unnecessary.

Key Principle: **A marriage may be annulled on the basis of a
mistake as to the nature of the ceremony or the identity of the
other party**

Mehta v Mehta 1945
The parties went through a ceremony of marriage in Hindi.
However, the petitioner, not a Hindi speaker, was under the
impression that the ceremony was to convert her to the Hindu
faith.

Held: The marriage was void, as the petitioner had not understood the true nature of the ceremony.

Commentary
It is understandable that the law offers redress in extreme cases of
this kind (although one cannot help but wonder how the mistake
came to be made, or what the bride's reaction was when she learnt
the truth). It is equally understandable that a mistake about the
other party's attributes does not invalidate the ceremony: if I
marry one person believing him to be another, the marriage is
voidable. By contrast, if I marry a person believing his assurances
that he is rich, honest and faithful, the fact that this turns out not
to be the case will not invalidate the marriage.

Key Principle: **A marriage is not invalid simply because the parties never intended to cohabit**

Vervaeke v Smith 1983
The plaintiff, who was domiciled in Belgium, married an Englishman in 1954 so that she could acquire British nationality. They never lived together, parting immediately after the ceremony.

Held: (HL) The marriage was valid. The parties had understood the nature of the ceremony, even if they had had no wish to live together as husband and wife.

Commentary
The facts of the case were far more complex than that brief summary might suggest, but for present purposes the key point was the confirmation by the court that even a "sham" marriage—entered into for the convenience of the parties—is a valid marriage. Thus the parties must have the ability to appreciate the rights and responsibilities that marriage entails, but not necessarily the intention to assume those responsibilities.

Consummation

A marriage may be annulled if one party is incapable of consummation or wilfully refuses to do so (see s.12(a) and (b) of the MCA 1973). There are no equivalent grounds in the CPA 2004.

Key Principle: **Consummation means sexual intercourse that is "ordinary and complete"**

D__e v A__g 1845
The marriage had not been consummated, due to the fact that the wife's vagina was malformed—in the words of one of the doctors who had examined her, "an impervious cul de sac." The evidence was that the malformation was incurable. The husband petitioned for nullity on the basis of his wife's incapacity to consummate the marriage.

Held: The marriage would be annulled. For a marriage to be consummated there must be sexual intercourse that was "ordinary and complete" intercourse, although this was a matter of degree as not "every degree of imperfection would deprive it of its essential character." (p.298). If—as here—the spouse was capable of no more than "an incipient, imperfect and unnatural coitus" the marriage would be a nullity.

Commentary

This case provides a useful reminder of the historical roots of much of the law of nullity, as well as a clear statement as to what is required for consummation of a marriage. At the time that the case was decided, the ecclesiastical courts still exercised jurisdiction over the issue of whether a marriage was valid (and did so until their jurisdiction was transferred to a new court by the Divorce and Matrimonial Causes Act 1857). It is difficult to imagine that a modern court would place so much emphasis on the purpose of consummation as "a lawful indulgence of the passions to prevent licentiousness." (p.298). Given that the legal definition of consummation is both rigid (requiring heterosexual penetrative sex) and minimal (requiring nothing beyond such penetration) one might wonder whether it really serves the ostensible purpose of diverting spouses from other, necessarily adulterous, liaisons.

Key Principle: **For the purposes of consummation, sex may be recreational rather than procreational**

Baxter v Baxter 1948

The parties married in 1934. The wife refused to have sexual intercourse with the husband unless he wore a condom, to which he reluctantly complied. He left her in 1944 and petitioned for nullity, arguing that she had wilfully refused to consummate the marriage.

Held: (HL) The marriage had been consummated, and so the husband was not entitled to a decree of nullity.

Commentary

The court endorsed the idea that the purpose of consummation is to foster the relationship of the couple rather than to produce children. As the judges pointed out, the procreation of children was not part of the classic definition of marriage in *Hyde*. Viscount Jowitt L.C. quoted Lord Stair to the effect that: "it is not the consent of marriage as it relateth to the procreation of children that is requisite; for it may consist, though the woman be far beyond that date; but it is the consent, whereby ariseth that conjugal society, which may have the conjunction of bodies as well as of minds, as the general end of the institution of marriage, [being] the solace and satisfaction of man." (p.289). One would hope that a modern judge would add "and woman", although given that only a single act of sexual intercourse is required in order for the marriage to be consummated, and that there is no requirement that either party enjoy it, it may not do much to satisfy either.

Key Principle: **A refusal to consummate the marriage is wilful if the respondent has come to a settled and definite decision without just excuse**

Horton v Horton 1947

The early years of the marriage were hardly conducive to consummation: the husband was in the Army, and the couple did not have a home of their own but lived in a room in the wife's parents' house. It was over a year before an attempt was made to consummate the marriage, and then the husband failed to penetrate the wife. No further attempt was made. The husband later sought to persuade the wife to consummate the marriage but she refused. The husband then petitioned for the marriage to be annulled on the basis of her wilful refusal to consummate.

Held: (HL) The husband's petition would be dismissed.

Commentary

The court emphasised the importance of looking at the whole history of the marriage in deciding whether one of the parties had come to a settled and definite decision not to consummate the marriage without good cause. The fact that the wife had refused to have intercourse with the husband on a particular occasion did not justify the decision that she had wilfully refused to consummate the marriage.

Key Principle: **A refusal to consummate the marriage that is attributable to a just cause is not "wilful"**

Ford v Ford 1987

The marriage took place while the husband was serving a five-year prison sentence. During his wife's visits the couple were left alone for periods of up to two hours, but the husband refused to consummate the marriage. On a home visit he demanded that his wife take him to his ex-girlfriend's house. The wife petitioned for the marriage to be annulled on the basis of the husband's wilful refusal to consummate it.

Held: The husband's refusal to have sex during his wife's visit to the prison did not amount to a wilful refusal to consummate the marriage, given that it was against the prison rules to engage in sexual intercourse during such visits. The husband's later conduct, did, however, constitute wilful refusal, and the marriage would therefore be annulled.

Commentary

The case provides a useful example of what constitutes a "just cause" to refuse to consummate the marriage, namely the fact that the husband would have been breaking prison rules had he done so.

Key Principle: **Refusing to take the necessary steps to set up home with one's spouse amounts to a wilful refusal to consummate the marriage**

A v J (Nullity Proceedings) 1989

A marriage was arranged between two Hindus and the civil ceremony took place. It had been agreed that a religious ceremony would follow, but the wife insisted on an indefinite postponement of the ceremony. The husband petitioned for nullity on the basis of her wilful refusal to consummate the marriage.

Held: The decree would be granted. The religious ceremony was an essential precondition of cohabitation of the parties, and so the wife's refusal to participate in such a ceremony amounted to a wilful refusal to consummate the marriage.

Commentary
The case illustrates that a "wilful refusal to consummate" may be based on a general refusal to live with the other party, as well as a direct refusal to have sex with one's spouse.

Bars to a Decree

Under s.13 of the MCA 1973, if the petitioner knew that the marriage could be annulled and acted in such a way as to give the other the impression that s/he would not seek to do so AND it would be unjust to the respondent to grant the decree, no decree will be granted (see also s.51 of the CPA).

Key Principle: **There is no public policy dimension to the statutory bar in s.13 of the MCA 1973**

D v D (Nullity: Statutory Bar) 1979
The parties married in 1966. The marriage was never consummated, as the wife was physically incapable of consummating it and refused to undergo the operation that could have cured this. The husband was aware that he could seek a decree of nullity but chose not to do so. In 1975 he agreed to adopt two children with the wife. He then changed his mind, left the wife for another woman and sought a decree of nullity.

Held: The decree of nullity would be granted. While the husband had led the wife to believe that he would not seek to have the marriage annulled, it would not be unjust to the wife to grant the decree, as she was willing for it to be granted and would have the same rights as upon divorce.

Commentary
This was the first—and, it would appear, only—case to consider the relationship between s.13 of the Matrimonial Causes Act 1973 and the common law doctrine of approbation that s.13 had replaced. The key difference between the two was that public policy had no role to play in s.13. As the judge pointed out, the Law Commission—whose recommendations had led to the law being changed—had noted that lawyers would be unable to advise

their clients with certainty "if there is a risk of individual notions of public policy being involved" (Law Com No.33 (1970) para.44). Thus the only relevant factors are those set out in the statute.

3. DIVORCE

The sole ground for divorce—that the marriage has broken down irretrievably—is set out in s.1(1) of the Matrimonial Causes Act 1973 (MCA 1973). However, as s.1(2) goes on to explain, "the court hearing a petition for divorce shall not hold the marriage to have broken down irretrievably unless the petitioner satisfies the court of one or more of the following five facts, that is to say—

(a) that the respondent has committed adultery and the petitioner finds it intolerable to live with the respondent;

(b) that the respondent has behaved in such a way that the petitioner cannot reasonably be expected to live with the respondent;

(c) that the respondent has deserted the petitioner for a continuous period of at least two years immediately preceding the presentation of the petition;

(d) that the parties of the marriage have lived apart for a continuous period of at least two years immediately preceding the presentation of the petition . . . and the respondent consents to a decree being granted;

(e) that the parties to the marriage have lived apart for a continuous period of at least five years immediately preceding the presentation of the petition. . . ."

Almost identical provisions are contained in s.44 of the Civil Partnership Act 2004 (CPA 2004), save that adultery is not a ground on which a civil partnership may be dissolved (the reasoning being that "adultery" specifically refers to heterosexual extramarital relations). A partner's infidelity could, however, be classed as behaviour with which the other could not reasonably be expected to live.

There are a number of cases on how the provisions of the Matrimonial Causes Act are to be construed. Many date from the 1970s, as the courts began the process of interpreting the new legislation. More recent authorities are relatively rare, since today over 99 per cent of all divorces are undefended.

The Relationship Between the "Breakdown Principle" and the Five Facts

Key Principle: **In order to establish that the marriage has irretrievably broken down it is necessary to prove one of the five facts listed in s.1(2) of the MCA 1973**

Buffery v Buffery 1988
The parties had been married 20 years but had grown apart, no longer had anything in common and could not communicate.

Held: A divorce could not be granted as the wife had failed to establish any of the grounds set out in s. 1(2), even though it was clear that the marriage had broken down.

Commentary
This case illustrates that, while in principle the irretrievable breakdown of the marriage is the sole ground for divorce under s.1(1) of the MCA, such breakdown can only be proved by establishing one of the five facts set out in s.1(2). Breakdown by itself is not sufficient. It should of course be borne in mind that the court will rarely have the opportunity to test the truth of the petitioner's allegations, since the vast majority of divorces (a) are undefended, and (b) may be granted without the judge ever seeing the parties. Since defending a petition is likely to be costly (and highly unlikely to save the marriage), it is perhaps more accurate to say that it must appear from the documents before the judge that one of the five facts in s.1(2) has been established.

Key Principle: **If the petitioner has failed to establish any of the five facts, a divorce cannot be granted even if the marriage was a sham**

Bhaiji v Chauhan, Queen's Proctor Intervening (Divorce: Marriages used for Immigration Purposes) 2003
The case concerned five divorce petitions. In each case a UK citizen had married an Indian citizen. Each couple had made a declaration that they intended to live together permanently as husband and wife. After one year, indefinite leave to remain had been granted to the Indian citizens. In each case, after indefinite leave had been granted a petition for divorce had

been presented by one of each of the couples under s.1(2)(b) of the MCA (the gap between the two events ranging from five days to sixteen months). The court's suspicions were raised by the fact that similar allegations were made in each petition: it was clear that the same person had drafted at least four of the five petitions. The petitions were undefended but the Queen's Proctor intervened to oppose the grant of a decree.

Held: The petitions would be dismissed, on the basis that the allegations made were false.

Commentary
The irony in this case was that although it would appear that the marriages were shams, entered into purely to secure leave to remain in the UK, the desire of the parties to divorce was presumably all the more real. But, as *Buffery v Buffery*, above, illustrates, the fact that a marriage has broken down—or indeed never existed in any real sense—does not by itself justify the grant of a decree. The judge acknowledged that denying the divorce would have little effect in the long term, since the parties could petition for divorce after they had been living separately for two years, but he emphasized that this did not justify a grant of a decree on the basis of fabricated allegations.

Key Principle: **The respondent has the right to oppose the divorce petition and to require the allegations made to be proved on the balance of probabilities**

Butterworth v Butterworth 1997
The wife petitioned for divorce, making a number of allegations against the husband, not all of which were made out in evidence. However, the recorder took the view that the marriage had broken down irretrievably and granted the petition.

Held: (CA) The appeal would be allowed and the case remitted for rehearing, as it was unclear what part of the wife's evidence had actually been accepted.

Commentary
While few divorce petitions are defended, and even a successful defence is unlikely to restore the marriage in any meaningful sense,

this case stands as a reminder that the statutory requirements still have to be fulfilled before a divorce can be granted. As Butler-Sloss L.J. noted in this case, the impression given by the decision of the recorder was "that it is unreasonable for husbands to object to divorces and that the evidence in support of the petition is something of a formality. That is far from the truth. All courts hope that spouses whose marriages fail will bury them decently and will not litigate the divorce in public with all the consequential adverse effect upon each of the parties and upon their children. But the present state of the English law of divorce gives the respondent to a divorce petition the right to oppose it and to have the allegations made in the petition against him properly proved to the satisfaction of the court to the civil standard of the balance of probabilities." (p.339)

Adultery

Key Principle: **Attempted adultery does not satisfy the requirements of s. 1(2)(a)**

Dennis v Dennis 1955
The wife petitioned for divorce, but the husband cross-petitioned on the basis of her adultery. The evidence was that although the wife had agreed to sexual intercourse with another man, intercourse had not in fact taken place owing to "a nervous disability from which he suffered."

Held: (CA) As penetration had not occurred, the wife was not guilty of adultery.

Commentary
The definition of adultery has parallels with the definition of consummation: something more than an attempt is required, and there must be penetration of the woman's vagina by the man's penis. Of course, in most cases the court will not require the details, and is entitled to presume that intercourse has taken place from circumstantial evidence. In this case, the evidence that the parties had gone to the wife's bedroom, taken off their clothes and lain down together would have been sufficient to infer that adultery had taken place, had there not been direct evidence of the man's impotency.

Key Principle: Under s.1(2)(a) it is necessary to establish that the respondent had committed adultery AND that the petitioner finds it intolerable to live with the respondent, but there does not have to be a link between the two

Cleary v Cleary 1974
The wife left the husband for another man, but then returned to him for a few weeks before leaving again, this time to stay with her mother. The husband petitioned for divorce.

Held: (CA) A divorce would be granted to the husband as he had established both her adultery and the fact that he found it intolerable to live with her.

Commentary
The significance of this case lies in the decision that the intolerability of living with the respondent need not be related to the respondent's adultery. In effect, the petitioner can obtain a divorce if the respondent has committed adultery, regardless of whether the adultery was the cause of the marriage breaking down. There is no need to show that a reasonable person in the petitioner's situation would have found it intolerable to live with the respondent: all that is needed is a statement that the petitioner finds it intolerable.

"Unreasonable Behaviour"

Key Principle: Whether or not it is reasonable to expect the petitioner to live with the respondent depends on the characteristics of both parties

Ash v Ash 1972
The wife's petition gave particulars of specific acts of violence and intoxication. The husband admitted some of the incidents but argued that the marriage had not broken down irretrievably.

Held: The decree would be granted. In construing the legislation, the "petitioner" referred to was the actual petitioner rather than a hypothetical reasonable person in the position of the petitioner. Thus the court had to consider the respondent's behaviour and the petitioner's character, personality and attributes in deciding whether it was unreasonable to expect the petitioner to continue to live with the respondent.

Commentary

As Bagnall J. observed in this case, while the legislation set an objective test, character is a subjective matter. While the test established in this case remains good law, it is unlikely that modern judges would apply the suggestion that a violent petitioner could be expected to live with a violent respondent, given the greater appreciation of the seriousness of domestic violence today (as well as the fact that its impact on the parties may be unequal).

Key Principle: **The reasonableness of expecting the particular petitioner to live with the particular respondent must be judged objectively**

Livingstone-Stallard v Livingstone-Stallard 1974

The wife petitioned for divorce on the basis that she could not reasonably be expected to live with her husband, who had constantly criticised her, telling her that wives had to be subservient to their husbands in order to be happy.

Held: The decree would be granted. The correct approach was to ask whether any right-thinking person would conclude that the respondent had behaved in such a way that the petitioner could not reasonably be expected to live with him or her, taking into account the whole of the circumstances and the personalities of the parties.

Commentary

The significant point to note is the emphasis on the objective element in the test applied by the courts: a decree will not automatically be granted simply because the petitioner believes that the respondent has behaved in a way that is unreasonable, but only if he or she can convince the court that it is objectively unreasonable to expect future cohabitation.

Key Principle: **The test is whether the respondent has behaved in such a way that the petitioner cannot reasonably be expected to live with the respondent, not whether the respondent is to blame for such behaviour**

Katz v Katz 1972

The husband was suffering from a manic-depressive illness and had spent four weeks in a mental hospital. This had had an impact on the wife, who was diagnosed as suffering from a severe anxiety state and had tried to commit suicide. She petitioned for divorce on the basis of her husband's behaviour.

Held: The decree would be granted. The test to be applied by the court was whether the character and gravity of the respondent's behaviour had been such that the petitioner could not reasonably be expected to live with him.

Commentary
The case illustrates how the courts were willing to interpret the provisions of the Divorce Reform Act in a way that reflected the underlying principle that a divorce should be granted if the marriage had irretrievably broken down, uninfluenced by the considerations of fault that had been central to the earlier law. It was clear in this case that the husband was not responsible for his behaviour: it was equally clear that his behaviour was adversely affecting the wife to such an extent that she could not reasonably be expected to live with him.

Thurlow v Thurlow 1976
The wife suffered from epilepsy and over the course of the marriage her condition deteriorated. She became bedridden and was occasionally aggressive, throwing objects at her mother-in-law. By 1972 it was clear that she required continuing institutional care. The husband petitioned for divorce under s.1(2)(b).

Held: The petition would be granted. The husband could no longer be expected to live with the wife, as his powers of endurance had been exhausted by her behaviour and his own health had been affected. The fact that the wife's behaviour resulted from her illness did not affect the fact that it was unreasonable to expect the husband to continue to live with her.

Commentary
This sad case is a further illustration of the fact that the key issue for the court is the effect of the respondent's behaviour on the petitioner, not the blameworthiness of the respondent. The judge did acknowledge that, if the behaviour complained of resulted from the "misfortune" of the respondent, the court "will take full account of all the obligations of the married state" including "the normal duty to accept and to share the burdens imposed upon the family as a result of the mental or physical ill-health of one member." (p.44). But even if spouses have promised—in the words

of the marriage service—to take one's spouse "for better, for worse, in sickness and in health", there is a limit to what a spouse can be expected to tolerate.

Carter-Fea v Carter-Fea 1987
The wife petitioned for divorce on the basis of the husband's financial irresponsibility over the last five years of the marriage, which had affected the family and had caused her stress, affecting her mental and physical health.

Held: (CA) The decree would be granted.

Commentary
The significant point in this case was the observation from Lawton L.J. that the husband's financial irresponsibility would not by itself have been a sufficient basis for the divorce to be granted: its relevance lay in the effect that it had had on the wife and family. Again, this illustrates the difference between a fault-based system and one based on the breakdown of the marriage: even if the respondent has behaved badly, s.1(2)(b) will not be satisfied unless the behaviour in question has had an impact on the petitioner.

Key Principle: **A petitioner may be able to show that it is unreasonable to expect continued cohabitation with the respondent even if the behaviour complained of has continued for some time**

Birch v Birch 1992
The parties were married for 27 years. Eventually the wife petitioned for divorce on the basis that she could not reasonably be expected to live with her husband, who was opinionated and chauvinistic and had belittled her throughout their marriage.

Held: The decree would be granted. Since the wife was of a sensitive nature and had resented her husband's behaviour for many years, it was not reasonable to expect her to continue living with him.

Commentary
The case further illustrates the fact that the test applied by the courts has a subjective element (could this person be expected to

live with his or her spouse?) as well as an objective element (is it reasonable to expect them to continue living together?). It also shows that the court is entitled to find that it is unreasonable to expect the parties to continue living together even if they have in fact been living together in a similar manner for a considerable period of time. If the husband had changed his ways, however, the wife might have found it more difficult to obtain a divorce, although under s.2(3) continued cohabitation for less than six months after the last incident relied upon in the petition is to be ignored, and longer periods may be ignored, in deciding whether it is reasonable to expect the petitioner to continue living with the respondent.

Key Principle: **A petitioner may be able to show that it is unreasonable to expect continued cohabitation with the respondent even if the parties have in fact continued to live together**

Bradley v Bradley 1973
The wife had six children from a previous marriage, and three children from the current marriage, all living together in a four-bedroom council house. The husband had been violent towards the wife, and she had obtained separation orders on the ground of his cruelty in 1969 and 1970 (under the previous law). The husband had, however, returned to the matrimonial home shortly after the making of these orders. When the Divorce Reform Act came into force the wife petitioned for divorce on the basis of the husband's behaviour. At first instance her petition was refused on the basis that she had continued to live with him.

Held: (CA) The appeal would be allowed, and the case remitted for rehearing. The fact that the wife had continued to live with the husband did not prevent her from petitioning for divorce on the basis of his behaviour.

Commentary
The decision of the Court of Appeal was a much more realistic approach to the issue than that of the judge at first instance. There was no statutory requirement that the parties had to be living apart in order for the court to find that it would be unreasonable to

expect them to continue living together. As Lord Denning M.R. pointed out, it was unreasonable to expect the wife to continue to live with the husband in the circumstances, but there was no other option open to her. Had the divorce been denied the wife would have been in a very difficult situation, as the local authority would not assist her with alternative accommodation while she remained married.

Key Principle: **The fact that the parties are no longer living together does not by itself mean that it is unreasonable to expect them to do so**

Stringfellow v Stringfellow 1976
After six years of marriage the husband told the wife that he no longer had any affection for her and left. Thereafter the parties lived apart. The wife petitioned for divorce under s.1(2)(b).

Held: (CA) The petition would be dismissed. Although the relationship between the parties had broken down, and the husband had deserted the wife, she had been unable to prove that the husband had behaved in such a way that she could not reasonably be expected to live with him.

Commentary
The case shows the court trying to maintain a distinction between the different facts from which the breakdown of the marriage could be inferred. If the mere fact that one party had left the other constituted behaviour with which the other could not be expected to live, then the specific periods of desertion or separation stipulated in s.1(2)(c), (d) and (e) would be circumvented. One might wonder, however, whether the case would be decided differently by the courts today: was the husband's declaration that he no longer had any affection for his wife any less damaging to the marital relationship than the husband's allegations in the following case?

Key Principle: **Defending the petition by criticising one's spouse is unlikely to save the marriage**

Hadjimilitis (Tsavliris) v Tsavliris 2003
After the parties had been married for eleven years the wife petitioned for divorce under s.1(2)(b), complaining of the hus-

band's criticisms, lack of warmth, controlling and undermining behaviour, public humiliation, and lack of respect for her, and alleging that this had resulted in her suffering depression and nervous strain. The husband denied the allegations, argued that the marriage had not broken down, and alleged that the wife was an adulteress, a drug taker, a bad wife and mother, irritable and erratic, and had merely married him for his money.

Held: The wife's petition would be granted. The husband's response to the petition bore out many of the wife's allegations: in particular, the allegation that she had merely married him for his money was thought to undermine the basis of the marriage to such an extent that the wife could not reasonably be expected to live with the husband.

Commentary
As well as providing a rare recent example of a reported divorce case, *Hadjimilitis* illustrates the futility of defending a divorce. As the judge pointed out, "it says much about his attitude towards his wife that he can even begin to think that after this there could be a reconciliation." (p.101). In this case, not only was the husband's defence hardly conducive to a reconciliation, but it also convinced the judge that the wife could not reasonably be expected to live with such a husband.

Desertion

Key Principle: **A respondent who has reasonable grounds for leaving the petitioner is not in desertion**

Quoraishi v Quoraishi 1985
The husband and wife were both Muslims. The husband wanted to take a second wife but the wife refused to give her consent. The husband subsequently married a second wife abroad (such marriage being valid because both parties were domiciled in a country that permitted polygamous marriages). The wife then left the husband, who subsequently petitioned for divorce on the basis of the wife's desertion.

Held: (CA) The petition would be dismissed. The wife had reasonable grounds for leaving the husband—namely the fact that he had taken a second wife against her wishes—and had therefore not deserted the husband.

Commentary

The case illustrates that the mere fact that one party has left the matrimonial home does not thereby make them guilty of desertion. Even though the wife had no valid complaint against the husband under Islamic law, the court took the view that she had reasonable grounds to leave him.

Key Principle: **If the conduct of one spouse effectively forces the other to leave the home, the former is in constructive desertion**

Saunders v Saunders 1965

The wife left the husband after almost five years of marriage, alleging desertion on the basis of his conduct towards her (expecting her to work long hours in their shop, even when she was heavily pregnant, failing to give her support when there was trouble between her and her parents-in-law, opening her mail against her wishes, and generally displaying a lack of consideration towards her).

Held: The conduct complained of was capable of amounting to constructive desertion. The test to be applied was whether the other spouse had "been guilty of such grave and weighty misconduct that the only sensible inference is that he knew that the complainant would in all probability withdraw permanently from cohabitation with him, if she acted like any reasonable person in her position." (p.504).

Commentary

The case illustrates that it is not necessarily the spouse who leaves the matrimonial home who is in desertion. The concept of "constructive desertion" dates back to the nineteenth century, but the need for such an expansive concept is reduced now that the grounds for divorce have been expanded. A spouse in this position would today be able to petition under s.1(2)(b) of the MCA. Today fewer than one per cent of petitions allege desertion.

Separation

Consent

Key Principle: **If a divorce is being sought under s.1(2)(d), it is necessary to show that the respondent consents to the divorce being granted**

McGill v Robson 1972

The wife petitioned for divorce on the basis of two years' separation plus consent. The petition was served on the husband but the wife's solicitors had sent the wrong form, which did not require him to state whether he consented to a decree being granted. A later letter from the husband's solicitors stated that "[o]ur client is not in the least concerned with the procedural problems that have arisen. Our client simply wants this affair to be brought to finality as soon as possible." (p.239).

Held: The husband's consent had to be given: it could not simply be inferred from the fact that he had not objected to the decree being granted.

Commentary

The judge in this case emphasized that the consent of the respondent is a positive requirement. Of course, the fact that such consent had not been provided in proper form did not pose an insuperable problem: the correct form was sent, the husband's consent given and the divorce granted.

Separation

Key Principle: **"Living apart" includes a mental element, and it is accordingly necessary to show that at least one of the spouses regarded the marriage as being at an end**

Santos v Santos 1972

The parties lived together in Spain until 1966, when the wife left the husband and returned to England. She went back to live with her husband in Spain on three occasions, but only for short periods (which even when added together were still less than six months). The husband consented to a divorce and the wife petitioned for divorce on the basis of two years' separation plus consent.

Held: (CA) In addition to the physical separation of the parties, at least one of them had to recognise that the marriage was at an end, although there was no requirement that this had to be communicated to the other spouse. The key issue was thus whether the wife had believed the marriage to be at an end during the two years that she had been living apart from the husband. The case was remitted for rehearing on this point.

Commentary
The decision in *Santos* was controversial as the legislation made no mention of any mental component to "living apart". The Court of Appeal noted, however, that other jurisdictions such as New Zealand, Australia and Canada had already enacted statutes making divorce available after a period of living apart and "the stream of authority ran uniformly and clearly in favour of mere physical separation not constituting 'living apart'." (p.257). One might well wonder why the courts felt it necessary to impose this requirement, especially given that the view of one spouse need not be communicated. Imagine a couple who have been separated for two years and, on being reunited, realise that they have drifted apart and that the marriage has broken down. Is there any justification for denying a divorce in such a case but granting it if one of the parties believed throughout the period that the marriage had broken down but did not inform the other until the two years had expired? The interpretation in Santos also poses problems of proof, as the Court of Appeal recognised: it is one thing to prove absence from one's spouse, quite another to prove a perhaps unarticulated and not necessarily communicated belief that the marriage is at an end. In practice, of course, the process by which divorces are granted means that the beliefs of the parties will not be investigated too closely.

Key Principle: **The parties may be living apart under the same roof, but only if they are living separate lives**

Mouncer v Mouncer 1972
The parties began to sleep in separate bedrooms in 1969 but continued to take meals together and to share the cleaning, although each did their own washing. The husband left in 1971 and petitioned for divorce on the basis of two years' separation plus consent.

Held: The petition was dismissed. The parties had continued to live in the same household. In the circumstances the statutory requirements had not been satisfied.

Commentary
It is possible for a couple to be living apart under the same roof, provided that they live separate lives. However, sleeping in separate bedrooms is not sufficient to show that the parties are leading separate lives. This of course means that the more co-operative a couple are, the less likely they are to be able to rely on this ground. As the judge pointed out, the fact that the parties in this case co-operated "from the wholly admirable motive of caring properly for their children cannot change the result of what they did." (p.323).

Fuller v Fuller 1973
The husband and wife lived together until 1964, when the wife moved in with another man. In 1968 the husband suffered a coronary thrombosis and was told by his doctor that he should not live on his own. Upon his discharge from hospital he went to live as a lodger in the house where his wife was living, paying a weekly sum. He ate some meals with the family, and the wife did the washing for the whole household. In 1972 the wife petitioned for divorce on the basis of five years' separation. The petition was dismissed on the basis that they were not living apart.

Held: (CA) The appeal would be allowed. The parties were not living with each other in the same household within the meaning of the statute, as they were not living together as husband and wife.

Commentary
Fuller is a somewhat unusual case, but it does illustrate that a husband and wife may be living apart for the purposes of the statute even if they are living under the same roof. While the wife was performing certain household tasks, she was not performing them for the husband *as a husband*, but as a lodger.

Grave Financial or Other Hardship

Under s.5 of the MCA 1973, "the respondent to a petition for divorce in which the petitioner alleges five years' separation may oppose the grant of a decree on the ground that the dissolution of the marriage will result in grave financial or other hardship to him and that it would in all the circumstances be wrong to dissolve the marriage." (See the equivalent s.47 of the CPA 2004). This provision has generated some litigation, but few attempts to oppose the divorce have been successful.

Key Principle: **The test is whether the grant of the divorce will result in grave financial hardship, not whether the respondent is in financial need**

Reiterbund v Reiterbund 1975
The parties had been living separately for some time and the wife received supplementary benefit (a means-tested benefit). The husband petitioned for divorce on the basis of five years' separation. The wife opposed the grant of the decree on the basis that she would suffer grave financial hardship because she would lose the right to a widow's pension.

Held: (CA) The grant of the decree would not result in grave financial hardship to the wife, as she would not be any worse off financially. She would still be entitled to supplementary benefit (and even if she had been entitled to a widow's pension this would simply have reduced the amount of supplementary benefit to which she was entitled).

Commentary
In this case the very fact that the wife was dependent on means-tested benefits indicates that she was not in a strong financial position, but the grant of the divorce would not have any effect on her actual income.

Key Principle: **A finding of grave financial hardship may justify a delay in the grant of the decree until acceptable proposals to mitigate that hardship have been put forward**

Le Marchant v Le Marchant 1977
The husband petitioned for divorce on the basis of five years' separation. The wife opposed the grant of a decree on the basis

that she would suffer grave financial hardship if it were granted, namely the loss of an index-linked widow's pension. The husband had sufficient assets to alleviate such hardship.

Held: (CA) The loss of such a pension was evidence of grave financial hardship within the meaning of s.5, and the appropriate course would be to dismiss the petition unless the petitioner could put forward an acceptable financial offer. Since the husband had done so (between the hearing at first instance and the appeal) the decree nisi would stand, but would not be made absolute until the offer had been implemented.

Commentary
The case shows that allegations of grave financial hardship may be more useful as a means of improving the financial provision for the respondent than as a means of preventing the divorce entirely. The court is now directed to take the loss of prospective pension rights into account when deciding what order to make under s.25 of the MCA and has greater powers to make orders relating to the pension rights of the parties.

Key Principle: **If it is not possible for the financial hardship to be ameliorated by the other spouse, it may be necessary to refuse to dissolve the marriage**

Julian v Julian 1972
The husband and wife were aged 61 and 58 respectively. The husband had left home several years earlier and when the Divorce Reform Act came into force petitioned for divorce on the basis of five years' separation. He wished to remarry. The wife, however, opposed the divorce on the basis that she would thereby lose her entitlement to a widow's pension under his police force pension scheme (which would otherwise amount to £790 per year). She was receiving £65 per month from her husband, who offered to increase this to £69 per month and to purchase her an annuity of £215 per year.

Held: Given the difference between the sum that the wife would lose upon divorce and the sum offered by the husband (part of which, the monthly allowance, would terminate upon his death), the loss of the pension would amount to grave financial hardship. In the circumstances it would be wrong to dissolve the marriage.

Commentary
The case illustrates that it is possible to mount a successful defence under s.5, although given that the court now has much greater powers to deal with the pension assets of the parties, it is open to question whether a court would reach the same decision today.

Key Principle: **It is necessary to show that the hardship alleged results from the grant of the divorce rather than the factual separation of the parties**

Rukat v Rukat 1975
The parties were both Roman Catholics. They had been separated for many years, and when the law was reformed in 1969 the husband petitioned for divorce on the basis of five years' separation. The wife opposed the grant of a decree on the basis that she would suffer grave hardship if it were granted, namely ostracism in her home country of Italy.

Held: (CA) In the circumstances, the wife had not been able to show that she would suffer grave hardship if a divorce were to be granted.

Commentary
While divorce may carry a stigma that separation does not, it is difficult to disagree with the result in this case, given that the parties had already been separated for 26 years. As Lawton L.J. commented, it was almost inevitable that her family had already realised that there was something amiss with her marriage.

Balraj v Balraj 1981
The parties had married in India in 1952. The husband had left the wife in 1963 and come to England, where in 1979 he filed a petition for divorce on the ground of five years' separation. The wife opposed the grant of a decree on the basis that she would suffer grave hardship if it were granted, namely social stigma, and that the divorce would adversely affect the marriage prospects of their child.

Held: (CA) The decree should be granted. The test under s.5 was objective, and given that the wife had already suffered stigma as a deserted wife, any increased suffering or social disadvantage resulting from the grant of a divorce in England would not constitute grave hardship and did not justify the refusal of a decree. The position of the daughter could be alleviated by the provision of a sum that could be paid to any future fiancé by way of compensation.

Commentary

Both *Rukat* and *Balraj* demonstrate the difficulty in establishing grave hardship under s.5 on the basis of the social stigma occasioned by divorce within certain cultures. The reasoning of the courts renders s.5 almost redundant. Since the parties will by definition have been living apart, the counter-argument that the respondent has already suffered social stigma as a result of the separation can be made in virtually every case to which s.5 applies. The breakdown principle endorsed in 1969 means that greater priority is given to the wishes of the spouse who wishes to bring a long-dead marriage to an end than to those of the spouse who wishes the marriage to continue, if only in name.

Decree nisi and Decree Absolute

Key Principle: **If the court does not have jurisdiction to grant a divorce, the marriage continues to exist as a matter of law**

Dennis v Dennis 2000

The wife petitioned for divorce. The husband did not defend the proceedings and a decree nisi was pronounced by the court. The wife was entitled to apply for the decree to be made absolute after six weeks had elapsed but failed to do so. An application was then made by the husband's solicitors, although as the respondent the husband was not entitled to apply for the decree to be made absolute until three months had elapsed. By mistake, the court treated the application as if it had been made by the wife and the decree was made absolute even though the three-month period had not expired. The husband then remarried.

Held: The court had had no jurisdiction to make the decree nisi absolute, and so the order was void. As a result, the husband had not been lawfully divorced, and his subsequent marriage was also void. The Human Rights Act 1998 had no effect on the outcome.

Commentary

The case provides a useful reminder of the formal two-stage process for obtaining a divorce. It also illustrates the limited scope of Article 12 of the European Convention on Human Rights: the right to marry is not an absolute one, but only the right to marry in accordance with the national laws governing the exercise of that right (which in this case had not been satisfied because the correct procedure laid down by law had not been followed). Nor does the right to marry extend to a right to divorce.

4. FAMILY ASSETS

The title of this chapter is a little misleading, in that there is no legal concept of "family assets" in English law. If it is necessary to ascertain the property rights of married or cohabiting couples, then a court will apply principles of property law. However, the topic is of considerable importance for family life (and therefore for family lawyers) for a number of reasons. First, if one member of the family becomes bankrupt or owes money to creditors, the ability of the family to keep their home may depend on whether any other family member has an interest in the property. Secondly, while the strict property interests of the parties are of little relevance in the context of divorce or dissolution, there is at present no adjustive regime for couples who are cohabiting. Thus the division of assets when a cohabiting relationship comes to an end will depend on who owns what. Thirdly, the property rights of cohabitants and other family members will be crucial in determining their rights under the Family Law Act 1996 in cases of domestic violence. Finally, if a person dies, then it will be necessary to determine what property forms part of his or her estate.

Key Principle: **Rights in the family home are to be determined by the application of orthodox property law principles**

Pettitt v Pettitt 1970
The matrimonial home had been purchased out of the proceeds of sale of a house owned by the wife, and was conveyed into the wife's sole name. The husband subsequently claimed to be entitled to a beneficial interest in the home on the basis of the work that he had done on the property.

Held: (HL) The husband was not entitled to any beneficial interest in the property. There was no common intention that he should acquire an interest in the property by making improvements to it.

Commentary
Pettitt v Pettitt put an end to the line of cases in which Lord Denning M.R. had adopted a creative interpretation of s.17 of the

Married Women's Property Act of 1882 to vary the property rights of the parties. The House of Lords held that s.17 was merely a procedural provision and did not confer on the courts any discretion to vary the property rights of the parties. The property rights of the parties in the family home were thereafter to be determined by the application of strict principles of property law.

In addition, the phrase "family assets" was also generally disapproved of as "devoid of legal meaning" by Lord Upjohn. It was accepted that a claim might be made where it had been agreed that the claimant should have an interest. But the majority were against the idea that the courts could impute an intention to the parties. At most the intention of the parties could be implied from their conduct.

The lack of any remedy in *Pettitt* did, however, lead Parliament to act, and s.37 of the Matrimonial Proceedings and Property Act 1970 accordingly provided that if a spouse made substantial improvements to the family home, he or she would thereby be entitled to a share (or increased share) in the property. In addition, the courts now have much wider powers to deal with the assets of the parties on divorce (see chapter 6). In other cases, as noted above, the strict principles of property law apply, as outlined below.

Formal Arrangements

Key Principle: **A written declaration of trust is conclusive as to the parties' shares in the property in the absence of force or fraud**

Goodman v Gallant 1986
The property in question was originally purchased in the name of the husband alone, although it was accepted that the wife had a half-share in it. After the marriage broke down, the husband conveyed the property to the wife and her new partner as beneficial joint tenants. The wife subsequently severed the joint tenancy and claimed that she was entitled to a three-quarters share.

Held: The wife was only entitled to a half-share. The declaration in the conveyance that the parties were to hold the property as beneficial joint tenants was binding, and upon severance a beneficial joint tenancy was converted into a tenancy in common in equal shares.

Commentary

Section 53(1)(b) of the Law of Property Act 1925 requires a declaration of trust to be evidenced in writing. The strict adherence to the principle that a written declaration of trust is binding even if it does not reflect the contribution that each party has made to the property may offer an incentive to the party who has contributed less to secure such a declaration. More fundamentally, it offers the incentive of certainty to both parties, and judges have urged conveyancers to ensure that their clients record how the beneficial interest in the property is to be held.

Key Principle: **A valid contract between cohabitants regulating their finances will be upheld by the courts**

Sutton v Mishcon de Reya 2003

A Swedish businessman and an air steward planned to enter into a master-slave relationship in which the former was subjugated to the latter and conferred on him a substantial proportion of his property. They sought legal advice to put this on a contractual footing and were advised that such an agreement might not be enforceable. In the event, the relationship did not develop and the intended "slave" sought the return of his property. Mishcon de Reya (a firm of solicitors) advised the intended "master" to negotiate a settlement, given the doubts as to whether the court would enforce the cohabitation deed. The latter later brought an action in negligence against both of the firms that he had consulted.

Held: The claim would be struck out. A contract along these lines would not have been upheld. Either the master-slave dimension was a fantasy, in which case there was no intention to create legal relations, or it was a reality, in which case the contract was vitiated for undue influence. In addition, such a contract was void as contrary to public policy as a contract for sexual services.

Commentary

For family lawyers, the main interest of the case lies in the distinction that Hart J drew between a contract for sexual relations (such as that between Sutton and Staal) and a contract between cohabiting parties. Some twentieth-century cases had suggested that a contract between cohabitants would be void as contrary to public policy, on the basis that such contracts would be encouraging sexual relationships outside marriage. Hart J., by contrast, held that while a contract for sexual relations would be void, a contract between cohabitants dealing with their finances—assuming the basic contractual requirements had been fulfilled—would be valid. *Sutton* has been welcomed as confirmation that a contract between cohabitants will be enforced by the courts, although as the point was *obiter* the Law Commission have rightly suggested that express statutory provision to this effect is necessary to put the matter beyond doubt. Whether cohabiting couples will choose to regulate their financial affairs by means of a contract remains to be seen.

Resulting Trusts

Key Principle: **A financial contribution to the purchase price of a property raises a presumption that the contributor is entitled to a proportionate share in the property**

Cowcher v Cowcher 1972
The matrimonial home was purchased in the name of the husband, who paid the purchase price of £12,000 by means of a £1,000 cash deposit, a £3,000 overdraft and a £8,000 mortgage. At the same time the wife paid approximately £1,000 to the husband and £3,000 to his business. She later paid some of the mortgage instalments.

Held: The wife was entitled to a one-third share, reflecting her initial financial contributions to the purchase price. However, the payment of mortgage instalments did not affect the beneficial interests of the parties.

Commentary
The principle that property belongs (or "results to") the person who paid for it is of long standing (see e.g. *Dyer v Dyer* (1788) 2 Cox Eq Cas 92; 30 E.R. 42). As this case shows, the principle also extends to a contribution to the purchase price: the contributor is entitled to a proportionate share in the property unless the contribution was made with the intention of benefiting the legal owner. It also illustrates that only contributions made at the time of the purchase give rise to a resulting trust, a point reinforced by the next case.

Key Principle: **Interests under a resulting trust crystallise at the time the property is purchased**

Curley v Parkes 2004
The male cohabitant claimed an interest in his partner's house under a resulting trust, based on his payment of a sum equal to the deposit after the property had been acquired and on his payment of the removal expenses and solicitors' fees.

Held: (CA) None of these contributions gave rise to a resulting trust, as none constituted a contribution to the purchase price.

Commentary
The restrictive nature of this decision can be seen as an attempt by the courts to return to a more orthodox conception of the resulting trust. The court stressed that contributions made after the property has been acquired cannot give rise to a resulting trust, which is determined once and for all at the time of the acquisition of the property. Thus the fact that the claimant had also made payments to the joint account out of which the mortgage repayments had been made was irrelevant for these purposes. The need for the courts to find a resulting trust on the basis of wider contributions to the property has largely been obviated by the expansion of the constructive trust (although it should be noted that in this case a claim on the basis of a common intention had been dismissed by the lower court).

Key Principle: **If the claimant can rely on a resulting trust, the fact that the property was conveyed into the other's name for an illegal purpose is irrelevant**

Tinsley v Milligan
A lesbian couple purchased a house together, but it was conveyed into the name of one of them alone, to enable the other to claim benefits. When they split up, the one whose name was on the title claimed that she was solely entitled to the property. The defendant counter-claimed on the basis that the property was held in equal shares.

Held: (HL) The defendant had established a half-share in the property under a resulting trust by virtue of her contributions to the property and there was therefore no need to rely on the illegal purpose.

Commentary

There are numerous examples in the case-law of couples seeking to set up arrangements to conceal the interest that one of them enjoys in the property—whether to prevent claims against that property or, as here, to make fraudulent benefits claims. The question for the court in such cases is how far the illegality of the arrangement should affect the rights of the parties. The long-standing principle of the court is *ex dolo malo non oritur actio*: the court will not lend its aid to a man who founds his cause of action upon an immoral act. In *Tinsley v Milligan* it was held that as the contributions of the defendant raised the presumption that she had an interest under a resulting trust she did not need to rely on the illegality.

Key Principle: **A transfer from a father to his child raises a presumption of advancement but this presumption can today be rebutted by relatively slight evidence**

McGrath v Wallis 1995

A father and son purchased a house together. The father contributed 70 per cent of the purchase price, the balance being provided by a mortgage taken out by the son. The property was conveyed into the son's sole name. A declaration of trust was drawn up but never executed, and the father later died without making a will. His daughter then claimed an interest in the home.

Held: (CA) The evidence in this case was sufficient to rebut the presumption of advancement (i.e. the presumption that a gift was intended): the property had been conveyed into the son's name because he was responsible for the mortgage, and the drafting of the trust deed showed that the father intended to retain an interest in the property. Moreover, no reason had been suggested as to why the father might wish to divest himself of all interest in the property. At the time of his death he had had a 70 per cent share in the property under a resulting trust, reflecting his contribution to the purchase price, and this interest formed part of his estate.

Commentary
The case illustrates the ease with which the presumption of advancement may be rebutted today. It is likely that even slighter evidence would be sufficient to rebut the presumption that a transfer from a husband to his wife, or a fiancé to his fiancée, was intended as a gift. However, the presumption of advancement may pose a problem if the transfer from the father, husband or fiancé was motivated by an illegal purpose: in such a case evidence of that illegal purpose would be necessary to rebut the presumption of advancement.

Constructive Trusts

Establishing a Constructive Trust

Key Principle: **A trust will arise if the owner of the property has induced the claimant to rely to his or her detriment in the expectation of thereby acquiring an interest in the property**

Gissing v Gissing 1971
The matrimonial home was purchased (for £2,695) in the name of the husband, who also assumed responsibility for the mortgage. The wife paid £220 for furnishings and the laying of a lawn: she also bought her own clothes and those of their son. After their marriage ended she claimed an interest in the property.

Held: (HL) The wife was not entitled to an interest in the property.

Commentary
If the facts of *Gissing v Gissing* were to be repeated today, the outcome would be very different, not because the law applied in that case has changed but, as noted above, because the courts now have much wider powers to deal with the assets of the parties on divorce. The importance of the decision lies in the test laid down by Lord Diplock, which laid the foundation for the subsequent development of the law of implied trusts. Lord Diplock stated: that "[a] resulting, implied, or constructive trust—and it is unnecessary for present purposes to distinguish between [them]— is created by a transaction between the trustee and the cestui que trust . . . whenever the trustee has so conducted himself that it would be inequitable to allow him to deny to the cestui que trust a

beneficial interest in the land acquired. And he will be held so to have conducted himself if by his words or conduct he has induced the cestui que trust to act to his own detriment in the reasonable belief that by so acting he was acquiring a beneficial interest in the land." (p.904). While Lord Diplock here conflated resulting, implied, and constructive trusts—distinctions with which later courts have struggled—it is now accepted that the circumstances he outlined will give rise to a constructive trust, as explained in the next case.

Key Principle: **A constructive trust arises if the claimant has relied to his or her detriment upon a common intention that the beneficial interest should be shared or if such a common intention can be inferred from the claimant's contributions to the purchase price**

Lloyds Bank v Rosset 1990

The property in question was purchased as the matrimonial home by the husband with money from his family trust. The trustees insisted on the property being registered in the husband's sole name. The property was in a semi-derelict condition, and the wife supervised the builders and carried out decorating work. However, she made no financial contribution to the purchase price or to the cost of the materials. The husband sought a loan from Lloyds Bank to finance the costs of renovating the property. When that loan was not repaid, the bank sought possession of the property.

Held: (HL) There was no common intention that the wife should have an interest in the property, and therefore she was not entitled to any such interest.

Commentary

As with *Gissing v Gissing*, the importance of the case lies not so much in the actual decision of the court but in the exposition of the circumstances in which a constructive trust would arise. According to Lord Bridge: "The first question is whether . . . there has at any time prior to acquisition, or exceptionally at some later date, been any agreement, arrangement or understanding reached between them that the property is to be shared beneficially. . . . Once a finding to this effect is made it will only be necessary for the partner asserting a claim to a beneficial interest against the partner entitled to the legal estate to show that he or she has acted to his or her detriment or significantly altered his or her legal position in reliance on the agreement in order to give rise to a constructive trust or proprietary estoppel." In the absence of such an agreement, "direct contributions to the purchase price . . . whether initially or by payment of mortgage instalments, will readily justify the inference necessary to the creation of a constructive trust. But, as I read the authorities, it is extremely doubtful whether anything else will do." (pp.132–3). The first part of this echoes Lord Diplock's words in *Gissing v Gissing* and reflected the consensus that some form of understanding on which a claimant had relied to his or detriment was necessary to the creation of a constructive trust. The second part—the idea that intentions could be inferred from direct contributions—was more problematic, since it raised the question of the relationship between the constructive trust and the resulting trust, a debate that continues to this day. It poses particular problems in deciding how the shares of the parties should be quantified in the absence of any discussions between the parties (contrast *Midland Bank v Cooke* and *Oxley v Hiscock*).

Common Intention Followed by Detrimental Reliance

Key Principle: **The relevant intentions of the parties are those that are expressed rather than their subjective intentions.**

Eves v Eves 1975
Stuart and Janet Eves began to live together in a house owned by the former. They then moved into a new house, but he told Janet that as she was under the age of 21 it would have to be in his name alone. He provided the purchase money, but she subsequently undertook a considerable amount of work on the property—stripping wallpaper, demolishing a garden shed, and breaking up concrete. After they split up she claimed an interest in the property.

Held: (CA) She was entitled to a one-quarter interest in the property under a constructive trust.

Commentary
From one perspective there would seem to be no common intention in *Eves v Eves*: Stuart Eves was simply providing an excuse as to

why his partner's name would not appear on the legal title. Yet his excuse led her to believe that she was to have *some* interest in the property. The court focused on how his words would have been understood rather than on his subjective intentions. In *Lloyds Bank v Rosset* (above), Lord Bridge cited *Eves v Eves* and the later case of *Grant v Edwards* [1986] Ch. 638 (in which the legal owner had told his cohabitant that her name could not appear on the title as it might prejudice her in divorce proceedings) as "outstanding examples" of what he meant by "agreement". Of course, not every excuse will give rise to an expectation of an interest in the property. The excuses in *Eves* and *Grant* could be construed as acknowledgements by the man that his cohabitant did have an interest in the property (else why would an excuse regarding the legal title be necessary?) By contrast, if the legal owner provided an excuse implying that the other party had no interest in the property, the latter would not be able to claim an interest. The other significant aspect of *Eves* is the fact that the court decided that Janet Eves had relied to her detriment in the expectation of an interest in the property by carrying out work on the property, work that it felt she would not have done if she had not been under the impression that she had or would have an interest in the property.

Key Principle: **Detrimental reliance may be established by unpaid work in a partner's business**

Hammond v Mitchell 1991

A second-hand car dealer met a Bunny Girl and they began to live together. He bought a bungalow in his sole name, telling his partner that this was due to tax reasons and assuring her that "when we are married it will be half yours anyway and I'll always look after you." In fact, they did not marry. She assisted him in his business as well as caring for their two children. When their relationship broke down she claimed an interest in the bungalow.

Held: She was entitled to a half share under a constructive trust, based on the express discussions between the parties and the fact that she had relied to her detriment on those discussions.

Commentary
The express discussions took the form of excuses rather than a promise, but as *Eves v Eves* (above) illustrates, it is the effect of the discussions rather than the subjective intentions of the parties that is important. With regard to the factors relied upon to establish detrimental reliance, it is interesting to note that the court referred to Ms Mitchell's contribution as mother, helper and unpaid assistant—the implication being that she did work that would normally be remunerated in addition to domestic work that would normally not be remunerated. There is an assumption that work that would not normally be remunerated is performed solely out of love and affection and not in the expectation of an interest in the property. If she had not assisted in his business ventures, it is unlikely that the court would have awarded her an interest in the property.

Key Principle: **Detrimental reliance may be established by work that is perceived as having a commercial value**

Cox v Jones 2004
The relationship between Miss Cox and Mr Jones began in 1997 but they retained separate homes. In 1999 a house in the country was purchased in the name of Mr Jones. Miss Cox played a role in the purchase by looking for suitable properties and then helping with the refurbishment of the property purchased.

Held: There had been an express common intention that Miss Cox was to have an interest in the property, upon which she had relied to her detriment by contributing her time and money to the refurbishment of the property in question. In the circumstances she should be awarded a 25 per cent share.

Commentary
There had been a dispute between the parties as to whether there had ever been any discussions relating to the ownership of the property, but the judge preferred the evidence of Miss Cox, partly because, as he suggested, it would be natural for there to be conversations about ownership in the context of the relationship, especially given that the parties were at the time intending to marry. (Although one might note that if it was common for couples to discuss their property rights many of the cases in this chapter might

have been avoided.) Even more interesting is his suggestion that Miss Cox's work had a commercial value, on the basis that in devoting time to the house "she was doing something that either Mr Jones would have had to have done himself (but which he had insufficient time to do) or it would have to have been done by a professional (who would have charged for it)." (para.73). Of course, precisely the same arguments could be made in respect of domestic work, but as yet the courts have not been willing to accept that domestic contributions are an indication of detrimental reliance.

Inferring a Common Intention

Key Principle: **No common intention can be inferred from domestic contributions**

Burns v Burns 1984

The couple began to live together in 1961. They were unable to marry, as Mr Burns was already married, but his cohabitant took his name. In 1963 Mr Burns purchased a property in his own name, with the assistance of a mortgage. "Mrs" Burns looked after their two children. In 1975 she began working as a driving instructor and used her earnings to pay bills and buy items for the house. In 1980 she left Mr Burns and claimed an interest in the property.

Held: (CA) There had been no express common intention that she should acquire an interest in the property, and no such intention could be inferred as she had not made a substantial financial contribution to the purchase of the house.

Commentary

Burns v Burns epitomises the problems with this area of the law: the fact that the parties had been together for almost twenty years, during which time Mrs Burns had brought up their children, looked after the home, and contributed, albeit in a modest way, to the family finances, was irrelevant to the question of whether she enjoyed any interest in the property that had been her home for so long. Had the parties been married, such contributions would have resulted in a generous award (see chapter 6). Had she made even a small direct contribution to the purchase price her other contributions could have been taken into account under existing property law rules (see e.g. *Midland Bank v Cooke* below). In the circumstances, she was left with nothing. The court noted that any remedy was a matter for Parliament. Over twenty years later, however, no reform has as yet been enacted.

Key Principle: **Making improvements to the property does not by itself give rise to an interest in the property**

Thomas v Fuller-Brown 1988

An unemployed builder carried out extensive work on his partner's property. He built a two-storey extension, installed a new staircase, rebuilt the kitchen and laid a new driveway, as well as replastering and redecorating the house. After the relationship broke down he claimed an interest in the property.

Held: (CA) He had no interest in the property. The mere fact that one person expends money or effort on another's property does not by itself entitle that person to an interest in the property.

Commentary

The case reaffirmed the long-standing principle that the owner of a property retains the benefit of any improvements made to that property. Matters would have been very different for Mr Thomas had he been able to substantiate his claim that his partner had promised him an interest in the property (or, alternatively, that she had promised to marry him). The case is also of interest because of the disparaging remarks directed by the judge at Mr Thomas, who was described as a "kept man" doing "the odd job here and there." (p.246). Clearly, the judiciary have certain expectations as to what the role of a man is, which are just as prescriptive as their expectations as to what a woman can be expected to do.

Key Principle: **A common intention to share the beneficial interest may be inferred from an indirect contribution that is referable to the purchase price**

Le Foe v Le Foe and Woolwich plc 2001

The wife paid for day-to-day domestic expenditure while the husband made the repayments under the mortgage. After she inherited a sum of money in 1995 she paid some of the mortgage arrears and also paid off a second mortgage that had been taken out.

Held: In the circumstances a common intention to share the property could be inferred from her contributions. The wife would be awarded a 50 per cent share.

Commentary
The facts of the case are more complex than the above summary might suggest, since there was also a dispute with a third party (which was why the spouses needed to rely on the principles of property law). The key point of interest of the case lies in the suggestion that a common intention may be inferred from indirect contributions to the purchase price. Lord Bridge in *Lloyds Bank v Rosset* had suggested that only direct contributions to the purchase price would justify the inference of a common intention, but the earlier authorities of *Gissing v Gissing* and *Burns v Burns* had accepted that contributions to the general household expenses might be sufficient to indicate that there was a common intention that the person paying them should have an interest in the property, assuming that the contribution was substantial and actually enabled the other party to make the mortgage repayments. Since Lord Bridge preceded his remarks in *Rosset* with the words "as I understand the authorities", it is arguable that he misunderstood, rather than intended to change, the law as it then was. The approach adopted in *Le Foe* is preferable both on the grounds of precedent and on considerations of policy. As the judge recognised, it was an arbitrary allocation of responsibility that the husband paid the mortgage and the wife paid for other expenditure. However, *Le Foe* has not been specifically endorsed by either the Court of Appeal or the House of Lords, and the point thus remains a matter of debate.

———————

Key Principle: **Even a direct financial contribution might not give rise to an interest in the property if it does not justify the inference of a common intention that the beneficial ownership is to be shared**

Lightfoot v Lightfoot-Brown 2005
The facts of the case were unusual. The parties had divorced, but both remained in the former matrimonial home. Mr Lightfoot had previously transferred his interest in the home to his former wife but had paid further sums while he was living there, including mortgage repayments to the value of £24,000 and a further lump sum of £41,000.

Held: (CA) In the circumstances there was no common intention that Mr Lightfoot should acquire an interest in the property by virtue of the financial payments that he had made. The mortgage repayments were "partly a substitute for the maintenance payments due under the consent order and partly as an acknowledgment that Mr Lightfoot was continuing to live in a house that was no longer his own." (para.9). In addition, his ex-wife had been unaware of the lump sum payment.

Commentary

While the decision may appear somewhat harsh, it is undoubtedly correct and does provide a useful reminder that a financial contribution does not automatically give rise to an interest in the property but is merely evidence from which the necessary common intention can be inferred. Given that the payment of the mortgage was explicable on other grounds, and that his ex-wife had been unaware of the lump sum payment, no common intention that he was to have an interest in the property could be inferred from the contributions.

Quantifying the Interest under a Constructive Trust

Key Principle: **If there is a common intention that the claimant is to have a specific share, then the court will give effect to it**

Crossley v Crossley 2005

The disputed property had been purchased in 1988 under the right-to-buy scheme. It was conveyed into the names of the claimant, her husband, and the defendant, who was their son. The parents paid the deposit, with the balance of the purchase price being raised by way of a mortgage for which all three assumed joint and several liability. The husband died in 1997. A dispute subsequently arose as to the ownership of the property.

Held: (CA) There was a common intention that the son was to have an interest in the property, and he had relied on this to his detriment by assuming joint and several liability under the mortgage. There was also a common intention that the beneficial interests of the three legal owners should be held under a joint tenancy, and the court would give effect to this intention.

Commentary

The case-law supplies few examples of express discussions between litigating parties as to whether each is to have a beneficial interest in the property (perhaps because those who have entered into clear agreements do not litigate) and fewer still of express discussions between such persons as to their respective shares. In the circumstances of this case, however, an intention to hold the beneficial interest as joint tenants was inferred from the facts that the parties were *legal* joint tenants and had all assumed joint and several liability under the mortgage, as well as from the parents' assurances that the son would have the property when they died, which was suggestive of the right to survivorship inherent in a joint tenancy.

Key Principle: **The shares of the parties under a constructive trust are not defined by their respective financial contributions, even where there is no agreement between the parties**

Midland Bank v Cooke 1995

The parties had married in 1971. Mr Cooke's parents had given them a sum of money as a wedding present, which was used to pay the deposit on their house. Mrs Cooke was therefore credited by the court with a notional contribution of 6.75 per cent towards the purchase price, representing her half of the wedding gift.

Held: (CA) Mrs Cooke was entitled to a 50 per cent share in the property under a constructive trust, despite the evidence that the parties had never discussed or even thought about their respective shares.

Commentary

Cooke is a case that arouses strong feelings: beloved by family lawyers on account of the fact that the court took into account the whole family history of the parties in deciding what shares each enjoyed in the property, and disliked by property lawyers for precisely the same reason. Before *Cooke* it had been assumed that, in the absence of any express discussions between the parties, their shares would be determined according to their financial contributions. Indeed, at first instance Mrs Cooke had been awarded a 6.75 per cent share in the property. The innovation of the Court of Appeal was to hold that once Mrs Cooke had established that she had a share in the property by virtue of her financial contributions, the extent of that share would be determined by the court in a broad-brush fashion.

Cooke is a perfect illustration of the tension between fairness and certainty in this area of the law. On the one hand, it is easy to agree that, in the light of their behaviour over the twenty years of their marriage, the Cookes probably did intend to share the property equally. But once the shares of the parties are no longer determined by the expressed intentions of the parties or their respective contributions, then how is the court to decide what shares are appropriate in any given case? A somewhat different answer to this question was provided by the next case.

Key Principle: **The shares of the parties under a constructive trust will be ascertained according to what is fair in the light of the whole course of dealing between the parties**

Oxley v Hiscock 2004

The parties initially began to live together in a rented property occupied by Mrs Oxley as a secure tenant. She then exercised her right to buy the property under the statutory scheme, the money for this purpose (£25,200) being provided by Mr Hiscock. When this house was sold, the proceeds (some £61,500) were put towards the purchase of a new home. This was registered in the name of Mr Hiscock alone, and the balance of the purchase price was provided by a £30,000 mortgage and a further contribution of £35,500 from Mr Hiscock. Mrs Oxley was advised to take steps to clarify her beneficial interest in the property, but told the solicitor that she felt that she knew Mr Hiscock "well enough not to need written legal protection in this matter." The relationship between the parties subsequently broke down, and she applied for a declaration as to their respective beneficial interests.

Held: (CA) Mrs Oxley should be credited with a contribution of £36,300 (the balance of the proceeds of sale of the first house) plus half of the £30,000 mortgage. A common intention that each should have a beneficial interest in the property could therefore be inferred from their respective financial contributions. This gave rise to a constructive trust. In ascertaining the shares of the parties, in the absence of specific evidence regarding their intentions, each would be entitled to that share which the court considered fair, having regard to the whole course of dealing between the parties. In the circumstances Mr Hiscock was entitled to a 60 per cent share and Mrs Oxley to a 40 per cent share.

Commentary

The principle articulated by Chadwick L.J.—that the shares of the parties should be ascertained according to what is fair—may appear to echo the broad-brush approach to quantification of *Midland Bank v Cooke*, but there are important differences between the two. The quantification of shares in *Cooke* was based on the court's view as to what the parties would have intended had they thought about the issue, while in *Oxley v Hiscock* the court adopted the view that the parties must have intended that the issue would be resolved when their relationship came to an end, and that at that point the court would ascertain their shares according to what is then fair. The more substantial difference between the two lies in the range of factors taken into account by the court. In *Oxley* the only factor taken into account in deciding what shares would be "fair" was the proportion that each party had contributed to the purchase price. Mr Hiscock's financial contributions amounted to 59.6 per cent of the purchase price and he was awarded a 60 per cent share in the property. This illustrates the problem in resorting to vague statements about "fairness": different judges may have very different conceptions of what is fair (contrast the interpretation of "fairness" in the context of the reallocation of assets on divorce in chapter 6). The broader range of factors taken into account in *Cooke* were simply not mentioned in *Oxley*.

Yet the principles to be derived from *Cooke* and *Oxley* can be reconciled by saying that the shares of the parties are not determined by a strict calculation of their respective financial contributions, but in deciding what is fair each party's financial contribution is an important consideration. Subsequent cases such as *Stack v Dowden* [2005] EWCA Civ 857 and *Supperstone v Hurst* [2005] EWHC 1309 reflect this: in these cases financial considerations played an important but not a decisive role in determining the shares of the parties.

Estoppel

Proprietary estoppel offers an alternative route to claiming a beneficial interest in the family home, although it is subject to many of the same limitations as the constructive trust.

Key Principle: **Vague assurances of financial security do not give rise to legally enforceable rights**

Coombes v Smith 1986
The relationship between the parties began when both were married to third parties. When she became pregnant, Mrs

Coombes moved into a house bought by Mr Smith. Mr Smith paid the bills and the mortgage, while Mrs Coombes decorated the property and improved the garden. Mr Smith refused to put the house in joint names but assured Mrs Coombes that he would always provide for her. When the relationship came to an end she claimed an interest in the property.

Held: The plaintiff was not entitled to any interest in the property, as she had not relied to her detriment on any belief that she had a legal right to occupy the house that would persist beyond the duration of the relationship.

Commentary
The case illustrates how the strict rules of property law may be too blunt to deal with the realities of family life. The vague assurances of financial support made by the defendant did not give rise to any enforceable legal rights: the court held that the claimant's belief that the defendant would always provide her with a roof over her head was something quite different from a belief that she had a legal right to remain there against his wishes. Even if the court had been willing to infer a promise that she could remain in the property, there was still the problem that her actions did not appear to be referable to any such expectation. Becoming pregnant, leaving her husband, and looking after their child, were not held to constitute detrimental reliance.

The Minimum Equity to do Justice

Key Principle: **The court may require an imperfect gift to be perfected**

Pascoe v Turner 1979
The parties began to live together as husband and wife in a house owned by Mr Pascoe. When he subsequently began a relationship with another woman, he told Mrs Turner that she could have the house and its contents, and she spent some of her modest capital on improvements. However, he took no steps to transfer the property to her formally and later requested her to leave the premises.

Held: (CA) The fact that the defendant had expended money on the property in reliance on the plaintiff's promise that it was her own gave rise to an estoppel. In the circumstances the minimum equity to do justice was to require the plaintiff to honour his promise by transferring the property to the defendant.

Commentary

In this case the minimum equity to do justice required the fulfilment of the plaintiff's promise, largely because of the need to secure her security of tenure as against a man who had, in the judge's words, tried to evict her "with a ruthless disregard of the obligations binding upon conscience." (p.438).

Key Principle: **The minimum equity to do justice may expire**

Sledmore v Dalby 1996

Mr and Mrs Sledmore purchased the property in dispute in 1962. In 1965 Mr Dalby married their daughter and moved in. Mr Sledmore indicated his intention to give the property to the young couple and Mr Dalby carried out substantial work on the property in reliance upon this. Mr Sledmore died in 1980 and his daughter in 1983. Mr Dalby continued to occupy the property rent-free. In 1990 Mrs Sledmore sought possession of the property.

Held: (CA) An order for possession would be made. While the facts of the case raised an estoppel, the equity had been satisfied by allowing the defendant to occupy the property rent-free for many years. In the circumstances it would not be inequitable for the plaintiff to enforce her legal right to possession.

Commentary

At the other end of the scale from *Pascoe v Turner*, the case illustrates that the mere fact that an estoppel has been established does not automatically mean that a remedy is appropriate. As the court noted, the minimum equity to do justice will not always require the expectations of the parties to be fulfilled. In the circumstances, Mr Dalby had enjoyed a benefit that was commensurate with the limited improvements that he had made to the property and no further remedy was necessary.

Key Principle: **There must be proportionality between the expectation and the detriment**

Jennings v Rice 2002
Mr Jennings was employed by Mrs Royle as part-time gardener from 1970. He ran errands for her, and carried out minor maintenance work. From the 1980s she did not pay him but told him that she would leave all her property to him. From 1993 he slept on a sofa in her house after a burglary. Mrs Royle died without making a will. At the time of her death the house was valued at £420,000 and the estate was worth £1.285m.

Held: The necessary elements of an estoppel—representation, detrimental reliance and unconscionability (in her not making a will) were all established. Jennings was awarded £200,000, which reflected the cost of providing full-time nursing care.

Commentary
The interest of the case lies in the court's approach to quantification. Robert Walker L.J. suggested that if there had been "assurances with a consensual character falling not far short of an enforceable contract" (para.45), then it might be appropriate for the expectations of the claimant to be fulfilled. If the expectations of the claimant were less precisely defined, then "their specific vindication cannot be the appropriate test." (para.47). Thus, "if the claimant's expectations are uncertain, or extravagant, or out of all proportion to the detriment which the claimant has suffered, the court can and should recognise that the claimant's equity should be satisfied in another (and generally more limited) way." (para.50). Proportionality was the key factor: since the value of the work done by Mr Jennings fell far short of the value of what he had been promised it was more appropriate to provide an award that reflected the value of what he had done. Two wider points should be made. First, there does seem to be a rather snobbish assumption that the house was not "suitable" for Mr Jennings: the court opined that he needed only £150,000 to purchase a property. Secondly, given that house prices have risen faster than earnings in recent years, the value of the work done by *any* claimant will probably fall far short of the value of any promised property. In the light of this, will it ever be "proportionate" to award a claimant the promised property?

Personal Property

Key Principle: **No formalities are required to create a trust over personal property**

Paul v Constance 1977
The case involved a dispute between the legal widow of Mr Constance and Mrs Paul, who had been living with him until his death, and concerned the ownership of a bank account in his name. He had frequently told Mrs Paul "this money is as much yours as mine" and had authorised her to withdraw funds from it. Their bingo winnings had been paid into the account, as well as the damages he had received on account of an injury at work.

Held: (CA) The bank account was held on trust for Mrs Paul and the estate of Mr Constance in equal shares.

Commentary
The case illustrates the ease with which a trust may be created in relation to personal property. Such a trust—unlike one relating to land—does not need to be evidenced in writing. The court acknowledged that the evidence that Mr Constance intended to create a trust was relatively slight but, bearing in mind the fact that the parties were unsophisticated people who knew nothing of the law and the fact that he had repeated his assurance to Mrs Paul on a number of occasions, held that it was justified in finding that a trust had been created.

Key Principle: **If both parties pay money into a bank account, the fund will be owned by both parties jointly, as will any investments made with money from the account**

Jones v Maynard 1951
The bank account was in the sole name of the husband, but both parties paid their income and earnings into it, and withdrew funds from it. The payments made by the husband were considerably larger than those made by the wife, and from time to time he withdrew funds to invest.

Held: The money in the account was jointly owned, and the wife was accordingly entitled to half of the money in the account and half of the value of the investments.

Commentary
In this case the judge was unwilling to unpick the respective contributions of the parties to a fund representing their pooled income, holding that to do so would be inconsistent with the purpose of a common pool. It is perhaps to be regretted that this robust approach to family finances is not adopted in the case of the common home.

Key Principle: **There is a presumption that an engagement ring is an absolute gift**

Cox v Jones 2005
In addition to the dispute over the ownership of the country home (see above), the parties gave conflicting accounts as to whether the engagement ring was intended as a conditional gift or not.

Held: The engagement ring was intended as an absolute gift, and there was no understanding that it would be returned if the relationship came to an end.

Commentary
The case breaks no new ground, being simply an application of the statutory presumption in s.3(2) of the Law Reform (Miscellaneous Provisions) Act 1970. The reasons that the judge gave for preferring the evidence of Miss Cox are, however, worthy of note: he opined that it was implausible that Mr Jones would have told her that the ring was a conditional gift in the context of a romantic holiday. This illustrates that the party giving an engagement ring will have a hard task persuading the court that the gift was conditional, since the context is, almost by definition, a romantic one.

5. PROTECTION FROM VIOLENCE AND HARASSMENT

The law in this area was revised and consolidated by Part IV of the Family Law Act 1996 (FLA 1996), which governs the circumstances in which a non-molestation order (preventing the respondent from molesting the applicant) or an occupation order (regulating the occupation of the family home) may be granted to an associated person (as defined by s.62 of the Act). The legislative scheme is lengthy and complex, and students are advised to consult the provisions of the Act, which have recently been amended by the Domestic Violence, Crimes and Victims Act 2004 (DVCVA 2004). In addition, anyone suffering harassment may invoke the provisions of the Protection from Harassment Act 1997 (PHA 1997), and this has often been used in a family context.

Non-Molestation Orders

Who Can Apply?

Key Principle: **The categories of "associated persons" should be construed purposively**

G v F (Non-Molestation Order: Jurisdiction) 2000

The relationship of the parties began in 1996. They maintained separate homes, but often stayed at each other's homes. At one point they planned to marry, and for a brief period they lived together in her flat. They also operated a joint bank account. After a number of violent incidents the applicant applied for a non-molestation order against the respondent. This was initially denied on the basis that the parties were not "associated persons".

Held: In the light of the fact that the 1996 Act was intended to provide swift and accessible protection to victims of domestic violence, a narrow interpretation of "associated persons" was not appropriate. There was evidence on which the justices could and should have found that the parties were former cohabitants and therefore associated persons.

Commentary
The facts of the case would now be covered by s.62(3)(ea) of the
FLA 1996, as amended by the DVCVA 2004, which added persons
who "have or have had an intimate personal relationship with
each other which is or was of significant duration" to the list of
associated persons. However, the case remains important in
illustrating the willingness of the courts to adopt a generous
construction of the legislation and to avoid disputes over jurisdiction in borderline cases (which may be particularly important in
the light of the potentially broad scope of the new category in
s.62(3)(ea)).

What Counts as "Molestation"?

Key Principle: **A campaign of harassment may constitute
"molestation" even if no violence is used or threatened**

Horner v Horner 1982
The husband had been violent to his wife, who obtained an
order restraining him from using or threatening to use violence
against her. He then began a campaign of harassment against
her: accosting her in public, handing her threatening letters,
repeatedly telephoning the school where she taught to make
disparaging remarks about her to anyone who answered, and
displaying scurrilous posters about her on the railings outside
the school. The wife applied for an injunction restraining him
from molesting her under the Domestic Violence and Matrimonial Proceedings Act 1976 (the predecessor of the FLA 1996).

Held: (CA) The injunction would be granted. The term
"molesting" was not confined to acts of violence but applied "to
any conduct which can properly be regarded as such a degree of
harassment as to call for the intervention of the court." (p.93).

Commentary
The court in this case approved a wide definition of molestation.
The scope of the legislation thus extends far beyond protection
from violence to include more insidious forms of harassment.
However, as the next case illustrates, the fact that one party finds
the other's conduct irritating or intrusive is not necessarily sufficient to justify the grant of a non-molestation order.

Key Principle: **Conduct that is merely irritating or embarrassing will not necessarily constitute molestation**

C v C (Non-Molestation Order: Jurisdiction) 1998

Articles were published in the *People* and the *Daily Mail* giving details of the husband's misbehaviour during the parties' marriage. The husband sought a non-molestation order to prevent the wife from making any further revelations.

Held: The wife's conduct did not constitute molestation and accordingly such an order could not be granted.

Commentary

The case illustrates that the broad definition of "molestation" adopted by the courts does have its limits. Sir Stephen Brown P noted that the term "implies some quite deliberate conduct which is aimed at a high degree of harassment of the other party, so as to justify the intervention of the court." (p.73). Just as the court in *G v F (Non-Molestation Order: Jurisdiction)* justified its broad interpretation of the term "cohabitant" by reference to the purpose of the legislation in dealing with domestic violence, so here a narrower interpretation of "molestation" was justified on the same basis. The wife's revelations might embarrass the husband or even damage his reputation, but conduct that amounted to no more than an invasion of one party's privacy did not constitute molestation.

When Should an Order be made?

Key Principle: **A non-molestation order should not be made to prohibit conduct over which the perpetrator has no control**

Banks v Banks 1999

The elderly husband applied for a non-molestation order against his 79-year-old wife, who suffered from a manic-depressive disorder and was verbally and physically aggressive.

Held: The application was refused. It would be wrong to make a non-molestation order as the wife's abusive conduct was a symptom of her illness and was not something over which she was capable of exercising control. In the circumstances, an order prohibiting such conduct would have no impact.

Commentary
This sad case illustrates the fact that the court has a discretion whether or not to grant a non-molestation order (under s. 42 of the FLA 1996). The fact that one party is abusive towards the other will usually be sufficient justification to grant such an order, but this is not automatic.

Occupation Orders

When will an Order be Granted?

Key Principle: **An occupation order must be made if the applicant (or any relevant child) would suffer significant harm that is attributable to the respondent's conduct if the order were not made and this harm is greater than the harm likely to be suffered by the respondent (or any relevant child) if the order is made (see s.33(7) of the FLA 1996)**

B v B (Occupation Order) 1999
The wife left her husband because of his violence. She and her baby were rehoused in temporary bed-and-breakfast accommodation, while her husband remained in the former matrimonial home—provided by the council—with his six-year-old son from a previous relationship. The wife applied for an occupation order.

Held: (CA) The harm that would be suffered by the boy in having to move home—and school—would be greater than that suffered by the baby in living in bed-and-breakfast accommodation. The balance of harm thus tipped against making an occupation order.

Commentary
The case illustrates that the application of the balance of harm test will not always result in the perpetrator having to leave the home, although the case did have a number of unusual features. If an occupation order had been made, the husband would have found it more difficult to obtain alternative accommodation from the council than the wife had done, since he would have been judged to be "intentionally homeless" on account of his violence. This would have meant that his son would have had to move to a different school. Another key factor was the relative ages of the two children: the judge opined that the essential security of the

baby lay with her mother, but that the boy was much more dependent on his day-to-day support systems such as home and school. Butler-Sloss L.J. was keen to stress that the court had no sympathy for the husband in this case, and that the occupation order had only been denied because of his son's needs. She stressed that the message of the case was "emphatically not that fathers who treat their partners with domestic violence can expect to remain in occupation of the previously shared accommodation." (p.724).

Key Principle: **If there is no question of either party suffering significant harm, the court has a discretion whether or not to grant an occupation order (see s.33(6) of the FLA 1996)**

Chalmers v Johns 1999
The parties began to live together in 1972. Their relationship was a tempestuous one (largely due to alcohol), and Ms Chalmers and her daughter finally left the family home in 1998. An application was made for an occupation order. An interim occupation order was made.

Held: (CA) The appeal should be allowed. Whether or not it was appropriate to grant an occupation order should be determined at the substantive hearing.

Commentary
The adjective "Draconian"—referring to the code of Draco under which the punishment for every crime specified was death—is much overused, and never more so than in the judgment of Thorpe L.J., where it appears four times in a single page. The message is clear: occupation orders are not to be made lightly. However, it is important to appreciate the context in which these comments were made: the court did not say that an occupation order was inappropriate on the facts of the case, merely that it was not a case in which the facts demanded that an occupation order should be made immediately. In the circumstances, regulating the occupation of the family home could wait until the final hearing.

How can an Occupation Order be Enforced?

Key Principle: **The FLA 1996 does not confer a power to commit a person to prison for failing to pay the ongoings on the property**

Nwogbe v Nwogbe 2000

In 1998 the wife successfully applied for a non-molestation order and an occupation order. The latter required the husband to leave the property and to pay the rent, council tax and bills, the court having the power to impose such conditions under s.40 of the 1996 Act. He failed to make these payments.

Held: (CA) The court had no power to commit the husband to prison for his failure to make these payments. Nor was it possible to make an attachment of earnings order, or for the wife to take action as a judgment debtor.

Commentary

The Court of Appeal reached this conclusion with regret, noting that the result was to render such orders effectively unenforceable. Butler-Sloss P pointed out that the person remaining in the property under the occupation order might not have sufficient resources to pay the ongoings on the property. As yet the calls for this lacuna to be addressed have not been heeded.

Key Principle: **In punishing a person for contempt of a court order, it is sufficient to show that the contemnor understood that an order was made prohibiting certain conduct and that punishment would follow if the order was breached**

P v P (Contempt of Court: Mental Capacity) 1999

Both parties to the marriage suffered various disabilities: the husband was deaf and dumb and had tunnel vision, while the wife was deaf. After they divorced, the wife remained in the former matrimonial home and an order was made prohibiting the husband from returning. He breached this order on 29 occasions, and then applied for the order to be discharged on the basis that he lacked sufficient understanding of the jurisdiction of the court.

Held: (CA) The husband was able to understand that an order had been made forbidding him to go to the matrimonial home and that if he did so he would be punished. This was all that was necessary. It was not necessary that he should have a full understanding of court procedure and the system of committing contemnors to prison.

Commentary

The case should be contrasted with that of *Banks v Banks* (above). There, the conduct of the wife was involuntary; here, the husband did at least understand that he was acting wrongly by returning to the matrimonial home.

Orders under the Protection from Harassment Act 1997

What Constitutes a Course of Conduct Amounting to Harassment of another?

Key Principle: **Even seemingly innocuous acts, if repeated, may amount to harassment**

King v DPP 2000

Mr King offered his neighbour a plant (which she refused) and sent her a letter. He subsequently filmed her without her knowledge and rummaged through her rubbish, removing her underwear from the bins. He was convicted of an offence under the 1997 Act.

Held: (CA) While K's initial gift and letter did not amount to harassment, his later conduct—filming his neighbour and rummaging through her bins—did.

Commentary

On the facts of the case there was little doubt that K's later conduct amounted to harassment. What is more interesting is the acceptance by the court that "the repeated offers of unwanted gifts or the repeated sending of letters could well amount to harassment." (para.22). This reflects the fact that harassment may take many forms, and that conduct that at first sight appears innocuous may be experienced as harassment if it is repeated (the British Crime Survey found that some victims of harassment had received unwanted letters on more than 50 occasions). However, the court refused to accept that the initial acts in this case could be treated as the first stages of a course of conduct. Given that there is some evidence that the actions of a perpetrator may become progressively more serious, it is perhaps unfortunate that these early indicators are not perceived as part of the overall course of conduct.

Key Principle: **There must be a link between the incidents alleged to constitute a course of conduct**

Lau v DPP 2000

After the relationship between Mr Lau and his girlfriend broke down, a number of allegations were made, but the only two to be substantiated were that he had slapped her and, some months later, had threatened her new boyfriend.

Held: In the circumstances there was no "course of conduct" of harassment. While it was unnecessary to prove more than two incidents, "the fewer the occasions and the wider they are spread the less likely it would be that a finding of harassment can reasonably be made." (p.801)

Commentary

The case illustrates both that the incidents alleged must be proved—no account could be taken of the unproved allegations in deciding whether there was a course of conduct—and linked in some way. As the next case shows, it may be even more difficult to establish any link between various incidents if the parties are in a continuing relationship.

R v Hills 2001

The parties cohabited for 19 months. After their relationship had broken down, the man was charged with harassment under the PHA 1997. The alleged course of conduct consisted of two assaults, both of these occurring during the relationship and separated by a period of six months, and regular hair pulling. The man was convicted and sentenced to six months' imprisonment.

Held: (CA) In the circumstances there was no "course of conduct". Since this was a basic ingredient of the offence, the appeal against conviction would be allowed.

Commentary
In allowing the appeal against conviction, it was not the intention of the court to downplay the seriousness of the assaults that had taken place: indeed, it was suggested that the prosecution might have been successful if it had focused on the two substantive counts of violence. The problem in this case was that the facts of the case did not seem to fit within the scope of the offence created by the PHA 1997. The couple had remained together—and indeed slept together—and the two incidents of violence, while serious in themselves, were unrelated. By contrast, the next case illustrates the circumstances in which the court may find a link between separate incidents.

Hipgrave v Hipgrave and Jones 2004
The claimant complained of 11 incidents of harassment by the three defendants, of which nine were found to be proved. Four of these involved the second defendant alone, three concerned the second defendant acting with the first, and two involved the second and third defendants acting together. These last two incidents were separated by a period of eight months. The second defendant was the first defendant's former partner and the third defendant was her sister.

Held: In the light of the family connection between the defendants, there was a sufficient link between the incidents that had occurred to constitute a "course of conduct" of harassment.

Commentary
The case illustrates that the mere passage of time between two incidents does not mean that those two incidents cannot be viewed as part of a course of conduct when viewed in context. However, had the third defendant not been part of a group that was harassing the claimant it is unlikely that her actions would have been construed as amounting to a course of conduct.

Key Principle: **Whether the perpetrator "ought to have known" that his conduct amounted to harassment is judged objectively**

R v Colohan 2001
Mr Colohan, who suffered from schizophrenia, wrote a number of abusive letters to his MP, who felt threatened by them.

Held: (CA) In construing the 1997 Act, it was important to bear in mind that it had been passed for the purposes of prevention and protection. In deciding whether the perpetrator ought to have known that the conduct complained of constituted harassment, the jury should apply the objective test of what a reasonable person would have thought.

Commentary

The purposive interpretation of the legislation in this case was seen as essential to ensure that it would afford adequate protection to victims of harassment. As Hughes J pointed out, the conduct from which it sought to provide protection "is particularly likely to be conduct pursued by those of obsessive or otherwise unusual psychological make-up and very frequently by those suffering from an identifiable mental illness." (p.761)

Sentencing

Key Principle: **Violence is no less serious if it occurs within a domestic context**

R v McNaughten 2003

The relationship between McNaughten and his cohabitant had been characterised by extreme violence: the trial judge described him as having "terrorised" her throughout their relationship. He was convicted of a number of offences and sentenced to a total of nine years' imprisonment (based on a number of separate sentences, some of which were to run concurrently and some consecutively).

Held: The sentence was appropriate in the circumstances, given the number of offences of which McNaughton had been convicted (which would if perpetrated against different persons justify consecutive offences) and the context in which the offences had taken place.

Commentary

While the court emphasised that it was not enunciating any new principle, it provides a very clear statement that domestic violence is taken seriously by modern courts. Indeed, Judge L.J. suggested that the fact that the violence occurred within a domestic context might even be seen as an aggravating factor: "given the bond of trust that should exist between people who live together or who

are members of the same family, repeated violence represents a
betrayal of that trust which is an aggravating feature of these
offences." (para.17).

***

Key Principle: **Sentences passed under the FLA and the PHA
should not be manifestly discrepant**

H v O (Contempt of Court: Sentencing) 2004

The father assaulted the grandmother in the presence of the
child (for whom she was caring), and a non-molestation order
was made against the father. Four breaches of that order were
alleged, including both verbal and physical abuse. The father
was sentenced to 12 months' imprisonment.

Held: (CA) A sentence of 9 months imprisonment would be
substituted.

Commentary

The importance of the case lies not in the actual sentence awarded
but in the comments of May L.J. as to the relationship between the
different ways of dealing with violence in a domestic context.
First, he noted how domestic violence was now taken extremely
seriously by the courts, and that older cases on the appropriate
level of sentencing would no longer provide a suitable guide.
Secondly, there should be some degree of consistency between
sentences passed for breach of a non-molestation order and
sentences passed under the Protection from Harassment Act. This
has now been facilitated by the passage of the Domestic Violence
Crimes and Victims Act 2004, which makes the breach of a non-
molestation order a criminal offence punishable by up to five
years' imprisonment.

6. MAINTENANCE AND FINANCIAL PROVISION ON RELATIONSHIP BREAKDOWN AND DEATH

This chapter examines the different ways in which the law makes provision for couples and their children if the relationship between the adults breaks down or is terminated by the death of one of the parties. The rules relating to provision for children, considered in the first part, apply whether the parents had formalised their relationship or not. By contrast, the court has specific powers to reallocate assets and order maintenance on divorce or dissolution which have no counterpart if the parties were merely cohabiting. (The rights of cohabiting parties on relationship breakdown are governed by property law, as chapter 4 explained). Finally, a range of family members and dependants are entitled to make a claim for provision from the estate of a deceased person, as the third section of this chapter explains.

Providing for the children

The Child Support Act 1991

In the vast majority of cases, maintenance for children is calculated according to a formula under the Child Support Act 1991. The jurisdiction of the courts is excluded in such cases, although they retain the power to make orders for capital provision (under Sch.1 of the Children Act 1989) in all cases, and to order maintenance in certain limited circumstances in which the Child Support Act does not apply.

Key Principle: **It is the responsibility of the Child Support Agency to enforce orders made under the Child Support Act 1991 and a parent has no right to do so**

R (Kehoe) v Secretary of State for Work and Pensions 2005
The parents divorced in 1993 and Mrs Kehoe sought maintenance for their four children under the Child Support Act 1991.

There were difficulties in obtaining payment from Mr Kehoe, and arrears built up from time to time. Mrs Kehoe claimed that the 1991 Act was incompatible with art.6 of the ECHR because it denied the parent with care the right to enforce maintenance payments.

Held: (HL) The parent with care had no personal right to receive maintenance from the non-resident parent, since that right had been removed by the 1991 Act and vested in the Child Support Agency. Consequently art.6 was not engaged.

Commentary
The fact that the parent with care does not have a right to enforce maintenance payments has been much criticised, and the recent report on the reform of child support suggests that it might be appropriate to confer such a right "if there was clear evidence that the administrative service had failed to do so effectively." (Department for Work and Pensions, *Recovering child support: routes to responsibility*, Cm 6894 (2006), para.67). Such a remedy would assist parents in the position of Mrs Kehoe, who observed sadly that her only remedy was "to constantly pressurise the CSA which takes no real responsibility for ensuring maintenance is paid and for whom I am just a nuisance."

Key Principle: **If a liability order is sought, the magistrates have no power to determine whether the initial maintenance calculation was properly made**

Farley v Secretary of State for Work and Pensions 2006
Mr Farley was assessed as owing sums in the region of £30,000 by way of child support, and an application was made to the magistrates' court for a liability order in order to enforce payment. Mr Farley argued that in the circumstances the Secretary of State had had no jurisdiction to make a maintenance assessment, since this was precluded by the agreement he had entered into with the mother of his children. The justices made the liability order on the basis that they did not have jurisdiction to enquire into the lawfulness of the maintenance assessment.

Held: (HL) The terms of the child support legislation precluded the magistrates from investigating whether a maintenance calculation had been properly made. There were other channels for challenging the decision of the Secretary of State.

Commentary
The case illustrates the strict demarcation of roles that exists under the child support legislation. Those who believe a maintenance calculation to be erroneous have the opportunity of appealing to a tribunal. As Lord Nicholls pointed out, it would have been odd if a parallel jurisdiction to examine the basis of the calculation had been conferred on the magistrates' courts, particularly at the late stage of an application for a liability order.

Provision under Sch.1 of the Children Act 1989

Key Principle: **The cohabitant of a child's parent cannot be required to make provision for the child under Sch.1**

J v J (A Minor: Property Transfer) 1993
A man and a woman cohabited in a council flat for ten years, together with the woman's daughter from a previous relationship. When the relationship broke down the woman applied for the tenancy of the flat to be transferred to her for the benefit of her child under Sch.1 of the 1989 Act.

Held: The court had no jurisdiction to make such an order, as the man was not a parent of the child.

Commentary
Under Sch.1 it is only parents who can be required to make provision for their children. While "parent" has an extended meaning—including not only adoptive parents but also a parent's spouse or civil partner who treated the child as a child of the family—it does not include the cohabitant of a parent, regardless of the length of time that the parties may have shared a home.

Key Principle: **The court may order capital provision for a child even if prohibited from making an order for periodical payments**

Phillips v Peace 1996
The relationship between the parents broke down shortly before the mother discovered that she was pregnant. After the birth the

mother applied to the Child Support Agency. The father was a wealthy man, who lived in a house worth £2.6m and owned cars with a total value of £190,000. He dealt in shares through a company that he owned and controlled. At the time of the mother's application to the Child Support Agency he was not receiving a salary or any other remuneration from that company. He thus had no "income" for the purposes of a child support assessment, and was therefore not liable to pay maintenance according to the formula applied. The mother then applied to the court for an order under Sch.1 of the Children Act 1989.

Held: If a child support officer has jurisdiction to make a maintenance assessment, the court is prohibited from awarding periodic payments for the support of a child. However, it retains the power to make orders for the transfer and settlement of property. Such powers should be used to meet the need of the child in respect of a particular item of capital expenditure rather than to provide a sum that is effectively capitalized maintenance. In the circumstances of this case the court would order the father to pay sums of £90,000 (for a house, which would revert to the father once the child reached adulthood), £15,000 (to furnish the house) and £14,370.51 (to cover such matters as medical, nursing and hospital costs and the money that the mother had already spent on clothing and baby equipment).

Commentary
The case illustrates both the deficiencies of the Child Support Act and the relationship between it and the statutory jurisdiction of the courts. On the first point, the absurdity of the nil assessment under the 1991 Act was the result of the strict formulaic approach that remains central to the Act. On the second point, the 1991 Act is clear in excluding the jurisdiction of the court to order periodic payments if the case falls within the Child Support Agency's jurisdiction (even if, as here, the result of a maintenance assessment is a nil assessment). The judge in this case therefore took the view that it was not the role of the court to order maintenance by an alternative means.

Key Principle: **A court cannot order a parent to make a further settlement or transfer of property**

Phillips v Peace 2004

Several years later, the mother in the above case applied for further orders under the 1989 Act. One of her arguments was that the property in which she was residing was now too small (as she now had another child by a different father) and that she needed funds to be able to purchase a larger property.

Held: The court had on a previous occasion ordered the father to settle a sum of money for the purchase of a house, and the terms of the 1989 Act prevented it from making a subsequent order of the same type. This meant that it could not make an order for either the settlement or the transfer of property. While it did have the power to order a second or subsequent lump sum, this power should not be used to circumvent the prohibition on a second order for the settlement or transfer of property.

Commentary

One might discern slightly less sympathy for the mother in this case than in the earlier litigation, although the actual decision turned on the construction of the legislation rather than the merits of the case. Just as the court will not exercise its powers to undermine the jurisdiction of the Child Support Agency, so too it will not make one type of order to circumvent restrictions on another. As the judge pointed out in this case, there is a clear distinction between a settlement of property (which reverts to the parent who settled it) and a lump sum that is intended either to reimburse past expenditure or to meet future needs. A lump sum that was subject to the condition that it should revert to the parent—as proposed by counsel for the mother in this case—was scarcely distinguishable from a settlement.

Key Principle: **It is generally more appropriate to require a parent to settle property for the benefit of the child until independence rather than to order an outright transfer**

A v A (A Minor: Financial Provision) 1994

The relationship between the parties had begun in the late 1970s, but they had never cohabited. The mother gave birth to three children (A, O and T). For a time the father supported them all but paternity tests later proved that O and T had a different father. He then tried to evict them all from the property that he had purchased for them to live in. The mother applied for orders against the father under Sch.1 of the Children Act, seeking provision for A.

Held: The obligation of the father was to provide for the maintenance and education of A until she had completed her education (up to tertiary level). Once she had reached independence, this obligation ceased. It would therefore not be appropriate to order him to transfer the property in which she was residing to her outright, but rather to order him to settle it on her until she reached independence.

Commentary

At the time of the decision the Child Support Act 1991 had not been brought into force, although as the father was resident overseas it would not have applied to him anyway, and the court would have retained its jurisdiction under the 1989 Act. The key issue in this case was how it should exercise that jurisdiction. The point decided was not that the court *could* not order the outright transfer of property under the 1989 Act, but that generally it *should* not. Although the father in this case was so rich that he could afford to transfer the property in which A was residing without even noticing that he had done so, this had no bearing on his legal obligation, which was simply to provide for A until she attained independence, rather than to set her up with a capital sum. It should also be noted that the order made by the court in effect required the father of A to provide a home for O and T as well, since A required accommodation that was suitable for occupation by her mother and her two sisters as well as herself.

Key Principle: **It is possible for the court to order a transfer of property for the benefit of the child**

Emmanuel Francis v Manning 1997

The parties began to cohabit in 1984 and their daughter was born in 1986. In the 1990s the relationship began to deteriorate, and in 1994 the mother applied for the father's interest in their home to be transferred to her for the benefit of their child. At the time the mortgage repayments were in arrears but there was some equity in the property.

Held: (CA) The property should be transferred to the mother, in consideration of which a sum of £6,000 would be paid to the father immediately (and a further £5,900 on the occurrence of certain specified events). The father would also be released from indebtedness under the mortgage.

Commentary

Two points stand out from this case. First, Thorpe L.J. was keen to emphasize that the court did have the power to order a transfer of property for the benefit of the child. In so doing he distinguished the earlier decision in *A v A (A Minor: Financial Provision)*, which involved parties who had never cohabited, on the basis that "[w]here a very rich man fathers a child on his mistress, she cannot by application under CA 1989 obtain an order which would have the effect of conferring capital on the child for use and enjoyment in later life. A completely different approach is necessarily adopted where a family unit is created without marriage and where on the disintegration of the family the court has the opportunity to preserve the family home for the benefit of a child and for the parent who happens to assume the responsibility for primary care." The second point to note is that the actual decision in the case was not as generous as that broad statement of principle might suggest. Thorpe L.J. went on to note that in the absence of consideration the father in this case might expect to realise his share when his daughter reached adulthood: here, however, consideration for the transfer was provided. In effect, the "transfer" in this case amounted to little more than the mother buying out the father's interest in the property. The case thus does not affect the key principle—endorsed by a long string of authorities—that the order for provision for a child should not subsist beyond the child's dependency.

Key Principle: **Maintenance ordered for a child may include an allowance for the child's carer**

Haroutunian v Jennings 1980

The father was a wealthy man and the mother was dependent on public funds. Weekly payments were ordered for their child, but the father challenged the amount of the order, arguing that it included a sum that was for the maintenance of the mother.

Held: Maintenance for a child had to cover not only food, clothing and accommodation but also care for the child. If the mother of the child had been unable to care for her, it would have been necessary to pay someone else to do so. It was thus appropriate to reflect the mother's care for the child in the level of maintenance ordered.

Commentary
While the actual case was decided under earlier legislation, the key principle remains the same. Provision by way of maintenance is now largely dealt with under the Child Support Act, but the courts have accepted that account may also be taken of the caring parent's need for accommodation in making capital orders under the 1989 Act (see e.g. *J v C (Child: Financial Provision)* [1999] 1 F.L.R. 152, below).

Key Principle: **A child is entitled to be brought up in circumstances that bear some relationship to the non-resident parent's standard of living**

J v C (Child: Financial Provision) 1999
The relationship between the parents broke down before the birth of their child. The father subsequently won £1.4m on the national lottery and the mother applied for orders under the 1989 Act.

Held: The father would be required to settle a sum of money on his child for the purpose of providing a home for her (which would revert to him when she reached the age of 21 or finished full-time education, whichever was the later), and to pay a lump sum for furnishings. While the father's wealth had accrued to him after the breakdown of his relationship with the mother, his child was entitled to be brought up in circumstances which bore some relationship to his current resources.

Commentary
In this case the mother was dependent on public funds, and the judge noted the public policy that "where resources allow, the family obligation should be respected in such a way as to reduce, or even eliminate, the need for children to be supported by public funds." (p.160). The standard of living of the parties during the relationship did not dictate the standard of provision that the non-resident parent should make for his child in this case.

Re P (Child: Financial Provision) 2003
A relationship between the parents, which continued intermittently for four years, resulted in the birth of a child in 2000. The

father was, in his own words, "fabulously wealthy." The mother applied for financial provision for the benefit of the child under Sch.1 of the Children Act 1989.

Held: (CA) It would be appropriate to order a housing fund of £1m, £100,000 to furnish the home and £70,000 per annum by way of periodic payments.

Commentary
The over-representation in the case-law on this topic of extremely wealthy fathers reflects the fact that families with less significant assets will be generally dealt with under the Child Support Act. The policy of awarding provision that reflected the father's means (rather than the child's needs) was in this case depicted as a means of fostering the relationship between father and daughter: according to Thorpe L.J., the daughter's prospects "of enjoying a relationship with her father in and beyond her minority may be strengthened rather than diminished by whatever enhanced familiarity with his world material benefits would provide." (para.69). Also of note in this case was the way in which the court assessed the mother's allowance: it was suggested that to relate this allowance to the cost of a nanny would be to "demean the mother's role" (para.54), given the commitment of time and effort that motherhood involves. However, the court was also quick to point out that the mother had no *personal* entitlement to any allowance from the father, and that the father was entitled to "reasonably detailed accounts of expenditure so that he can be satisfied that . . . all is spent to meet the needs for which it is provided and none goes to the personal or exclusive benefit of the mother." (para.54).

Dividing the Assets on Divorce, Dissolution or Annulment

Private Ordering

Key Principle: **The right to apply to the court cannot be excluded by private agreement between the parties**

Hyman v Hyman 1929
Upon separation the husband and wife entered into an agreement whereby he promised to pay maintenance and she agreed

not to seek maintenance from the court. She subsequently obtained a divorce and petitioned for maintenance.

Held: (HL) The agreement between the parties did not prevent the wife from petitioning the court for maintenance.

Commentary
The principle in *Hyman v Hyman* still holds good, despite the fact that private ordering is today encouraged by the courts. The parties may agree between themselves that neither of them will apply to the court, and if both remain of the same mind the court will have no occasion to consider their financial arrangements. But if either party changes their mind, he or she has the right to apply to the court. As Lord Hailsham L.C. pointed out, there is an important public interest in the reallocation of assets on divorce, since inadequate provision will leave the weaker party dependent on the state.

Key Principle: **A pre-nuptial agreement is not binding but may be taken into account by the court as part of all the circumstances of the case**

K v K (Ancillary Relief: Pre-nuptial agreement) 2003
The marriage between the parties had been precipitated by the wife's pregnancy: she had told the husband that unless he married her she would have an abortion. Prior to the marriage the parties entered into a pre-nuptial agreement in order to limit any claim that she might otherwise have against his substantial assets. The marriage broke down after a year.

Held: In the circumstances of the case, it would be unjust to the husband to ignore the terms of the agreement regarding the division of the capital assets. However, the agreement had made no mention of maintenance for the wife or of provision for their child. Periodical payments of £15,000 per year would be awarded to the wife to reflect her ongoing responsibilities for child-care. In addition, the husband should pay a sum of £1.2m in order to provide a home for the child during his minority. The property would revert to the husband when his son had finished full-time education.

Commentary
The case provides a perfect example of the circumstances in which a pre-nuptial agreement may be accorded significant weight: a

wealthy (and somewhat reluctant) husband, a short marriage, and an agreement entered into only after independent legal advice had been provided to both parties. It also illustrates the circumstances in which such an agreement is likely to be disregarded, namely if children are born.

Key Principle: **A separation agreement is likely to be upheld unless there are clear and compelling reasons not to do so**

Edgar v Edgar 1980

A separation agreement was negotiated between the parties' solicitors whereby the wife agreed to accept assets worth £100,000 from her multimillionaire husband and not to seek any further provision from him. She subsequently petitioned for further provision.

Held: (CA) Although the court had jurisdiction to hear the petition, in the circumstances of the case it should not go behind the agreement entered into by the parties. Formal agreements that had been entered into freely, and on the basis of competent legal advice, should be given effect by the courts "unless good and substantial grounds were shown for concluding that injustice would be done by holding the parties to the terms of the agreement" (p.1417).

Commentary

There is an important distinction between a pre-nuptial agreement and a separation agreement. In the first case the parties are making provision for the end of the marriage before it has even begun, and cannot know what the circumstances will be if the marriage does in fact come to an end. In the latter case the marriage has come to an end and the parties are simply making their own arrangements. The courts are understandably keen to encourage private ordering in such cases. From the parties' point of view, the test established in *Edgar* provides some reassurance that a properly negotiated agreement will be respected by the courts. It should be noted that the emphasis is on procedural rather than substantive fairness: Mrs Edgar clearly agreed to accept less than a court would have ordered, but since this was not the result of any procedural impropriety it was not unfair for the agreement to stand. The corollary of this is of course that an agreement may not be given

effect if it was the result of duress or undue influence, or if one
party did not have independent legal advice.

Key Principle: **An order made by consent is effectively an
order of the court, not simply an agreement between the
parties**

De Lasala v De Lasala 1980

Upon divorce a consent order was made by the judge, approv-
ing the financial arrangements that the parties had made. The
wife subsequently challenged the provision that had been made.

Held: (PC) There was no subsisting maintenance agreement to
be varied by the court. Once the financial arrangements had
been made the subject of a consent order, their legal effect
derived from the order of the court, not from the agreement of
the parties.

Commentary

Edgar v Edgar (above) shows that the circumstances in which an
agreement between the parties can be set aside are narrowly
prescribed. *De Lasala* illustrates that once any such agreement has
been enshrined in a court order, it can only be challenged in the
even more narrowly defined circumstances in which an order of
the court may be set aside (see further below).

Key Principle: **Inadequate legal advice is not a ground on
which a consent order may be set aside**

Harris v Manahan 1997

The parties agreed that the wife would receive a share of the
proceeds of the former matrimonial home in lieu of periodical
payments. A consent order was made in those terms. Unfor-
tunately, it proved difficult to sell the property, the mortgage
arrears mounted and any surplus was wiped out. The wife, who
had been left with no assets and who was dependent on income
support, applied to set aside the consent order on the basis of
inadequate legal advice.

Held: (CA) The wife's application would be dismissed. While bad legal advice was a factor that could be taken into account as part of all the circumstances of the case, "only in the most exceptional case of the cruellest injustice will the public interest in the finality of litigation be put aside." (p.225). This was not such a case.

Commentary

The case illustrates the potential danger in making a consent order: it is more difficult to challenge if events do not turn out as expected. The assumption underlying the differential treatment of separation agreements and consent orders is that in the latter case the court will have had the opportunity to scrutinise the agreement between the parties and address any obvious inequities—although whether all consent orders are subjected to an adequate level of scrutiny is perhaps open to doubt.

Key Principle: **An agreement reached in the course of a Financial Dispute Resolution appointment and approved by the court constitutes an order from which the parties cannot resile**

Rose v Rose 2002

The parties reached agreement in the course of a Financial Dispute Resolution appointment, and the judge indicated that he was happy with the outcome. The husband subsequently changed his mind.

Held: (CA) The FDR appointment had resulted in an order of the court, and the husband was therefore not entitled to change his mind.

Commentary

The scope for a dispute arose in this case on account of the fact that the outcome of the FDR appointment had not been formally recorded in an order of the court. The Court of Appeal decided, by a process of elimination, that what had transpired did constitute an order of the court: since there had been no directions for an adjournment, or directions for a trial, the matter must have been resolved by way of an order.

The Exercise of the Court's Discretion: General Principles

The court has extensive powers on divorce, dissolution or indeed annulment: it may order that assets be reallocated between the parties by means of property adjustment orders; it may require one party to make provision for the other by ordering periodical payments or a lump sum; and it also has the power to make pension sharing orders. The relevant legislation (Part II of the Matrimonial Causes Act 1973, and the similarly-worded Sch.5 of the Civil Partnership Act 2004) confers a broad discretion on the court, but two recent decisions of the House of Lords attempt to lay down some general principles governing the exercise of that discretion.

Key Principle: **The role of the court is to achieve a fair outcome, and fairness requires that there should be no discrimination between the breadwinner and the homemaker**

White v White 2001
Mr and Mrs White were both farmers, and had worked in partnership throughout their long marriage. They had amassed assets of £4.6m. At first instance Mrs White was awarded one-fifth of the assets on the basis of her reasonable requirements. The Court of Appeal increased this to two-fifths.

Held: (HL) The role of the court was to achieve a fair outcome, although "fairness" would depend on all the circumstances. There should be no discrimination between husband and wife, and no bias against the homemaker. Judges should check their provisional view against the yardstick of equality of division, and "[a]s a general guide, equality should be departed from only if, and to the extent that, there is good reason for doing so." (p.605). In this case the wife should be awarded two-fifths of the assets.

Commentary
The decision in *White* was highly significant for a number of reasons. First, it held that there was no ceiling of "reasonable requirements" on a claim for financial provision, thus putting an end to a line of cases involving wealthy husbands in which the

claimant-wives had been awarded a relatively small proportion of the overall assets—sufficient to meet their reasonable requirements—leaving the husbands with the surplus. Equally, however, there was no presumption of equal division. Lord Nicholls emphasized that the introduction of any such principle was a matter for Parliament, being beyond the permissible bounds of judicial interpretation. He also stressed that all the factors listed in s.25 should be taken into account. Yet even if *White* does not establish that equal division is the appropriate starting point, it does hint that it might be a desirable end result, in that any departure from equal division needs to be justified.

Of course, this raises the question as to why Mrs White did not receive half of the assets, given that she had worked in partnership with her husband for many years. The only justification provided was that Mr White's father had assisted the couple with a loan in their early days (and Lord Cooke of Thorndon expressed his doubts as to whether this really justified the difference in outcome). The real reason lies in the nature of the appellate jurisdiction: the amount awarded by the Court of Appeal was not so far outside the acceptable range of orders to justify the House of Lords substituting its own view. This reflects the fact that the courts are keen to discourage appeals in this contentious and highly discretionary area (and *Piglowska v Piglowski*, below, illustrates why). Ironically, had Mrs White been less successful in the Court of Appeal she might have been more successful before the House of Lords.

White v White raised a number of questions, not all of which have been resolved in the most recent case to come before the House of Lords, which involved the conjoined appeals in *Miller v Miller* and *McFarlane v McFarlane*.

Key Principle: **The key principles underpinning the discretionary jurisdiction of the court are need, compensation and sharing**

Miller v Miller; McFarlane v McFarlane 2006

The Millers' marriage had lasted only two years and nine months when Mr Miller left his wife for another woman. During that period his assets had significantly increased in value, with shares valued at between £12m and £18m. The issue between them concerned the level of capital provision that should be made. The McFarlanes had been married for 16 years, during which time Mrs McFarlane had given up her lucrative career as a City solicitor to look after their three children. They had agreed to divide their assets equally and the sole remaining issue was the level and duration of the periodical payments order in favour of Mrs McFarlane.

Held: (HL) Mrs Miller's award of £5m was upheld by the House of Lords. Mrs McFarlane's appeal was allowed, with the result that no term was set on the periodical payments of £250,000 p.a. that she was to receive from her former husband.

Commentary
The significance of *Miller*; *McFarlane* lies less in the final sums awarded than in the underlying principles articulated by the House of Lords, although given the differences between the judgments it is sometimes a little difficult to work out exactly what principles the case establishes.

First, the House of Lords was significantly more willing to spell out the principles underlying the discretionary jurisdiction of the courts than previous judges had been. Both Lord Nicholls and Baroness Hale identified three key features to the law: need, compensation, and sharing, although Lord Nicholls described them as "strands" and Baroness Hale saw them as justifications for redistributing resources. This apparently slight difference in terminology was symptomatic of a deeper division: the whole tenor of Baroness Hale's judgment was that redistribution needed to be clearly justified, given that English law operates on the principle of separation of property during a marriage, while Lord Nicholls spoke in terms of "entitlement". There were also differences between their respective interpretations of these three elements: in relation to need, Baroness Hale noted that redistribution could be justified on the basis that the "relationship has generated needs which it is right that the other party should meet" (para.138). while Lord Nicholls made reference to needs not arising from the relationship (e.g. as a result of the disability of one of the parties). Similarly, in relation to sharing, both described marriage as a partnership but differed as to what exactly should be shared.

This leads on to a second point. Both were agreed that there was a difference between property acquired by the joint efforts of the parties and other property (whether it had been acquired before the marriage or by gift or inheritance during the marriage). However, they differed on the question of what property should be seen as being acquired by the joint efforts of the parties. Lord Nicholls drew no distinction between business assets and other assets, maintaining his view that a domestic contribution could be seen as a contribution to the former. Baroness Hale held that business assets should be treated differently to those assets acquired for the use of the family, referring to them as assets generated by the efforts of one of the spouses alone (although it is difficult to reconcile this with her description of Mr McFarlane's earning capacity as a "family asset"). The view of Baroness Hale would seem to have prevailed in the House of Lords, since Lord Mance delivered a judgment agreeing with her on this point, and Lord Hoffman briefly concurred with the reasons she gave. It should be noted that she did not suggest that business assets should be excluded from consideration, nor that they should never be shared between the parties, but rather that they should be treated in the same way as assets acquired by way of gift or inheritance, or before the marriage, and that the shortness of the marriage might justify a departure from equality of division. It remains to be seen how the lower courts will interpret this aspect of *Miller*; *McFarlane* (see e.g. *Charman v Charman* below).

A third point to note is that the House of Lords rejected the suggestion made in the lower courts that Mr Miller's conduct in leaving his wife for another woman should be taken into account in determining the appropriate level of the award to his wife. It emphasised that the conduct of either party should be taken into account only if it was obvious and gross, as had been the approach of the courts for the previous 30 years.

Finally, an important point was established in relation to periodical payments. Since there were not adequate capital assets to compensate Mrs McFarlane for the disadvantage that she had suffered as a result of giving up her career, such compensation would be achieved by way of periodical payments. The Court of Appeal had imposed a five-year term on such payments. The House of Lords allowed Mrs McFarlane's appeal on this point, noting that there was a distinction between periodical payments aimed at addressing the needs of the recipients and periodical payments intended to compensate the recipient. There was no need for the courts to strive for a clean break in relation to the latter. Indeed, Mrs McFarlane could be entitled to periodical payments on a compensatory basis even if she no longer needed them, although her husband would be able to apply for them to be reduced or terminated if her circumstances changed.

First Consideration to the Welfare of any Children

The court is required to "have regard to all the circumstances of the case, first consideration being given to the welfare while a minor of any child of the family who has not attained the age of eighteen" (see s.25(1) of the MCA 1973 and Sch.5 para.20 of the CPA 2004).

Key Principle: **The children's welfare is the first consideration for the court, but it is not the paramount consideration**

Suter v Suter and Jones 1987
The parties had been married for 15 years and had two children. After the divorce, the wife remained in the former matrimonial home with the children and her lover. The husband was ordered to transfer his interest in the home to his former wife, to make periodical payments of £200 per month for the children and £100 per month for the wife.

Held: (CA) The judge had misdirected himself in construing s.25(1). The true meaning of this section was that the welfare of children was to be regarded as of first importance, but not overriding all other considerations pointing to a just result. The task of the court was therefore "to consider all the circumstances, always bearing in mind the important consideration of the welfare of the children, and then try to attain a financial result which is just as between husband and wife." (p.238). The periodical payments for the wife would accordingly be reduced to a nominal £1 per year, as her new partner could be expected to make a contribution to the household expenses.

Commentary
The implication of this case is that there is a fundamental difference between litigation in which the upbringing of the child is in issue (in which case the welfare of the child is paramount) and cases in which the dispute centres on the financial resources of divorcing parents (in which case the welfare of the child is the first but not the paramount consideration). One might wonder why fairness to both of the adult parties is deemed to be a more important consideration in the latter context. In any case, it should be noted that the priority for the courts in exercising their

jurisdiction under s.25 will always be to ensure that the children and their primary carer are provided with adequate accommodation, as the next case demonstrates.

B v B (Financial Provision: Welfare of Child and Conduct) 2002

The parties divorced after six years of marriage. The husband then abducted the child of the marriage, and was subsequently sentenced to eighteen months' imprisonment for the offence of child abduction. The only assets of the parties were the former matrimonial home (which had a net value of £124,000) and a building society account (from which the husband had removed £37,000, which he sent to his mother in Sicily). It was ordered that the proceeds of sale of the former matrimonial home should be transferred to the wife, who was by then reunited with and caring for the child.

Held: The order was justified. The proceeds of sale would only be sufficient properly to rehouse the child and his mother. Bearing in mind the substantial contribution that the wife would be making as the child's carer, a departure from equality was justified. A *Mesher* order (see below) was not appropriate given the respective contributions of the parties, the husband's conduct, and the fact that it was unlikely that any maintenance would ever be forthcoming from the father.

Commentary

The case illustrates that, despite the concern of the courts to ensure that both parties are adequately housed, the emphasis on fairness to both parties in *White v White*, and the fact that the welfare of any child of the marriage is not the paramount consideration for the court, there may still be cases in which it is appropriate for all of the available assets to be used for the benefit of the children and their carer. While the facts of this particular case were exceptional, the point made by the judge—that *White v White* only applies where there are surplus assets—is of wider relevance. In less exceptional cases the courts may attempt to balance the need of the children and primary carer for accommodation during the children's minority with fairness to the other spouse by ensuring that the latter will receive at least some benefit from the property, perhaps by means of the type of order described in the next case.

Key Principle: **It is possible to secure the former matrimonial home as a home for the children during their minority while ensuring that both parties retain an interest in it**

Mesher v Mesher 1980

Upon divorce an order was made whereby the former matrimonial home would be transferred to the wife. The husband appealed on the basis that it was unfair that he should be deprived of the whole of his interest in the property.

Held: (CA) Given the respective economic positions of the parties, it was wrong to strip the husband of any interest in the home, and the court would substitute an order that the house was held in equal shares but was not to be sold until the child of the marriage reached the age of 17 or the court gave leave.

Commentary

The case gave its name to the *Mesher* order, whereby the home would be retained by the primary carer until the children reached a specified age. (Of a similar nature was the *Martin* order, which allowed the primary carer, usually the wife, to retain the home until she remarried or cohabited: see *Martin v Martin* [1978] Fam 12). The order rapidly became popular—so much so that it proved necessary to issue a reminder that there was no automatic presumption that the house should be sold once the children reached their majority. However, later courts became aware of the problems that such an order might cause: sale at this point might leave the primary carer with insufficient assets to buy a new property at a time when she had been out of paid employment for a considerable period of time.

The Duty to Consider "all the Circumstances" of the Case

As noted above, the court is required to have regard to all the circumstances of the case, but it is specifically directed to eight specified factors in s.25(2) of the MCA:

(a) the income, earning capacity, property and other financial resources which each of the parties to the marriage has or is likely to have in the foreseeable future, including in the case of earning capacity any increase in that capacity which it would in the opinion of the court be reasonable to expect a party to the marriage to take steps to acquire;

(b) the financial needs, obligations and responsibilities which each of the parties to the marriage has or is likely to have in the foreseeable future;

(c) the standard of living enjoyed by the family before the breakdown of the marriage;

(d) the age of each party to the marriage and the duration of the marriage;

(e) any physical or mental disability of either of the parties to the marriage;

(f) the contributions which each of the parties has made or is likely in the foreseeable future to make to the welfare of the family including any contribution made by looking after the home or caring for the family;

(g) the conduct of the parties if it is such that it would in the opinion of the court be inequitable to ignore it;

(h) in the case of proceedings for divorce or nullity of marriage, the value to each of the parties to the marriage of any benefit which, by means of the dissolution or annulment of the marriage, that party will lose the chance of acquiring.

The same factors are set out in Sch.5 para.21 of the CPA 2004. There is a wealth of case-law on this topic but earlier cases may be of limited utility in the light of the fundamental shifts effected by *White v White* and *Miller; McFarlane*. This section focuses on those cases that remain relevant and those illustrating the application of the general principles discussed above.

Key Principle: **The court is entitled to infer the availability of undisclosed assets if a spouse fails to supply the necessary information**

Al-Khatib v Masry 2002

After the parties separated, the husband refused to supply evidence about his assets or to attend court. The wife alleged that the husband was worth about $200m and sought £24m. The husband was warned that inferences might be drawn about the extent of his wealth, but the information that he eventually supplied contained a number of inconsistencies and failed to disclose certain assets.

Held: This was a case in which it was appropriate to draw the inference that the husband's assets were vastly greater than he was prepared to admit. While it was obviously impossible to estimate the extent of his wealth, the evidence justified the inference that the family assets were comfortably in excess of £50m and therefore justified the level of award that the wife was seeking.

Commentary

The ability of the court to draw adverse inferences about the extent of undisclosed assets owned by one of the spouses will in many cases operate as a powerful incentive to ensure full disclosure. As the judge observed, the amount awarded to the wife in this case was probably no more than half of the family assets, and even if it were the husband had no one to blame but himself.

Key Principle: **The court is entitled to take into account the potential availability of wealth from sources owned or administered by others**

Thomas v Thomas 1995

The husband was the joint managing director of a successful family business (managed on a day-to-day basis by himself and his brother) but received only a relatively low monthly salary, as a result of the company policy of ploughing back profits into the business. The judge made an order for maintenance for the children of the marriage at a level that, combined with other expenses, would leave the husband with a deficiency of income, on the assumption that the husband would be able to make good such deficiency by bringing about a change in company policy and securing a higher level of remuneration for himself.

Held: (CA) The husband's appeal was dismissed. The court is entitled to take into account that resources are available to one of the spouses from sources owned or controlled by third parties, although it will not put undue pressure on those third parties to act in a way that enhances the financial position of the spouse. In this case the decision of the court did not place improper pressure on the husband's family.

Commentary

As Waite L.J. pointed out in this case, "if justice is to be achieved between spouses at divorce the court must be equipped, in a society where the forms of wealth-holding are diverse and often sophisticated, to penetrate outer forms of wealth and get to the heart of ownership." (p.670). The principle articulated in this case is equally applicable to the situation in which one spouse enjoys an interest under a discretionary trust (see e.g. *Browne v Browne* [1989] 1 F.L.R. 291) or has been supported by the family for a considerable period of time (see e.g. *M v M (Maintenance Pending Suit)* [2002] EWHC 317).

Key Principle: **The source of the assets may be a relevant consideration in deciding how they should be divided**

P v P (Inherited Property) 2004

Both parties were farmers, and their nineteen years of married life had been spent working on the family farm, which had been in the husband's family for several generations.

Held: In the circumstances of the case the appropriate solution was to meet the wife's reasonable needs and ensure that the husband was able to retain the family farm. The wife was awarded 25 per cent of the assets, reflecting the fact that the family farm constituted the bulk of those assets.

Commentary

Munby J. was quick to stress that he was not deciding that inherited property should always be treated differently from other assets, nor that it would always be appropriate for one spouse to retain the family farm in farming cases. As he pointed out, each case turns on its own facts: "[f]airness may require quite a different approach if the inheritance is a pecuniary legacy that accrues during the marriage than if the inheritance is a landed estate that has been within one spouse's family for generations and has been brought into the marriage with an expectation that it will be retained in specie for future generations." (para.37). And even in the latter type of case an estate may need to be broken up if this is necessary to meet the needs of the parties.

A further illustration of the principle that the source of the assets may be a relevant consideration in deciding how they should be divided is provided by *Miller; McFarlane* (above), which considered the point in relation to business assets.

Key Principle: **The nature of the assets should be taken into account in deciding what constitutes a fair division**

Wells v Wells 2002

For most of the marriage the husband's business had provided a good standard of living for the family but in recent years it had been less successful. The wife was awarded the entire proceeds of the value of the matrimonial home, while the husband retained the value of his shares in the company.

Held: (CA) The division of the assets was unfair as it left the husband with assets that were substantially more risk-laden and illiquid than those awarded to the wife. In the circumstances the husband's share of the risk-free realisable assets should be increased, as the earlier award did not adequately address his needs.

Commentary

It was noted by Thorpe L.J. that fairness would usually require "a fair division of both the copper-bottomed assets and the illiquid and risk-laden assets." (para.24). In this case, however, neither party had sought an increase in the wife's shareholding, and given that any transfer to the wife would attract liability to capital gains tax it would be inappropriate to impose such a solution. The only solution was therefore to increase the husband's share of the risk-free assets.

Key Principle: **The shortness of a marriage may be of little significance if there are children of the relationship**

Re G (Financial Provision: Liberty to Restore Application for Lump Sum) 2004

The marriage of the parties lasted only four years, but two daughters were born in that period. Both parties remarried (although at the time of the application the wife was in the process of getting a second divorce). The original consent order had adjourned the wife's claims for a lump sum and secured provision, with liberty to restore, in order that the husband's anticipated inheritance from his uncle might be taken into account. The assets available to the husband, largely as a result of that inheritance, were £2.1m.

Held: Had there been no children of the marriage, the wife would not have had a claim, but her contribution to their welfare should be recognised. It was reasonable that the husband should be required to meet her needs from the resources that had become available to him.

Commentary

In this case the wife (who suffered from multiple sclerosis and was not in paid employment) was in a poor financial situation and did not expect to receive any capital assets from her second husband (although she was in receipt of maintenance from him). However, the court made it clear that her illness would not by itself have justified a claim against the husband's anticipated inheritance. Equally, the fact that she had entered into a second marriage did not change the fact that she continued to care for the children of the first marriage and so was making an ongoing contribution to the children's welfare. It was this contribution that justified the award.

Key Principle: **The fact that the parties have cohabited before the marriage should be taken into account by the court**

CO v CO (Ancillary Relief: Pre-Marriage Cohabitation) 2004

The parties lived together for nearly eight years before they married, and their two daughters were born in this period. The marriage itself lasted only four years.

Held: The time that the parties had lived together before the marriage should be taken into account by the court, as part of all the circumstances of the case or under either s.25(2)(f) or (g).

Commentary

Although s.25(1)(d) refers specifically to the duration of the *marriage*, the courts have proved increasingly willing to consider the overall duration of the *relationship* in exercising their discretion. In this case, Coleridge J. noted that where a committed cohabiting relationship "seamlessly and immediately" preceded the marriage, it was a relevant factor. (By contrast, the fact that the parties were "dating"—as in the *Miller* case, above—is unlikely to be given any weight).

Key Principle: **the disability of the parties is only one factor to take into account**

Wagstaff v Wagstaff 1992
The husband had been awarded damages as compensation for loss of amenity and pain and suffering. The question for the court was whether the sum awarded should be treated in the same way as any other asset.

Held: (CA) The damages formed part of the husband's financial resources and should be regarded as an asset available for redistribution. While the fact that the sum had been awarded by way of damages was relevant, it did not mean that the money was therefore secure against any application by the other spouse. In the circumstances, the disparity in the financial position of the parties justified a lump sum being awarded to the wife.

Commentary
As the court emphasized, all of the factors in s.25 must be taken into account, and the husband's disability should not be treated as the paramount consideration, although it was undoubtedly relevant in assessing his needs.

Key Principle: **The contributions of the homemaker and breadwinner should be regarded as being of equal value**

Lambert v Lambert 2002
The parties had been married for 23 years, during which time they had built up assets in excess of £20m. The children of the marriage had reached adulthood and a fund had been set aside to provide for them. At first instance the judge held that the husband's contribution in building up the business from which

the bulk of the assets derived justified a departure from equality.

Held: (CA) The wife should be awarded an equal share. To hold that the scale of the husband's success justified a departure from equality would inevitably lead to discrimination in big-money cases since there was no equivalent opportunity for the homemaker to demonstrate that she had made a special contribution. However, it would still be possible for one spouse to argue that he or she had made a special contribution justifying a departure from equality in "exceptional" circumstances.

Commentary
The decision in *Lambert* was highly significant, as it was the first "big money" case decided in the wake of *White v White* in which a wife was awarded half of the assets, bringing to an end a line of cases in which judges had held that success in business constituted a special contribution to the marriage justifying a departure from equal division (see e.g. *Cowan v Cowan* [2001] EWCA Civ 679). It should however be noted that although Thorpe L.J. laid great stress on the equal value to be accorded to the contributions made by each of the spouses, he also emphasised that a finding that the parties had made equal contributions would not automatically lead to a finding that equal division was appropriate, as all of the circumstances had to be taken into account. Yet two developments have already cut down the scope of the principle established in *Lambert*. First, if the assets are significantly greater than those in *Lambert*, the courts may well decide that a departure from equality in favour of the breadwinner is justified (see e.g. *Sorrell v Sorrell* and *Charman v Charman*, below). Secondly, in the case of shorter marriages, the decision of the House of Lords in *Miller; McFarlane* may well justify a different approach to assets accrued through one spouse's business efforts.

Key Principle: **In exceptional circumstances it may be found that one party has made a "special contribution" justifying a departure from equality**

Sorrell v Sorrell 2005
A fortune in excess of £100m had been generated by the husband's business during the marriage.

Held: The wife was entitled to 40 per cent of the assets. A departure from equality was justified on the basis of the husband's exceptional contribution.

Commentary

After *Lambert v Lambert* left open the possibility of finding that one spouse had made a "special contribution" in exceptional circumstances, it was only a matter of time before such an "exceptional" case came before the court. The judge tried to emphasise that his decision was not simply based on the size of the family fortune, noting instead that the husband was widely regarded as an exceptionally talented businessman. It hardly needs to be pointed out that an individual who has amassed a fortune of over £100m is almost bound to be regarded as an exceptionally talented businessman.

Charman v Charman 2006

The parties had been married for almost thirty years, and during that period the husband had built up a fortune of £150–160 million.

Held: The wife was entitled to 37 per cent of the assets. Exceptional wealth creation was a factor that could be taken into account in justifying a departure from equality.

Commentary

Charman made legal history as the largest award in favour of a wife to date—although this was on account of the sheer size of the husband's fortune rather than the percentage awarded to her. It was also the first "big money" case to be decided after the House of Lords' decision in *Miller; McFarlane*, and offered an ideal opportunity to test how business assets should be treated. Perhaps understandably, Coleridge J decided not to engage with the subtleties of the different judgments in that case, simply holding that however one approached the issue, the husband's exceptional wealth creation had to be taken into account. The fact that *Miller; McFarlane* has done little to clarify the law is also reflected in the judge's suggestion that it might be helpful to establish "some generally accepted tariff" which "might prove to be helpful guidance and, ultimately no less fair than the current expensive uncertainty." (para.136)

Key Principle: **The conduct of the parties should only be taken into account where it is "obvious and gross"**

Wachtel v Wachtel 1973

The parties divorced after eighteen years of marriage. The judge noted that each was equally responsible for the breakdown of the marriage. It was contended by counsel for the husband that this should have a negative impact on the provision to be made for the wife.

Held: (CA) The conduct of the parties should not influence the court's decision unless it was "obvious and gross."

Commentary

Wachtel marks the transition from the old law to the new. Under the old law fault was relevant, and even the equal blameworthiness of the wife (as opposed to her complete innocence) might be seen as a justification for awarding her a smaller share of the assets. *Wachtel* confirmed that the shift from fault to breakdown in the obtaining of a divorce would be reflected in the way that the courts exercised their jurisdiction over the assets of the parties. To have allowed couples to argue about responsibility for the breakdown of the marriage in this context would have undermined the purpose of the 1969 Divorce Reform Act, which aimed to ensure that marriages could be ended as amicably as possible. As Lord Denning M.R. explained, "there will obviously be a residue of cases where the conduct of one of the parties is . . . 'both obvious and gross', so much so that to order one party to support another whose conduct falls into this category is repugnant to anyone's sense of justice. . . But, short of cases falling into this category, the court should not reduce its order for financial provision merely because of what was formerly regarded as guilt or blame." (p.90). The limited role of fault established by the decision in *Wachtel* received Parliamentary approval in 1984, when the legislation was amended to emphasise that conduct would only be taken into account if it was inequitable to disregard it. The fact that fault will not be taken into account save in these limited circumstances was recently reasserted by the House of Lords in *Miller; McFarlane* (see above).

Key Principle: **Conduct that it is inequitable to disregard should not result in a punitive award but acts as a potentially magnifying factor when considering the other criteria listed in s.25**

H v H (Financial Relief: Attempted Murder as Conduct) 2006

The husband had viciously attacked the wife in front of their two young children, for which he had been imprisoned. The question for the court was how this should affect the division of the assets.

Held: in the circumstances of the case, the wife's needs should take priority over those of the husband, since he was responsible for the situation in which she found herself. She should therefore receive a substantially greater proportion of the assets.

Commentary

The discretionary nature of the law in this area is such that no mathematical formula can be derived from the result in this case. The fact that the wife received substantially more than half of the assets does not mean than in a similar case a wife would automatically be entitled to more than half. One would hope that few cases of this gravity occur: the judge agreed that this was conduct "at the very top end of the scale" (p.43) and it is difficult to imagine a clearer example of conduct that it "would be inequitable to disregard". The significance of the case lies in the approach to s.25(2)(g) adopted by Coleridge J., who emphasised that the court "should not be punitive or confiscatory for its own sake." (p.44). Instead, the husband should bear the responsibility for the situation he had created, and the needs of the wife should be prioritised. The higher proportion of the assets granted to her reflected not only her ongoing responsibility for the children of the marriage, but also the fact that she was no longer able to follow her career as a police officer and had a much diminished earning capacity. It also reflected the fact that the award was on a "clean break" basis: unsurprisingly, the wife wanted no further link with the husband even in the form of maintenance for herself or the children.

A Clean Break?

Key Principle: **The court is required to consider whether a clean break is appropriate, but should not strive to achieve it regardless of all other considerations**

Clutton v Clutton 1990

The former matrimonial home was the sole capital asset of the parties, and the wife's earning capacity was considerably less than that of the husband. The husband appealed against an order transferring the property to the wife.

Held: (CA) In the circumstances it was appropriate to make a *Martin* order, allowing the wife to remain in the property until she died, remarried, or cohabited.

Commentary

In this case fairness to the husband (in retaining some interest in the former matrimonial home) was seen to outweigh the importance of achieving a clean break between the parties (A *Martin* order was preferred to a *Mesher* order on the basis that the wife might not have sufficient assets to rehouse herself when her daughter reached the age of 18.) More recently, in *Miller; McFarlane*, the House of Lords emphasised that s.25A did not dictate a clean break.

Reconsidering the Division of Assets

Key Principle: **A periodical payments order does not automatically come to an end if the payee cohabits**

Atkinson v Atkinson 1988

A consent order had been made under which the husband was to pay the wife periodical payments of £6,000 per year. She subsequently began to cohabit with another man. The husband applied for the order to be varied.

Held: (CA) Although the wife's new relationship could be taken into account by the court in deciding whether to vary the periodical payments order, in the circumstances it was not appropriate to order any reduction.

Commentary

While periodical payments automatically terminate if the payee remarries, the court has a discretion in determining how far a cohabiting relationship should be taken into account. In this case the husband was a successful businessman earning £40,000 per year, while her new partner was earning a modest wage as a nurseryman. Without the periodical payments, the parties would have been

unable to pay the mortgage. Had the financial positions of the two
men been reversed, it is highly likely that the court would have
ordered a reduction or cessation of the periodical payments.

Key Principle: **If the original agreement was that the payer's
obligations would terminate on a particular date, the exercise
of a power to extend those obligations will require exceptional
justification**

Fleming v Fleming 2003

The parties separated in 1995 after 17 years of marriage and
divorced in 1997. A consent order provided for the division of
the assets and for the payment of £1,000 per month to the wife
by way of periodical payments. The order stated that the
periodical payments would be paid until December 20, 2002 but
there was no express provision prohibiting the wife from
applying for an extension of the term. Shortly before the date on
which the payments were to come to an end she applied for an
extension. At first instance the application was allowed.

Held: (CA) In the circumstances it was inappropriate to order
an extension. There was an enhanced duty on the court to bring
financial relationships between the parties to an end where the
payer had a legitimate expectation that his obligations would
cease on a certain date. There was no evidence that the
termination of the payments would cause financial hardship to
the wife.

Commentary

As the House of Lords noted in *Miller; McFarlane,* this means that
any person applying for the extension of an order for periodical
payments must surmount a high threshold. Of course, the reaction
of the court in that case was that it was inappropriate to impose a
term on the order for periodical payments, thus placing the onus
on the payer to apply for a variation if the circumstances of either
party changed.

Key Principle: **An appellate court should exercise caution in
granting leave to appeal and is only entitled to interfere if the
decision was plainly wrong**

Piglowska v Piglowski 1999

The case involved a dispute over the appropriate distribution of relatively modest assets (totalling £127,000).

Held: (HL) An appellate court should only grant leave to appeal if the decision of the lower court was plainly wrong. The appellate court should bear in mind the advantage which the first instance judge had in seeing the parties and the other witnesses, forbear from engaging in "narrow textual analysis" of judgments, and recognize that value judgments might differ.

Commentary

Limitations have now been imposed on the granting of leave to appeal (see r.52 of the Civil Procedure Rules). One situation in which leave may be granted is where the appeal would raise an important point of principle or practice. In *Piglowska*, however, the House of Lords counselled caution in granting leave even in such cases if the parties were of limited means. As Lord Hoffmann noted, there should be some degree of proportionality "between the amount at stake and the legal resources of the parties and the community which it is appropriate to spend on resolving the dispute." (p.785). After all, the result of the repeated appeals in *Pigslowska* had been to produce legal costs that exceeded the actual assets of the parties, an unsatisfactory result inviting comparisons with *Jarndyce v Jarndyce* in Charles Dickens' *Bleak House*.

Key Principle: **Leave may be granted to appeal out of time if the basis of the order has been falsified by a change in circumstances within a relatively short time of the order being made, as long as the application for leave was made promptly and third parties would not be unfairly prejudiced**

Barder v Barder (Caluori Intervening) 1987

After the divorce the wife remained in the former matrimonial home with the two children of the marriage. A consent order was made under which the husband was to transfer his share in the home to her, subject to her undertaking responsibility for the mortgage. Before the transfer was completed the wife killed the two children and committed suicide. Under her will, all of her property would go to her mother. The husband sought leave to appeal out of time against the order, on the ground that the basis of the order had been undermined by subsequent events.

Held: (HL) A court could properly grant leave to appeal against an order out of time if four conditions were satisfied: (1) that new events had occurred since the making of the order that so fundamentally undermined the basis on which the order was made that any appeal was likely to be successful; (2) that those events occurred within a relatively short time of the order (usually within a few months); (3) that the application for leave was made reasonably promptly; and (4) that the grant of leave to appeal would not prejudice third parties who had acquired interests in the relevant property in good faith and for valuable consideration. In this case all of the necessary conditions were satisfied and leave would be granted.

Commentary

As Lord Brandon of Oakbrook noted, the issue in this case was a difficult one because it involved a conflict between two principles: the first that there should be finality in litigation and the second that cases should be decided on the true facts, as far as possible. The conflict was resolved in this case by allowing leave to be granted only in certain tightly defined circumstances.

Key Principle: **An order may be set aside on the basis of a material non-disclosure**

Livesey v Jenkins 1985

The parties agreed that the husband would transfer his share in the former matrimonial home to the wife in lieu of periodical payments. The wife then became engaged to Mr Livesey, but did not disclose this fact. A consent order was made in the terms agreed, and the husband transferred his share to his wife. Shortly afterwards she married Mr Livesey. When he learnt of this, the husband sought leave to appeal out of time against the order.

Held: (HL) Leave would be granted and the consent order would be set aside on the basis of material non-disclosure.

Commentary

Had the consent order made provision for periodical payments, such payments would have ceased on the wife's remarriage. Thus the fact that the wife gave up any right to such payments was, in the circumstances, a poor exchange for the transfer of the husband's share in the former matrimonial home. The mere fact that the transaction was less advantageous to the husband than he had thought would not have justified the setting aside of the consent order. The House of Lords noted that unless the parties provided the court with all relevant information, the court would not be able properly to exercise its discretion as required by s.25. Each party therefore had a duty to make full and frank disclosure of all material facts, and in the circumstances the wife's failure to disclose her engagement justified the consent order being set aside. Lord Brandon of Oakbrook did, however, end his judgment with a warning that not every failure to disclose information would lead to an order being set aside: "it will only be in cases when the absence of full and frank disclosure has led to the court making, either in contested proceedings or by consent, an order which is substantially different from the order which it would have made if such disclosure had taken place that a case for setting aside can possibly be made good." (p.445). This reflects a theme that pervades much of the case-law in this area: the need for finality in litigation.

Dividing the Assets on Death

If an individual dies, the disposition of his or her estate may be regulated either by a will or, if no will was made, by the intestacy rules laid down by statute. In either case, it is possible for certain specified family members and dependants to apply for provision from the estate under the Inheritance (Provision for Family and Dependants) Act 1975. As the following cases show, there has been some litigation on the definition of particular categories of claimants (set out in s.1 of the Act), on the circumstances in which the provision made for the claimant will be deemed to be unreasonable, and on the level of provision that is appropriate.

In 1995, the 1975 Act was amended to allow a claim by a cohabitant who had been living with the deceased in the same household immediately before the date of the death, and for at least two years before that date, as the husband or wife of the deceased (s.1(3)(1A) of the 1975 Act). Each of these elements has been the object of judicial consideration.

Key Principle: **In deciding whether a particular couple were living together as husband and wife the court applies an objective test but takes into account the variety of spousal relationships that may exist**

Re Watson (deceased) 1999

The relationship between the parties began in the 1960s, and at one point they had been sexually involved, but it was not until 1985 that the applicant, Miss Griffiths, then aged 54, moved into the deceased's house. By this time their sexual relationship was over and they slept in separate rooms. Miss Griffiths looked after the house and cooked and cleaned for Mr Watson, as well as paying half of the day-to-day household expenses. In 1996 Mr Watson fell ill and died a few weeks after his admission to hospital. He left no will and no known surviving relatives, with the result that his estate would in default of any claims pass to the Crown as *bona vacantia*. Miss Griffiths claimed that she was entitled to bring a claim under the 1975 Act.

Held: In deciding whether a couple were living together "as husband and wife" the court "should ask itself whether, in the opinion of a reasonable person with normal perceptions, it could be said that the two people in question were living together as husband and wife; but when considering that question, one should not ignore the multifarious nature of marital relationships." (p.883). In the circumstances, such a person would take the view that the parties had been living together as husband and wife. She was thus entitled to bring a claim.

Commentary

Perhaps predictably, the newspapers reported this case with headlines such as "Chores make woman a wife" (*The Times*, November 28, 1998). Of course, it was the entire relationship between the parties that led the judge to conclude that their relationship had been one akin to that between husband and wife rather than an arms-length home-sharing relationship. Their care and concern for each other was demonstrated by his invitation to her to share his home, and by the fact that when Mr Watson learnt that he was dying he left the hospital to bid farewell to Miss Griffiths, whose own health made it impossible for her to travel to the hospital. The judge also emphasized that it would not be possible to hold that a couple were living together as husband and wife merely because their relationship was one that a husband and wife *might* have, since this would mean that virtually any relationship between a man and a woman living in the same household would fall within the legal definition. The requirement that the relationship be one that the ordinary person would recognise as spousal is reminiscent of the test applied to determine whether one person is a member of another's family, considered in chapter 1. It should also be noted that same-sex cohabitants can now claim on the basis that they had been living together as civil partners, to which a similar test will no doubt apply.

Key Principle: **A couple may be deemed to be living in the same household even if they reside in separate properties, but only if there is a significant degree of sharing and support between them**

Churchill v Roach 2002
The relationship between the parties began in the early 1990s, but although they spent weekends and holidays together they did not share a home. In 1998 the male partner sold his house and bought the cottage adjoining hers. The two properties were subsequently turned into one. He died early in 2000.

Held: The parties had not been living in the same household for two years and thus Ms Churchill could not claim as the cohabitant of the deceased.

Commentary
The issue in this case was whether the parties had been living in the same household for the requisite two-year period. The problem was that the deceased had died less than two years after buying the next-door property. While the judge accepted that it was possible to have one household and two properties, he decided that on the facts of this case there were in fact two separate domestic economies. He helpfully set out the sorts of factors that would be relevant in deciding whether a couple were "living in the same household", suggesting that this connoted "elements of permanence, to involve a consideration of the frequency and intimacy of contact, to contain an element of mutual support, to require some consideration of the degree of voluntary restraint upon personal freedom which each party undertakes, and to involve an element of community of resources." (p.1004). As he was quick to emphasise, none of these

factors is decisive, but each may be relevant. This approach means that those couples who genuinely have a shared life—who are, in effect, living apart together—will be able to bring a claim under this provision even if they have not been sharing a roof for two years, while those whose relationship is less developed will not. The latter may, however, be able to claim on the basis that they were dependent on the deceased (as indeed Ms Churchill successfully did in this case).

Key Principle: **A couple may be regarded as living together even if separated by a temporary absence**

Gully v Dix 2004

The parties had lived together since 1974. After the man sustained an accident their relationship came under strain, and there were a number of temporary separations of up to a week. In August 2001 he threatened to kill himself and a doctor advised his partner to leave for her own safety. His messages asking her to return were not passed on, and he was found dead in his bed in October 2001.

Held: The parties were still living together in the same household immediately before the death of the deceased. The female partner was accordingly entitled to bring a claim as his cohabitant.

Commentary

Even though the separation that preceded the male partner's death was longer than their earlier separations, it still seemed appropriate in the circumstances of the case to regard the parties as members of the same household (and not merely because under the intestacy rules the estate would have passed to the brother of the deceased, whom he had not seen in 30 years). Neither party regarded the relationship as being at an end: he clearly wanted her back, as his telephone messages showed, and as she had only taken a small suitcase of clothes she was clearly not intending to leave him permanently. In addition, the judge felt that the concealment of the deceased's messages was a significant factor, opining that the female partner would have returned if asked: "The very fact that her daughter concealed the telephone calls from her is an indication that, to those who knew her, it was obvious that she would have returned to live with the deceased the moment he asked her to do so." (p.29). It is clearly easier to satisfy the courts that an established cohabiting relationship has continued until death than that a nascent relationship has become a co-residential one.

As noted in the context of *Churchill v Roach* [2002] EWHC 3230, above, a claim may also be made by a person who was dependent on the deceased—i.e. a person who can show that he or she "was being maintained, either wholly or partly, by the deceased" immediately before the latter's death (s.1(1)(e) of the 1975 Act, and note the definition of "being maintained" in s.1(3)).

Key Principle: **A person was "being maintained" by the deceased if the deceased was making a substantial contribution to that person's reasonable needs other than for full valuable consideration**

Bishop v Plumley 1991

The parties had been living together for ten years prior to Mr Plumley's death in 1984. During the early years of their relationship he had been the primary breadwinner but by the end of 1983 both were in receipt of benefits and pooled their resources. Mr Plumley then inherited a sum of money from his uncle, which he used to purchase a house, and there they lived together until his death nine months later. At first instance it was held that she was not eligible to apply for provision under the 1975 Act as the financial benefits provided by the deceased were equalled by the domestic contributions provided by his cohabitant.

Held: (CA) In the circumstances, the provision of a home by Mr Plumley was a substantial contribution to the reasonable needs of the appellant, and her contribution to his needs by way of her love and support did not constitute "full valuable consideration" so as to prevent her from bringing a claim.

Commentary

A claimant in the situation of the appellant in this case would now be able to claim as a cohabitant, but at the time no such claim was possible. The case illustrates that a claim may be brought if the flow of benefits from the deceased to the claimant was greater than *vice versa*, a question that Butler-Sloss L.J. emphasised should be looked at "in the round, applying a commonsense approach, and avoiding fine balancing computations involving the value of normal exchanges of support in the domestic sense" (p.126). If both contribute equally to the relationship no claim is possible: as the judge noted, it could not be said that the appellant was being maintained by the deceased while both were pooling their benefits.

Even those eligible to bring a claim are still required to demonstrate that the disposition of the estate did not make reasonable financial provision for them, and some claims may fail at this stage, as the next case illustrates.

Key Principle: **A failure to make financial provision will not necessarily be unreasonable**

Re Jennings 1994

The claimant in this case was a 50-year-old man, whose parents had divorced when he was very young. There had been no continuing relationship between him and his father, who subsequently left his estate to charity. The son himself was in reasonably comfortable financial circumstances.

Held: (CA) In the circumstances, the father's failure to make provision for his son was not unreasonable. Although s.3(1)(d) required the court to take into account "any obligations and responsibilities which the deceased had towards any applicant for an order", this referred only to those obligations that the deceased had had immediately before his death, not to obligations that he might have had in the past. Although the father had failed to discharge his legal obligations to his son during the latter's minority, at the time of his death he had no legal or moral obligations towards his son.

Commentary

The case illustrates that it is not the purpose of the 1975 Act to enable the courts to rewrite a will to make provision for the deserving. As Henry L.J. emphasized, the powers of the court "to order financial provision to those of full age in good health and economically self-sufficient . . . should be exercised . . . circumspectly and in relatively rare circumstances" (p.546). It is not a precondition of a claim that the deceased should have owed a legal or moral obligation to the applicant, but even so a claim by an adult with an established earning power is likely to fail in the absence of special circumstances.

The final stage is to determine what provision is appropriate for the claimant. The legislation draws a distinction between the level of provision that should be made for a bereaved spouse (and now civil partner) and that which is appropriate for other claimants.

Key Principle: **Provision for a surviving spouse should take into account what the applicant might have received had the relationship been ended by divorce rather than death, but this does not determine the level of the award**

P v G, P and P (Family Provision: Relevance of Divorce Provision) 2004

The parties had been married for twenty years, but the marriage had been in difficulty for some years. The husband died following an attempted reconciliation, leaving an estate valued at over £4.5m. His will provided that the matrimonial home should be held on trust for his widow until her death or remarriage, and that the remainder of the estate should be held on trust for her and for his three children. The terms of the trust conferred on the trustees a discretion as to how much should be awarded to each of the beneficiaries, but a memorandum left by the husband stated that the wife had been adequately provided for by her entitlement to remain in the matrimonial home and the pension provision that had been made for her and discouraged the trustees from exercising their discretion in her favour unless she was suffering unforeseen hardship. The widow applied under the 1975 Act, and it was conceded that reasonable financial provision had not been made for her.

Held: Had the marriage ended by divorce rather than death, it is likely that the assets would have been divided equally. However, to award the wife only half of the assets would in this case not constitute reasonable provision. There is a difference between divorce (when there are two spouses for whom provision must be made) and death (when there is only one). The widow would accordingly be awarded a further £2m in addition to the pension provision that had already been made for her.

Commentary

The case is of significance for two reasons. First, it illustrates the way in which the courts approach their task under the 1975 Act—

a task that requires rather different questions to be asked in the wake of *White v White* (see above). Secondly, it demonstrates the limitations of the analogy that the statute requires them to draw. The judge in this case was clearly sensitive to the artificial nature of comparing provision on divorce to that appropriate on death, refusing to engage in an "entire fictional ancillary relief case" and recognising the salient difference between the two situations, namely the necessity of providing for both parties out of the assets if the relationship ends *inter vivos*.

Fielden v Cunliffe 2005
Mrs Cunliffe initially worked as the deceased's housekeeper. Six months later they married, and within 12 months he was dead. It was accepted that his will did not make reasonable financial provision for her.

Held: (CA) The widow should be awarded £600,000 (out of an estate valued at £1.4m). The shortness of the marriage was a factor that should be taken into account in deciding what level of provision should be ordered, just as it would be if the marriage had ended in divorce.

Commentary
The case confirmed both the applicability of the principles set out in *White v White* (and now, of course, those articulated in *Miller; McFarlane*) and the caution that should be exercised in applying those principles to a different context. In this case the facts— largely the shortness of the marriage—justified a departure from equality downwards rather than upwards.

Key Principle: **An applicant other than a spouse or civil partner is only entitled to receive such provision as is required for his or her maintenance**

Re Watson (deceased) 1999
The facts of the case are described above. A further point arose in this case as to the level of the provision that should be made for Miss Griffiths, who owned her own home and had an income of £5,000 per year.

Held: In the circumstances, the reasonable requirements of the claimant were for a home that was suitable in the light of her increasing frailty, and an extra £2,400 per year.

Commentary
Two points should be noted: first, although Miss Griffiths was the
only claimant and the deceased had left no relatives, she did not
receive the entire estate. Secondly, however, the relatively generous interpretation of "maintenance" should be noted: as in this
case, maintenance needs may include a need for housing rather
than being confined to day-to-day expenses.

7. LEGAL PARENTAGE AND PARENTAL RESPONSIBILITY

Establishing Parentage at Common Law

The basic principle at common law is that the child's biological parents are the child's legal parents. Litigated cases have largely concerned the circumstances in which biological parentage may be presumed or proved.

Key Principle: **The importance of establishing the truth outweighs the risk that a marriage will be destabilised by proof that the husband is not the father of the wife's children**

Re H and A (Children) 2002
The wife had been having sex with her husband and another man around the time that the twins were conceived. The other man then applied for parental responsibility and contact. The husband stated that if he was not the father then he would leave his wife and children.

Held: (CA) Tests should have been ordered. Establishing the truth was to be preferred to continuing uncertainty.

Commentary
The case confirms the trend away from protecting the family unit against potentially disruptive truths evidenced in earlier cases. The fact that biological paternity can now be established with virtual certainty by DNA profiling—rather than by a process of elimination through the comparison of blood groups—has undoubtedly been a factor in encouraging the courts to favour certainty over stability.

In any case, as Thorpe L.J. noted in this case, it could not automatically be assumed that the marriage of the parties would survive even if tests were not ordered, given the evidence of the wife's adultery. As a result, if there is a dispute as to whether a blood test should be ordered, the court will almost certainly hold that it is in the best interests of the child for the test to be carried out.

Key Principle: **If a man refuses to submit to a blood test there is a virtually inescapable inference that he is in fact the father**

Secretary of State for Work and Pensions v Jones 2003

The mother was living with Mr Jones at the time of conception but returned to her husband before the birth of her child, K, who was registered as the child of the mother's husband. The mother subsequently named Mr Jones as the father when seeking a maintenance assessment under the Child Support Act 1991. Mr Jones ticked the "Yes" box on the enquiry form in answer to the question of whether he was the father but added a question mark and wrote "maybe". He then failed to comply with the court's direction that he take a DNA test and did not attend the hearing.

Held: Mr Jones was the legal father of the child. The mother's evidence, combined with Mr Jones' answer on the CSA form and his failure to take the DNA test, suggested that on the balance of probabilities he was the child's legal father. In any case his refusal to undergo testing would by itself raise a virtually inescapable inference that he was the father.

Commentary

The willingness of the courts to draw adverse inferences from a refusal to undertake a blood test means that a man has no incentive to refuse to submit to a paternity test: if he does refuse he will be presumed to be the father anyway, and if he goes ahead with the test the evidence might show that he is not the father. As with the desirability of ordering such tests, a key influence on the law in this context is the certainty that such tests offer. In this case the evidence outweighed the presumption that the husband of the mother is the father of the child, as well as the presumption that the man registered as the father on the birth certificate is in fact the father.

Establishing Parentage under the Human Fertilisation and Embryology Act 1990

The Human Fertilisation and Embryology Act 1990 established special rules for determining legal parentage in cases of assisted reproduction. It should be borne in mind that in most cases of assisted reproduction the genetic materials of the couple who intend to bring up the resulting child are used. There is, however, a significant minority of cases in which the genetic material of a third party or parties (donated sperm, eggs or embryos) are used. The rule is that the woman who gives birth to a child is that child's legal mother. The provisions relating to legal fatherhood (contained in s.28 of the 1990 Act) are more complex and have given rise to litigation.

Key Principle: **A husband who does not consent to another man's sperm being used to treat his wife is not the legal father of any resulting child**

Leeds Teaching Hospital NHS Trust v A 2003

Two couples—one black, one white—had been receiving treatment at the same IVF clinic. Due to a mix-up Mrs A's eggs were mixed with Mr B's sperm, and Mrs A subsequently gave birth to mixed-race twins.

Held: Mr A was not the legal father of the twins. Under s.28(2) of the Human Fertilisation and Embryology Act the husband of a woman who is artificially inseminated or who has been implanted with an embryo not created from the husband's sperm will be treated as the legal father unless it is clear that he did not consent. In this case Mr A had himself provided sperm, and had only consented to his sperm being mixed with his wife's eggs. He had thus not consented to what had actually happened—i.e. her eggs being mixed with the sperm of a third party—and thus could not be treated as the legal father under s.28(2). The court further held that Mr B was the legal father, on the basis that he was the biological father of the child and that his position was not analogous to that of a sperm donor as he had not consented to his sperm being used to treat others.

Commentary

The complex reasoning in the case reflects the difficulties that arise if legislation has to be construed to meet unforeseen circumstances. The court adopted a very narrow meaning of "consent": it was not sufficient that the husband had consented to his wife receiving IVF treatment, since he had not consented to her receiving IVF treatment using donated sperm.

Key Principle: **A man and a woman are receiving treatment services "together" for the purposes of s.28(3) if at the time that the embryo was placed in the mother they are engaged in a joint enterprise that is intended to result in the birth of a child**

Re R (a child) 2005

A cohabiting couple had been trying for a child. They embarked upon IVF treatment, using sperm provided by an anonymous male donor. After the first cycle of treatment proved unsuccessful, the relationship between the parties came to an end. The mother did not inform the hospital of this and went through a second, successful cycle of treatment.

Held: (HL) Her former cohabitant was not the legal father of the child, as treatment services were not being provided to him and the mother "together" at the time that the embryo was placed in the mother.

Commentary

It was clear that the former cohabitant was not the biological father of the child. It was equally clear that the anonymous sperm donor was not the legal father of the child, by virtue of s.28(6)(a) of the 1990 Act. The question was whether the mother's former cohabitant could be treated as the legal father by virtue of s.28(3), which provides that where a course of treatment services is provided for "a man and a woman together" then the man is to be treated as the child's father. At first instance it was held that he was the legal father, on the basis that he and the mother had consented to two cycles of treatment and that as far as the clinic knew the parties were still together at the time the second cycle was carried out. However, the Court of Appeal, in reasoning endorsed by the House of Lords, came to a different conclusion. The test to be applied was not whether the parties were together at the time the treatment commenced, but whether they were together at the time that the embryo that resulted in a birth was placed in the mother. The different outcomes at different levels reveal conflicting policy considerations: should the court construe the legislation as widely as possible, to ensure that the child is not legally fatherless, or more narrowly, on the basis that creating legal relationships other than by blood or marriage is a serious matter? The Court of Appeal and House of Lords adopted the latter approach.

Key Principle: **A female-to-male transsexual who has gone through a (void) ceremony of marriage with a woman is not the legal parent of a child later born to that woman.**

J v C and E (a child) 2006

J, a female-to-male transsexual, went through a ceremony of marriage with C, a woman. C gave birth to two children as the result of artificial insemination by donor. Long after the parties had separated and the "marriage" had been declared void (see *S-T (formerly J) v J* [1997] 1 F.L.R. 402), J sought a specific issue order and prohibited steps order to regulate what the children were told about his gender and the reasons for the breakdown of the marriage. Whether he was entitled to apply for such orders without the leave of the court depended on whether he was a parent of the children in question.

Held: (CA) J was not a parent. Although s.27 of the Family Law Reform Act 1987 (the legislation that preceded the 1990 Act) provided that the other party to a void marriage would be treated as the father of a child conceived by artificial insemination by donor (as long as at least one of the parties believed the marriage to be valid), as a woman J could not be said to be a party to a marriage with a female.

Commentary

As Wall L.J., delivering the main judgment of the Court of Appeal, noted, the legal concept of a "parent" is not fixed, but depends on the context in which it is used. In this case the relevant statutory provision was s.27 of the Family Law Reform Act 1987. This statute, rather than the current governing legislation, was applicable as, while the child in question had been born after the Human Fertilisation and Embryology Act 1990 came into force, the critical date was the date on which artificial insemination must have occurred. Since this preceded the coming into force of the 1990 Act, the earlier legislation applied. Wall L.J. did suggest, however, that the same interpretation would apply to the equivalent provisions of the 1990 Act.

The decision of the court indicates that, despite the passage of the Gender Recognition Act 2004, the dictum of Lord Penzance in *Hyde v Hyde* (1865) LR 1 P & D 130 and the first instance decision of Ormrod J. in *Corbett v Corbett* [1971] P 83 (discussed in chapter 2) continue to exert an influence over English law. While a literal reading of the statute supported J's claim to be a parent, the court accepted the argument that marriage was exclusively the union of one man and one woman and that therefore there could not be a marriage of any kind between two women. Wall L.J. explained that s.11(c) of the Matrimonial Causes Act 1973—which provides that a marriage in which the parties are not respectively male and female is void—merely gave statutory expression to the decision in *Corbett*.

The decision does appear to be a harsh one. It is one thing to develop a category of "non-marriage" to deal with those ceremonies that fall outside the scope of the statute. It is quite another to hold that a marriage that a statute declares to be void is in fact in effect not a marriage at all. It should be noted that J subsequently acquired a Gender Recognition Certificate from the Gender Recognition Panel and is now legally a man. If he should subsequently marry a woman, such a marriage would be valid, and J would be the legal father of any child born as the result of artificial insemination by donor at a licensed clinic.

Key Principle: **A determination of legal parentage under the Human Fertilisation and Embryology Act is good for all purposes**

Re CH (Contact: Parentage) 1996
The husband had had a vasectomy during a previous marriage and it proved impossible to reverse the operation. The couple then decided to undergo fertility treatment and were advised that the best way for them to achieve parenthood would be for the wife to be artificially inseminated with donated sperm. The husband gave his written consent to the procedure and a child was subsequently born to the parties. The marriage between the parties broke down less than a year later and the wife sought to deny contact between her former husband and the child on the basis that he was not the child's biological father and therefore there was no presumption of contact in his favour.

Held: The husband was the legal father of the child under the 1990 Act and there was no reason to treat him any differently from a man who was the biological father of a child.

Commentary
The case illustrates that legal parentage is good for all purposes. The husband may have acquired his status as the child's father

because he was married to the mother, but the ending of the marriage did not cause him to lose that status. As the judge pointed out, the birth of the child in this case was the result of what was essentially a joint enterprise between the husband and the wife: both had wanted the child to be conceived.

It should however be noted that courts today are wary of stating that there is a *presumption* in favour of contact with any parent, legal or biological, particularly in the circumstances of violence that led to the separation in this case (see further chapter 8).

Should the court make a parental responsibility order?

There are a number of ways in which a father may acquire parental responsibility (by being married to, or subsequently marrying, the mother, by entering into a parental responsibility agreement with the mother, or, after December 2002, by registering the birth jointly with the mother). In other cases it will be necessary for him to apply for a parental responsibility order, and there have been a number of cases in which the propriety of making such an order has been questioned. Since 2005 a step-parent has also been able to apply for a parental responsibility order (and to enter into a parental responsibility agreement).

Key Principle: **In deciding whether to make a parental responsibility order, the court will have regard to the degree of the father's commitment and attachment to the child and his reasons for seeking the order**

Re H (Minors) (Local Authority: Parental Rights) (No. 3) 1991
The issue was whether a parental rights order—the predecessor to the parental responsibility order introduced by the Children Act 1989, which was not in force at the material time—should be granted to the father. The parents had never married and had ceased to cohabit, but the father had remained in regular twice-weekly contact with the children even after they had been received into care by the local authority.

Held: (CA) In considering whether to make a parental rights order in favour of an unmarried father, the court will take into account, among other factors, the degree of the father's commitment and attachment to his child and his reasons for seeking an order. In the circumstances it was appropriate to make a parental rights order in the father's favour.

Commentary
Although the case was decided under the legislation that preceded the 1989 Act (hence the reference to "parental rights" rather than the concept of "parental responsibility" introduced by the 1989 Act), the courts have continued to rely on the three factors identified by the court in this case as a guide in deciding whether parental responsibility should be granted. These three factors do not, however, determine the issue: other factors may be relevant, and the welfare of the child, rather than the father's desire to have his status recognised, will be the paramount consideration, as *Re H (Parental Responsibility)* [1998] 1 F.L.R. 855, below, shows.

The case also illustrates that granting parental responsibility may have little effect in practice, since the court also decided that on the facts the father was unreasonably refusing his consent to the children being adopted by third parties.

Key Principle: **In deciding whether to make a parental responsibility order, the welfare of the child is the paramount consideration for the court**

Re H (Parental Responsibility) 1998
The relationship between the parents broke down but the father continued to have contact with his son. After one visit the boy was found to have bruises on his body (including the inner ear, penis and scrotum). The father denied inflicting these injuries but in the context of his application for a parental responsibility order it was concluded that he had done so, and that the nature of the injuries indicated deliberate cruelty and possibly sadism. The order was therefore refused.

Held: (CA) Parental responsibility should not be awarded to the father. The three factors set out in *Re H (Minors) (Local Authority: Parental Rights) (No.3)* provided the court with a useful starting point but were not exhaustive. The court was under a duty to take all of the circumstances of the case into account, bearing in mind that the welfare of the child was paramount.

Commentary

There has been some debate as to whether s.1(1) of the Children
Act applies to applications for parental responsibility orders, but
the consensus is that it does. As Bulter-Sloss P noted there is no
presumption that a father who fulfils the factors set out in *Re H
(Minors) (Local Authority: Parental Rights) (No.3)* should be
granted parental responsibility, and in individual cases there may
be factors that tip the balance against making an order. In this case
the court suggested that it was the father's failure to acknowledge
the harm that he had done to his son, as well as the harm itself,
that indicated that parental responsibility should not be granted to
him.

Key Principle: **Whether or not parental responsibility should
be granted is a distinct and separate question from whether
the father should have contact with his child**

Re C and V (Contact and Parental Responsibility) 1998

The father applied for parental responsibility and contact after
his relationship with the mother broke down. His application
for contact was refused on the basis that the stress that would be
caused to the mother would have a detrimental impact on her
ability to care for her son, who was ill and needed regular care,
and his application for parental responsibility was refused on
the basis that it was linked to the application for contact.

Held: (CA) An application for parental responsibility should
be treated as separate from an application for contact, and the
refusal of one should not mean the automatic refusal of the
other. In the circumstances parental responsibility would be
granted to the father.

Commentary

The court emphasised that a parental responsibility order was
designed to confer a status on the father rather than to enable him
to exercise his role as a parent. Any potential misuse of his
parental responsibility could be controlled by orders under s.8 of
the Children Act (as to which see further chapter 8). Despite the
references to status, the reasoning of the court was child-focused
rather than parent-focused, it being argued that it would generally
be in the best interests of a child for a father to have parental

responsibility. Thus, according to Ward L.J., "a child needs for its self-esteem to grow up, wherever it can, having a favourable positive image of an absent parent; and it is important that, wherever possible, the law should confer on a concerned father that stamp of approval because he has shown himself willing and anxious to pick up the responsibility of fatherhood and not to deny or avoid it." (p.397). One might wonder whether the conferral of parental responsibility will suffice to create such a favourable image, particularly if the exercise of parental responsibility is constrained by orders under s.8.

Key Principle: **A parental responsibility order may be refused if the parent intends to use the order for improper and inappropriate means**

Re P (Parental Responsibility) 1998

The relationship between the parents had begun when the father was in his 60s and the mother was in her mid-teens. The relationship lasted for seven years, and even after separation the father continued to enjoy considerable contact with his daughter. However, when the mother discovered obscene photographs of children (including his own grandchildren) in the father's possession she took steps to restrict contact. The father then applied for parental responsibility. The judge refused to make the order on the basis that the father would make inappropriate use of it.

Held: (CA) The judge had been right to refuse the parental responsibility order. While his commitment and attachment to his daughter were not in question, the irresponsibility of his behaviour and the likelihood that he would abuse his parental responsibility justified its refusal.

Commentary

The choice in this case lay between, on the one hand, granting a parental responsibility order but constraining the father's exercise of parental responsibility by orders under s.8 and, on the other, refusing to grant parental responsibility in the first place. The fact that the court chose the second option reflects the seriousness of the father's behaviour in the present case (a clinic had assessed him as being deeply confused over sexual boundaries and his history of pestering his daughter's school and making unfounded allegations about the mother's care to social services raised concerns about how he would use parental responsibility). As the court pointed out, it was not the law that a parental responsibility order would automatically be granted to a committed father on the basis that any manifestation of irresponsibility could be addressed by a s.8 order.

Key Principle: **A parental responsibility order may be made subject to conditions**

B v A, C and D (Acting By Her Guardian) 2006

Ms A and Ms C, a lesbian couple, advertised for a man who would be interested in fathering a child. Mr B responded, and D was conceived following sexual intercourse between Ms A and Mr B. Mr B then sought to be involved in D's life, seeking a contact order (which was granted) and a parental responsibility order (which was deferred). When the latter application came to be heard, Mr B offered undertakings not to interfere in certain areas of D's life.

Held: A parental responsibility order would be made subject to the undertakings offered by Mr B.

Commentary

The dilemma facing the court in this case was a familiar one: should a parental responsibility order be granted if there was a risk that the father would disrupt the child's upbringing? In earlier cases the issue had been dealt with by either refusing the order (see *Re P*) or granting it upon the understanding that the father's exercise of parental responsibility could be controlled by orders under s.8 of the Children Act. Here, however, a more creative solution was available in the light of the undertakings offered by Mr B.

Other Means of Conferring Parental Responsibility

The Children Act sets out a number of ways in which parental responsibility may be obtained by specified persons—for example adoptive parents, special guardians, guardians and a local authority. Parental responsibility is also conferred automatically on any person in whose favour a residence order is made, and such orders may be used deliberately to confer parental responsibility.

Key Principle: **A residence order may be made to confer parental responsibility**

Re G (Residence: Same-Sex Partner) 2005

CG, who was in a long-term lesbian relationship with CW, conceived their two children by anonymous donor insemination. Both women played an equal role in the children's upbringing. After the relationship between the two adults broke down, CG attempted to exclude CW from the children's lives.

Held: (CA) A shared residence order would be granted in order to recognise the role of the co-parent, since this was the only means by which parental responsibility could be conferred upon her.

Commentary

As the court noted, the children in this case required "firm measures to safeguard them from diminution in, or loss of, a vital side of family life." (para.27). Making a shared residence order primarily to confer parental responsibility is not unprecedented, but this would appear to be the first case in which this option was used to secure the children's ongoing relationship with a former same-sex partner of a parent (for the sequel see *In re G (children)* [2006], discussed in chapter 8). It should be noted that it is now possible for civil partners to enter into a parental responsibility agreement, although this of course only assists those who wish to formalise their relationship and would not offer a solution once the relationship between the parties had broken down.

Losing Parental Responsibility

Key Principle: **Parental responsibility may be revoked by the court, whether granted by agreement or order**

Re P (Terminating Parental Responsibility) 1995

When P was nine weeks old she was admitted to hospital with a combination of injuries that had evidently been inflicted deliberately and over a period of time. As a result of these injuries P was permanently disabled, both mentally and physically. The mother subsequently entered into a parental responsibility agreement with the father, to whom she was not married, in the belief that he was not responsible for the child's injuries. The father subsequently admitted that he was guilty of harming P, and was convicted of a number of offences, for which he served a prison sentence. The mother then applied for the parental responsibility agreement to be terminated.

Held: It was clear that the court had jurisdiction to terminate the parental responsibility of an unmarried father under the Children Act 1989 (see now s.4(2A) of the Act). In general, it should be slow to do so: parental responsibility "once obtained should not be terminated . . . on less than solid grounds, with a presumption for continuance rather than for termination." (p.1052). In the circumstances, however, parental responsibility should be terminated. The father had forfeited parental responsibility by his actions and the continuance of the parental responsibility agreement would be unsettling for the other parties involved—the mother, the foster-parents who were caring for the child, and the local authority.

Commentary
The case illustrates that in an appropriate case the court may bring the parental responsibility of an unmarried father to an end. While one can have little sympathy for the father in this case, it is worth noting that no such jurisdiction exists in the case of a *married* father, or indeed the married or unmarried mother. Such persons cannot forfeit parental responsibility whatever their behaviour, unless their child is adopted by a third party.

The Scope of Parental Responsibility

Key Principle: **Rights are conferred on parents and persons with parental responsibility for the benefit of the child, and must be exercised in this way**

Re A (Minors)(Conjoined Twins: Medical Treatment) 2001
Conjoined twins were born. The medical evidence was that if an operation was not carried out to separate them both would eventually die. If such an operation were to be carried out, the weaker twin would die almost immediately but the stronger

twin had a good chance of survival. The parents, who were devout Catholics, did not want the operation to go ahead.

Held: (CA) The operation to separate the twins should be carried out, as the least detrimental option.

Commentary
This sad case raised many complex issues, but for present purposes its significance lies in the willingness of the courts to override parental wishes in the best interests of the child. One consequence of parental responsibility is the right to consent to the child receiving medical treatment, but as Ward L.J. noted, this right exists "for the performance of their duties and responsibilities to the child and must be exercised in the best interests of the child." Their opposition to the operation could thus be overridden.

Key Principle: **There are limits on the extent to which a parent or person with parental responsibility may use physical punishment to discipline a child**

A v UK (Human Rights: Punishment of Child) 1998
A nine-year-old boy was discovered to have severe bruising, and his stepfather admitted caning him on a number of occasions. The stepfather was subsequently charged with assault occasioning actual bodily harm but pleaded in his defence that a parent was entitled to administer moderate and reasonable punishment. He was acquitted of the offence. The case was then taken to the European Court of Human Rights.

Held: (ECHR) The step-father's treatment of the child amounted to a violation of art.3 of the ECHR ("inhuman or degrading treatment or punishment"), and UK law had not provided adequate protection for the child.

Commentary
The decision of the European Court of Human Rights that UK law violated the Convention did not immediately lead to reform. Eventually the defence of "reasonable chastisement" was abolished by s.58 of the Children Act 2004 and replaced by one of "reasonable punishment."

This new defence cannot be used to justify an assault or battery of a child that caused actual bodily harm, wounding or grievous bodily harm, but can be invoked in relation to the less serious charge of assault.

Sharing Parental Responsibility

Key Principle: **There are some issues that should not be determined by a unilateral exercise of parental responsibility**

Re G (Parental Responsibility: Education) 1994
The children remained with their father after their parents divorced. The boy, aged nine, became difficult at school and it was arranged that he should attend a local education authority boarding school. When the mother learned of these plans she opposed the move.

Held: (CA) The mother should have been consulted about the decision to send her son to boarding school. However, in the circumstances it was not possible to say that the judge had been wrong to decide that it would be in the best interests of the boy to attend the boarding school.

Commentary
The decision by the court that the mother should have been consulted would seem to contradict the express provision in s.2(7) of the Children Act that each person who enjoys parental responsibility "may act alone and without the other . . . in meeting that responsibility." Despite this, the courts have adopted the view that there are certain decisions that one parent should not take alone, and that the approval of the court is required if the other parent or person with parental responsibility does not agree, as the following case further illustrates.

Re J (Specific Issue Orders: Child's Religious Upbringing and Circumcision) 2000
The parents of J separated when he was two-and-a-half years old. He was brought up by his mother, a non-practising Christian, in an essentially secular household. When he was five years old his father—a non-practising Muslim of Turkish origin—sought a specific issue order that J be circumcised. The mother opposed the application, and the judge held that circumcision was not in J's best interests.

Held: (CA) The appeal would be dismissed. It was noted that s.2(7) of the Children Act did not entitle a parent to arrange for the circumcision of a child without the consent of the other. In the words of Dame Elizabeth Butler-Sloss P there is "a small group of important decisions made on behalf of a child which, in the absence of agreement of those with parental responsibility, ought not to be carried out or arranged by a one-parent carer although she has parental responsibility under s.2(7) of the Children Act 1989. Such a decision ought not to be made without the specific approval of the court. Sterilisation is one example. The change of a child's surname is another. Some of the examples, including the change of a child's surname, are based upon statute (see s.13(1) of the 1989 Act) . . . The issue of circumcision has not, to my knowledge, previously been considered by this court, but in my view it comes within that group." (paras 31–2).

Commentary
The interest of the case lies not in the precise point decided but in the useful list provided by the then President of the Family Division of the circumstances in which the consensus of those with parental responsibility, or the approval of the court, will be necessary. Immunisation has since been added to the list (see *Re C (Welfare of Child: Immunisation)* [2003] EWCA Civ 1148). In a sense, however, the principle developed in these cases is unnecessary. If one parent disagrees with the way in which the other is exercising parental responsibility, then the appropriate course is an application under s.8 of the Children Act 1989 (see further chapter 8). It is irrelevant for these purposes whether that parent was consulted, and any disagreement between parents that results in an application to the court will require resolution by the court.

Children's Rights and Parental Responsibility

Key Principle: **A child of sufficient maturity and understanding is entitled to take certain decisions**

Gillick v West Norfolk and Wisbech Area HA 1986
The case was sparked off by guidance on family planning issued by the Department of Health and Social Security to area health authorities. Mrs Gillick, a mother of five, objected to the suggestion that in exceptional cases a doctor could, in the exercise of his clinical judgment, prescribe contraception for a girl under the age of 16 without the knowledge or consent of her parents. Mrs Gillick accordingly sought an assurance that no

contraceptive advice or treatment would be given to any of her daughters while under 16 years of age without her knowledge and consent. The area health authority refused to give such an assurance, and Mrs Gillick sought a declaration that the DHSS advice was unlawful and wrong. At first instance the declaration was refused, but the Court of Appeal allowed Mrs Gillick's appeal.

Held: (HL) The appeal would be allowed and the declaration refused. While it would be unusual for a doctor to give contraceptive advice and treatment to a girl under the age of 16 without the knowledge or consent of her parents, there would be circumstances in which it might be desirable for doctors to exercise their discretion to do so. A girl under the age of 16 would be able to consent to such treatment provided that she was of sufficient maturity and intelligence.

Commentary
Mrs Gillick's crusade to reinforce parental rights and to ensure that her daughters would not be given contraceptive advice without her knowledge backfired spectacularly. Her name has in fact become synonymous with adolescent autonomy: "*Gillick*-competent" children of sufficient age and understanding are entitled to take at least some decisions pertaining to their welfare. The exact scope of adolescent decision-making is not entirely clear, largely because even the judges who agreed on what the outcome of the case should be did not speak with one voice. The majority agreed that parental rights exist for the benefit of the child rather than for the benefit of the parent, but while Lord Fraser stated that parental rights do not disappear until the child reaches the age of 18 (suggesting, however, that wise parents relax their control and allow increasing independence), Lord Scarman, by contrast, suggested that as soon as a child is competent to make certain decisions, a parent loses the right to make those decisions for the child.

While *Gillick* has often been hailed as a milestone for children's rights, it should be noted that considerations of welfare also played an important role. The provision of contraceptive advice and treatment without parental knowledge or consent was seen as a lesser evil than unwanted teenage pregnancies. This is most apparent in the decision of Lord Fraser, who set out a number of conditions regarding which a doctor should satisfy himself before providing contraceptive advice or treatment to a girl under the age of 16, including, in addition to the ability of the girl to understand the relevant advice, the likelihood that the girl would begin or continue to have sexual intercourse with or without such advice, the likelihood that the girl's mental and/or physical health would suffer if she did not receive such advice, and, most telling of all, "that her best interests required him to give her contraceptive advice, treatment, or both without the parental consent." (p.239).

Twenty years after the decision of the House of Lords in *Gillick*, revised guidance issued by the Department of Health sparked a fresh legal challenge:

R (ota Axon) v Secretary of State for Health 2006

Mrs Axon challenged the lawfulness of guidance issued by the Department of Health, claiming that it misrepresented the decision in *Gillick*. She argued that doctors were under no obligation to keep the provision of contraceptive advice and treatment to a child under the age of 16 confidential and therefore that such advice and treatment—in particular abortion—should not be provided without parental knowledge and consent.

Held: The declaration would be refused. It would be inappropriate and unacceptable to retreat from the guidelines laid down in *Gillick*, which were equally applicable to abortion.

Commentary

There were two factors that distinguished *Axon* from *Gillick*: first, the fact that the challenge focused on the more serious issue of abortion, and, secondly, the passage of the Human Rights Act and subsequent scope for the reinvigoration of arguments based on parental rights. But of course the test established in *Gillick* is one that adapts to the seriousness of the issue at stake: a higher level of maturity and intelligence is likely to be required to undergo an abortion than to begin using contraception. As Silber J. pointed out, the requirement that a minor understand properly "'what is involved' . . . would constitute a high threshold and many young girls would be unable to satisfy the medical professional that they fully understood all the implications of the options open to them." (para.90). On the second point, the passage of the Human Rights Act made no difference to the outcome, because the parent had no right to family life once the child attained sufficient maturity to make the decision.

Key Principle: **A person under the age of eighteen has no power to refuse medical treatment if consent has been given by someone who has parental responsibility or by the court**

Re E (A Minor) (Wardship: Medical Treatment) 1993

A young man was diagnosed with leukaemia a few months before his sixteenth birthday. As a devout Jehovah's Witness he refused to agree to the blood transfusion treatment that the doctors regarded as the most appropriate treatment for him and which might in certain circumstances become essential to save his life. His parents, also Jehovah's Witnesses, similarly refused their consent. The hospital sought the leave of the court to treat him as they saw fit.

Held: Leave would be granted to enable the blood transfusions to go ahead. The young man did not have a full understanding of what his refusal of treatment would involve and his refusal was therefore not decisive. It was the responsibility of the court, exercising its wardship jurisdiction, to act in the best interests of the child. In this case his best interests required that the hospital should be at liberty to treat him as it saw fit.

Commentary

The decision in this case indicates that children's autonomy is more limited than that of adults. A competent adult may refuse medical treatment, a child, even one on the verge of adulthood, may not. While the boy in this case was under the age of sixteen, it is clear from other decisions that the jurisdiction of the court to override a child's refusal of treatment lasts until the child's eighteenth birthday (see e.g. *Re W (a minor) (medical treatment: court's jurisdiction)* [1993] Fam. 64). While it is understandable that the courts are reluctant to allow a child to refuse potentially life-saving treatment, the result is that children are only allowed to make those decisions which are deemed to be in their best interests anyway (i.e. to consent to life-saving treatment), which can only be regarded as a very limited form of autonomy.

There are, however, some indications that the courts may be more willing to respect children's autonomy if issues of life and death are not at stake.

Key Principle: A Gillick-competent child should be able to share otherwise private information with the world at large

Re Roddy (A Child) (Identification: Restriction on Publication) 2003

The case concerned a girl who had become pregnant at the age of 12. Her child was subsequently taken into care and adopted. An injunction prevented the newspapers from disclosing the identity of any of the parties involved. Later, aged almost seventeen, the girl approached the *Mail on Sunday* with her story. The newspaper sought a variation of the injunction to enable it to publish the girl's story.

Held: The injunction would be varied to allow publication while protecting the identity of the father and the child. The mother should be able to tell her story as she wished.

Commentary
The key interest of the case lies in Munby J.'s robust defence of children's rights. For him, the main issue in the case was the girl's right to tell her own story, which engaged both art.10 (freedom of expression) and art.8 (the right to private and family life—in this context the right to decide what information should be shared with others). It was the responsibility of the court "not merely to recognise but . . . to defend . . . the right of the child who has sufficient understanding to make an informed decision." (para.57). As in all these cases, the ability of a child to act as he or she wishes will depend on the court's assessment of the child's maturity and ability to understand the issues at stake.

8. CHILDREN: PRIVATE DISPUTES

Under s.8 of the Children Act 1989, courts have the power to make a number of different types of orders regulating the upbringing of children: residence orders, contact orders, specific issue orders and prohibited steps orders. A number of key issues relating to such orders are addressed in this chapter: first, who can apply for an order; secondly, what is the scope of the various orders; thirdly, in what circumstances will such orders be made; and, fourthly, how may orders be enforced in the case of breach? The Children Act also contains certain specific restrictions on unilateral action by a parent: under s.13, if a residence order is in force one parent may not change the child's surname, or remove the child from the jurisdiction, without the written consent of every person with parental responsibility or the leave of the court. The way in which the court has resolved disputes over these matters is considered at the end of the chapter.

Who May Apply for an Order?

Under s.10 of the Children Act 1989, certain persons are entitled to apply for any s.8 order automatically. Parents are included within this category, which may raise questions about the reality of claimed parentage or the meaning of the word "parent" (see e.g. *J v C and E (a child)* [2006], discussed in chapter 7). Other specified persons may only apply for certain orders, and a further category of persons must seek the leave of the court in order to apply for an order. It is this last category, by definition, that has given rise to litigation.

Key Principle: **The decision whether or not to grant leave is governed by the factors set out in s.10(9), and the welfare of the child is not the paramount consideration for the court in this context**

Re A and others (Minors) (Residence Orders: Leave to Apply) 1992
In 1989 the local authority placed the four children with a foster mother. Two years later the children were removed from her care and she applied for leave to apply for a residence order.

Held: (CA) On the basis of the factors listed in s. 10(9), leave would be refused.

Commentary

The case illustrates the limited role of the welfare principle, which only applies where the court is determining a substantive issue with respect to the upbringing of the child concerned. The court pointed out that the specific factors listed in s.10(9) would be otiose if the welfare principle applied, and that any application for leave had to be determined in accordance with those specific factors (namely (a) the nature of the proposed application for the s.8 order; (b) the applicant's connection with the child; (c) any risk there might be of that proposed application disrupting the child's life to such an extent that he would be harmed by it; and (d) where the child is being looked after by a local authority (i) the authority's plans for the child's future; and (ii) the wishes and feelings of the child's parents). In refusing leave on the facts of the case, the court was particularly influenced by the wishes of the children involved, all of whom were opposed to any return to the foster mother, and by the potential disruption that would be caused if the foster mother's application were to proceed.

Key Principle: **It is not necessary for the applicant to show 'a good arguable case' for leave to apply for an order to be granted**

Re J (Leave to issue application for residence order) 2002

The case concerned a child born in 2001. Her mother suffered from psychiatric illness and was unable to care for the child. The local authority assessed the mother's own mother as a potential carer but decided that she was too old to bear the burden of bringing up a young child and that the best solution would be a care order leading to adoption. The grandmother applied for leave to apply for a residence order.

Held: (CA) Leave to apply for the order would be granted. Applications should be determined by the application of the statutory factors set out in s.10(9) of the Children Act. That checklist contained no requirement that the applicant should show a "good arguable case", and protection of the applicant's rights under art.6 of the ECHR required, as a minimum, that applications should not be dismissed without full enquiry.

Commentary
The court in this case rejected an earlier line of cases that had advanced the view that an applicant for leave would need to show "a good arguable case", and reasserted the importance of the statutory list of factors set out in s.10(9). Indeed, Thorpe L.J. stated categorically that the statutory language was "transparent" and that "[n]owhere does it import any obligation on the judge to carry out independently a review of future prospects." (para.14). Subsequent cases have, however, held that a judge is permitted to take the prospects of a claim succeeding into account in deciding whether or not to grant leave (in that it is relevant to the nature of the proposed application) and is only prohibited from dismissing an application *solely* on the basis that it has no reasonable prospects of success (see *Re R (Adoption: Contact)* [2005] EWCA Civ 1128). The latter view is sustainable, since s.10(9) is not an *exhaustive* list of the factors to which the court must have regard in deciding whether to grant leave.

Key Principle: **A person otherwise automatically entitled to apply for a s.8 order may be required to obtain the leave of the court if such a restriction is deemed to be in the best interests of the child**

Re P (Section 91(14) Guidelines) (Residence and Religious Heritage) 1999

The child of Orthodox Jewish parents, who were unable to look after her, was placed with Roman Catholic foster parents. The placement was intended to be a temporary one, but no foster parents of the same religious background could be found. The foster parents applied for, and were granted, a residence order. The parents subsequently applied for the order to be varied.

Held: (CA) The parents' application was dismissed and a leave requirement was imposed to prevent them from making any future applications without the leave of the court.

Commentary
The case illustrates that the key consideration for the courts in deciding whether to impose a leave requirement under s.91(14) of the Children Act is the welfare of the child concerned, not the reasonableness of the previous applications. The court in this case

felt that any future litigation, even if motivated by genuine parental concern, would be damaging to the child. The highly-charged proceedings had already taken their toll on all of the parties. It was emphasised that any restriction had to be proportionate to the harm that it was intended to avoid. The case also confirms that the imposition of a limited restriction on access to the courts is not seen to be inconsistent with art.6 of the ECHR.

Key Principle: **The court has a discretion to refuse to grant leave to a child who wishes to apply for a s.8 order, even if the child has sufficient understanding to make the application**

Re H (Residence Order: Child's Application for Leave) 2000

The parents of a twelve-year-old boy, S, were divorcing. S sought leave under s.10(8) to apply for a residence order in favour of his father. Two solicitors confirmed that he was of sufficient understanding to do so.

Held: Leave would be refused, even though S had sufficient understanding to make the application. As S's wishes coincided with those of his father, there was no need for S to make a separate application. S's wishes would be taken into account by the courts in determining the substantive issue.

Commentary

The case illustrates the difficulties facing a child who is seeking leave to apply for a s.8 order. Under s.10(8) leave can be granted if the court is satisfied that the child has sufficient understanding to make the proposed application. This in itself poses a significant hurdle to be surmounted. While no other conditions are stipulated, the courts have consistently adopted the view that there is a discretion to refuse the application for leave even if the child does have sufficient understanding.

As the next case shows, the court may refuse to grant leave even if the child's views conflict with those of *both* parents.

Re C (A Minor) (Leave to Seek Section 8 Order) 1994

C, who was almost 15 years of age, became unhappy at home and, with her parents' permission, went to stay with a friend, initially for a short holiday. At the end of the holiday she refused to return to her parents, and sought leave to apply for a residence order in favour of her friend's family, and also for a specific issue order in order to go on holiday with them.

Held: In the circumstances there would be no advantage in making a residence order, and this application would therefore be adjourned. Leave to apply for the specific issue order would be refused, as the jurisdiction to entertain applications by children should be reserved for serious cases. The issue was one that should be resolved by discussion between the parties rather than by the intervention of the court.

Commentary

At one level, the judge's unwillingness to grant leave to apply for a s.8 order is understandable. No one would wish to see the courts clogged with applications by children disputing the way in which their parents exercised parental responsibility (bedtimes, choice of food etc). Yet, as pointed out above, the granting of leave is in any case dependent on the child being able to demonstrate sufficient understanding to make the application. While the judge opined that the issue in dispute was "not a matter that I regard as important" (p.29), it is difficult to escape the suspicion that the issue was deemed to be trivial simply because the person applying for leave was a child. Certainly the courts have been willing to adjudicate on the holiday plans of disputing *parents* (see e.g. *Re N (A Child)* [2006] EWCA Civ 357). Moreover, it can be argued that in most family disputes it is better for the parties to sort matters out for themselves rather than involve the court, but, again, this does not deter the court from adjudicating between disputing adults.

It should be noted, however, that at the time of the case C was still living with her friend's family. While the court refused to formalise this arrangement, it equally did not envisage that it would be appropriate to force C to return to her parents. To this extent the autonomy of C was respected.

Key Principle: **Once "family proceedings" are before the court, the court has the power to make an order, even if no application has been made for it**

Gloucestershire CC v P 1999

The child at the centre of the case had been taken into care by the local authority and had been living with foster parents for two-and-a-half years. The local authority felt that it was in the best interests of the child to be adopted, while the paternal grandparents wished to apply for a residence order. The guardian *ad litem* took the view that a residence order in favour of the foster parents would be the best option. However, under the terms of s.9(3) of the Children Act the foster parents were unable to apply for such an order as they were not related to the child, the child had not been living with them for the requisite three years, and nor did they have the consent of the local authority. The preliminary issue for the court was whether it had the power to make a residence order in favour of the foster-parents.

Held: (CA) The court had the power to make a residence order in favour of the foster-parents. Under s.10(1)(b) of the Children Act 1989, once "family proceedings" are before the court it has jurisdiction to make an order if it "considers that the order should be made even though no such application has been made." This broad discretion to exercise its powers in the best interests of the child was not curtailed by the restrictions in s.9(3) on the ability of a foster-parent to apply for an order.

Commentary
It is clear that if there are "family proceedings" before the court, the court has the power to make an order under s.8 even if no application has been made for that specific order. *Gloucestershire CC v P* took this principle a step further, in that the Court of Appeal made an order in favour of persons who were specifically debarred from seeking an order. The case stands as a reminder of the wide discretion of the court, although it was emphasised that the court would need to be satisfied that there were good reasons for making a residence order in favour of persons who were not entitled to apply for such an order. Butler-Sloss L.J. in particular noted that this would be an exceptional course, particularly given that the foster-parents did not have the support of the local authority.

The Scope and Availability of the s.8 Orders

The wording of s.8 is relatively straightforward, but this has not prevented litigation about the scope of each of the orders listed. The manner in which the court may exercise its discretion to

impose conditions upon the parties under s.11(7) has also been
the topic of debate.

Key Principle: A contact order might be an order for no contact

Nottinghamshire County Council v P 1993

An investigation had found that the father had sexually abused
his eldest daughter and that the two younger daughters were
also at risk of abuse. The local authority applied for a prohibited
steps order. This was refused by the judge (see chapter 9), who
instead made a residence order in favour of the mother and
imposed restrictions on contact between the children and their
father.

Held: (CA) The order could not stand. The mother was not
willing to accept the conditions imposed by the judge, which
raised questions as to who would be able to enforce them. It
could not be enforced by the local authority, as the order was
not expressed to be made in favour of it and in any case the
court was precluded (by s.9(2) of the 1989 Act) from making
either a residence order or a contact order in favour of a local
authority. Nor could a prohibited steps order be made in favour
of the local authority with the purpose of prohibiting contact,
since s. 9(5)(a) prevents the court from making a prohibited
steps order that achieves the same effect as a residence order or
contact order and order for 'no contact' falls within the concept
of a contact order.

Commentary

The case illustrates how the courts have delineated the scope of s.
8 orders in order to maintain distinctions between such orders and
those available in public law disputes (as to which see further
chapter 9). The real problem in this case was the local authority's
refusal to make use of the public law provisions. It is clear that a
prohibited steps order *may* be made to prevent contact in private
law disputes. It is equally clear that the court in this case wished to
discourage the local authority from relying on a prohibited steps
order to resolve the problem in this case and that this influenced
its view of the scope of a contact order.

Key Principle: **The court may impose conditions requiring the residential parent to facilitate contact with the other parent**

Re O (Contact: Imposition of Conditions) 1995

An unmarried couple separated before their child was born. The mother subsequently opposed contact between the child and his father. As the child was distressed during his visits to the contact centre, it was accepted that direct contact would cease for the time being. The judge ordered that the mother should pass on photographs of the child to the father, along with any reports on his progress from nursery or playgroup, should inform the father if the child suffered any illness, and should accept cards and presents from the father for the child.

Held: (CA) The court had the power to compel the mother to pass on such information in order to promote meaningful contact between the father and his child.

Commentary
The court was keen to stress the importance of direct contact between parent and child in the wake of parental separation. Indirect contact was seen as a temporary substitute for such contact, a means of sustaining the relationship until direct contact could be ordered. It was also emphasised that each parent had certain obligations in relation to such contact: the non-residential parent had an obligation not to bombard the child with presents or long, obsessive letters, while the parent with whom the child was living had an obligation to pass on relevant material. It is clear from the terms of both s.8 (defining a contact order) and s.11(7) (which sets out that conditions may be attached to such an order) that the court has the power to require positive action by a parent in order to facilitate contact. The ways in which the courts can enforce contact if the residential parent remains opposed to it are considered further below.

Key Principle: **A shared residence order may be made where this is in the best interests of the child**

D v D (Shared Residence Order) 2001

After the parents divorced, the three girls lived with their mother but had substantial contact with their father (140 days per year at the time of the hearing). The father complained that there had been difficulties with the girls' schools attributable to the fact that he did not have a residence order in his favour.

Held: (CA) A shared residence order was appropriate in the circumstances. The children were in effect living with both of their parents and the order simply reflected the "reality of these children's lives" (para.34).

Commentary

This case marked a significant shift in the courts' attitude towards shared residence orders. Previous cases had held that such orders should only be made in exceptional circumstances, or where there was a positive benefit in making such an order (as opposed to a residence order in favour of one parent and a contact order in favour of the other). In this case, by contrast, the Court of Appeal held that there were no such limitations on the making of a shared residence order. The overriding consideration, in disputed cases, was the welfare of the child or children in question. In this case, as the court pointed out, a shared residence order was entirely appropriate as it reflected the underlying reality of the situation: the children were in effect living with both parents. Despite the clear refusal by Hale L.J. to "add any gloss on the legislative provisions, which are always subject to the paramount consideration of what is best for the children concerned" (para.32), subsequent judges have focused on the idea of the "underlying reality" of the situation, as the next case illustrates.

Key Principle: **A residence order may be made where this reflects the underlying reality of the situation (and is in the best interests of the child)**

Re A (Temporary Removal from the Jurisdiction) 2004

The mother planned to move to South Africa with her daughter for two years, and sought the authorisation of the court.

Held: Leave to remove the child from the jurisdiction was granted. It was appropriate to make a shared residence order in favour of both parents, as it reflected the underlying reality that both parents had parental responsibility and would continue to exercise it.

Commentary

The case illustrates the new willingness of the courts to make shared residence orders. By no stretch of the imagination could it be claimed that the child was effectively living with both parents in this case, as during her sojourn in South Africa her contact with her father would necessarily be limited. The case appears to be parent-focused rather than child-focused in its identification of what constituted the "underlying reality" of the case. If a shared residence order can be justified on the basis that both parents have, and continue to exercise, parental responsibility, there will be few cases in which a shared residence order will be not be made. In this respect the shared residence order is performing the role that parental responsibility was intended to fill: the symbolic involvement and valuing of both parents. It is clear, however, that such an order will not be made *solely* for symbolic reasons: thus a shared residence order would not be appropriate if the child had no contact with the other parent.

Key Principle: **A prohibited steps order may only be made to prohibit conduct that falls within the scope of a parent's parental responsibility**

Croydon LBC v A 1992

The local authority sought interim care orders in respect of two young children. The father had admitted causing non-accidental injuries to the elder and had been convicted of actual bodily harm. The court subsequently made two prohibited steps orders, the first preventing the father from having contact with the children, and the second preventing the mother from having contact with the father.

Held: The court did not have the jurisdiction to make the second order, since one adult having contact with another for their own purposes was not a "step which could be taken by a parent in meeting his parental responsibility for a child". An interim care order was substituted.

Commentary

The extent to which a s.8 order may be used to constrain parental actions is a contentious issue. Contact with one's child is an aspect of parental responsibility and thus may be constrained by a prohibited steps order. Contact between the parents is not an exercise of parental responsibility and so falls outside the scope of such an order. The decision also reinforces the distinction between private disputes and state intervention.

Key Principle: **A specific issue order may require a parent with parental responsibility to take positive steps**

Re C (Welfare of Child: Immunisation) 2003

The case involved two separate disputes. In each an unmarried father was arguing that his child should be vaccinated, a process to which the mother, the primary carer, was opposed.

Held: It was in the best interests of the children to be vaccinated, and a specific issue order would be made to require the mothers to ensure that this was done.

Commentary

The length of the judgment in this case is largely attributable to the judge's careful consideration of the medical evidence. His task was eased somewhat—or at least rendered less politically sensitive—by the fact that the mothers were opposed to all vaccinations, not just the MMR vaccine that at the time was the subject of unwarranted media controversy. Under the terms of the specific issue order granted, the mothers were required to subjugate their own objections in the interests of their children's welfare.

Key Principle: **Conditions attached to a s.8 order must be subsidiary to the order itself**

Birmingham CC v H 1992

The local authority was seeking an interim care order in respect of a baby. It was argued on behalf of the fifteen-year-old mother that a residence order should be made in her favour, subject to conditions designed to secure the baby's protection (for example requiring the mother to reside at a particular institution, comply with all reasonable instructions from the staff, and even to hand over the child to the care of the staff if so required).

Held: It would be inappropriate to make a residence order accompanied by conditions that effectively envisaged that parental responsibility would be exercised by another person.

Commentary
In the circumstances of the case, the suggested conditions were so extensive that they would effectively have negated the making of the residence order. The very making of a residence order envisages that the person exercising it will enjoy a level of autonomy and exercise parental responsibility. However, this is not to say that conditions cannot constrain the choices of the residential parent, as the next case illustrates.

———————

Key Principle: **In exceptional circumstances, the court may impose a condition on a residence order requiring the parent in whose favour it has been made to refrain from moving out of a specified area**

B v B (Residence: Condition Limiting Geographic Area) 2004
The mother initially sought leave to remove her child from the jurisdiction as part of a planned move to Australia, but then changed her mind. A second application was later made and again withdrawn. She then decided to move from the south to the north of England, despite the fact that she had no friends or family in the area where she was planning to live. The father opposed the mother's plans.

Held: A residence order would be made in the mother's favour, but with a condition that she should reside within the area bounded by the A4, A3 and M25.

Commentary
The willingness of the judge to take what he acknowledged to be the "exceptional" step of imposing a condition as to where the mother should reside was largely due to his perception of the personalities of the parties involved. He opined that the mother was an unimpressive witness, "so hostile to the father that she often lost all sense of reality" (para.16), and that the move to Newcastle was intended at least in part to frustrate contact with the father. The approach taken by the courts when the residential parent proposes a move out of the jurisdiction is considered at the end of the chapter.

In What Circumstances will a s.8 Order be made?

If the court is required to determine any issue relating to the upbringing of a child, the welfare of the child is the paramount consideration under s.1(1) of the Children Act. The scope and content of the "welfare principle" is considered further in chapter 11, and the following examples should be read with the provisions of s.1 in mind.

Contact

Key Principle: **There is no presumption against the making of a contact order in cases of domestic violence, but such violence is a factor to take into account in deciding whether or not to order contact**

Re L; Re V; Re M; Re H (Contact: Domestic Violence) 2000
The case concerned four separate and unrelated contact disputes. In each case there had been a history of domestic violence between the parents, and after the parents had separated the father had made an application for a contact order. In each case the application for direct contact had been refused (although orders for indirect contact were made), and in each case the father appealed.

Held: (CA) The appeals would be dismissed. In the circumstances of each of the individual cases it would not be in the best interests of the child to have contact with the father. In *Re L*, there was a history of serious violence and the mother had a genuine and reasonable fear of the father. The anxiety that direct contact would cause her would undoubtedly be transmitted to the child. In *Re V*, the child had witnessed a knife attack by the father on the mother. While the father had expressed remorse for his conduct and had undergone counselling, the boy's own opposition to contact was such that it was not in his best interests to order direct contact. In *Re M* the boy had had contact with his father for five years after the relationship between the parents had come to an end, but then refused to see his father in the wake of an argument between his parents. In the circumstances it was hoped that the father would be able to rebuild his relationship with his son through indirect contact. In

Re H the father had threatened to kill the mother and she remained afraid of him. The father had a overbearing personality and would be likely to use direct contact to try to impose his own views on the children, which would undermine the care provided for them by their mother.

Commentary

The case is of significance for a number of reasons. It marked a shift in the way that the courts approach the issue of domestic violence in contact cases. It reflected an increased awareness of the seriousness of domestic violence, emphasising the impact of such violence on the children as well as the primary victim. As part of this it instigated a change in practice, requiring allegations of domestic violence to be resolved before the contact dispute could be adjudicated. A further point of significance—which contributed to the first—was the court's reliance on expert evidence. Two consultant child psychiatrists provided a report for the court on the issue of contact in the context of domestic violence. While the court was undoubtedly influenced by the report, it should be noted that it did not accept its central recommendation that there should be an assumption against contact in cases of domestic violence. At the same time, it was emphasised that there was no presumption in *favour* of contact, and that each case must be resolved according to the best interests of the child. In the event of a clash between the rights of the parent and the best interests of the child, the latter must prevail.

Residence

Key Principle: **It is likely to be in the best interests of the child to reside with the person who has been his or her primary carer**

Re H (Agreed Joint Residence: Mediation) 2004

The parents separated when their son was three years old. For the first nine months after the separation he lived with his father. The mother then wished for residence to be transferred to her. At one point she removed her son to another location without his father's knowledge, but the father applied to the court for his son to be returned to him and a residence order was made in his favour. The parties worked out a co-parenting routine whereby the son would live primarily with his father but would see with his mother on alternate weekends and two nights during the week. The father then decided that he needed to relocate for the purposes of his employment. Both parents were agreed that there should be a joint residence order and that the parent with whom the child did not have his main home would enjoy generous contact. The issue was with whom the child's main home should be.

Held: It was in the child's best interests to remain with his father, as his primary attachment was to his father, who had been his primary carer since the separation.

Commentary

The main interest of the case lies not in the well-established (if not, in the eyes of some advocates of fathers' rights, uncontentious) principle that a child should remain with his or her primary carer, but in the fact that the primary carer was in this case a father. The fact that residence orders are more usually made in favour of mothers reflects the reality that mothers continue to shoulder the majority of the burden of providing practical care for their children.

Key Principle: **While there is no presumption in favour of the natural parent, the biological relationship must be given due weight in deciding with whom the children should make their home**

In re G (children) 2006

CG, who was in a long-term lesbian relationship with CW, conceived their two children by anonymous donor insemination. Both women played an equal role in the children's upbringing. After the relationship between the two adults broke down, CG attempted to exclude CW from the children's lives. A shared residence order was made, in part to ensure that CW could continue to play a parenting role (see chapter 7). CG then moved from the Midlands to Cornwall, in defiance of a court order. CW applied for residence to be transferred to her, and was successful at first instance and in the Court of Appeal.

Held: (HL) The appeal would be allowed. The primary residence of the children should be with the biological mother, CG, although they would continue to visit CW.

Commentary
Baroness Hale's temperate judgment offers little to please those in search of a ringing endorsement of the importance of the 'natural' parent. While suggesting that the appeal should be allowed on the basis that the lower courts had failed to attach sufficient importance to the status of the mother, she emphasised that there was no presumption in favour of the natural parent in such cases. The status of CW as the children's psychological parent was fully accepted. By contrast, Lords Nicholls and Scott, in concurring, stated the importance of biological parenthood in more forceful terms. The former decried any tendency to diminish the significance of biological parenthood, while the latter suggested mothers were "special". It would appear that, all other factors being equal, it is still seen as more "natural" for a child to reside with a biological parent than one who lacks this link. While the court studiously avoided attaching any significance to the fact that the parents had been in a same-sex relationship, it might be pertinent to ask whether the response to the case would have been the same had the dispute involved a biological mother and an infertile husband.

Enforcing s.8 Orders

Of all the section 8 orders, those relating to contact raise the biggest problems in terms of enforcement. This is largely due to the nature of the order: specific issue orders and prohibited steps orders often deal with one-off issues, whereas a contact order aims to regulate the on-going relationship between the parents and the child. In recent years the courts have considered a number of ways in which contact orders may be enforced.

Key Principle: **In deciding how a contact order should be enforced, the child's welfare is not the paramount consideration for the court**

A v N (Committal: Refusal of Contact) 1997
An unmarried couple separated when their daughter was 20 months old. Initially, the mother did not object to the father having contact with his daughter, but subsequently she vigorously opposed his application for a contact order on the basis of his lack of commitment and his violence. She also made

allegations—later disproved—that he was not in fact the father of the child. The court ordered that the child have contact with her father, such contact to be supervised by her grandmother. The mother refused to let contact take place. After the eighth order for contact had been flouted, the father applied to commit for breach of the order. The judge imposed a six-week suspended sentence upon the mother, stipulating that the sentence would be enforced if the mother did not obey the contact order. The mother still refused to let contact take place and was committed to prison.

Held: (CA) In the circumstances an order committing the mother to prison was appropriate. She had flagrantly disregarded the court's orders, and the due administration of justice required that enforcement measures be taken. Since the question as to whether there should be committal for breach of the court's order did not directly concern the child's upbringing, the child's welfare was not the paramount consideration, although it remained a material factor.

Commentary
Whether it is appropriate to commit a parent to prison for flouting a contact order will depend on the circumstances of the case. Punishing one parent might not lead to the desired result: indeed, as Butler-Sloss P recognised in *Re S (Contact: Promoting Relationship With Absent Parent)* [2004] EWCA Civ 18, it may worsen the situation between the child and the other parent as "[i]t will hardly endear the father to the child who is already reluctant to see him to be told that the father is responsible for the mother going to prison." (para.28). Other options for enforcement must therefore be considered.

Key Principle: **A costs order may be made against a parent who acts unreasonably in the conduct of litigation**

Re T (Order for Costs) 2005
The parents had been in continuous dispute about contact between the father and his son since their separation. The mother had made a number of allegations against the father but it was held at a fact finding hearing that her concerns were unwarranted and that it was in the best interests of the child to

have contact with his father. After contact between the father and the child had been resumed, the mother made further allegations that the father had sexually abused his son, which necessitated a further fact finding inquiry. Once again, it was decided that the allegations could not be substantiated. The father subsequently sought an order for costs in relation to the second fact-finding inquiry. The judge made an order that the mother should pay the costs of those hearings.

Held: (CA) The judge had been right to decide that the mother's conduct in relation to the litigation had been unreasonable, and had been entitled to make the costs orders.

Commentary
While an order for costs is not in itself a means of enforcing a contact order, the fact that a parent who persists in making allegations against the other with the aim (deliberate or subconscious) of impeding contact may be required to pay the costs of subsequent proceedings does provide an incentive to comply with a contact order. As Wall L.J. noted, there is a distinction between "legitimate litigation over reasonable disagreements, and irrational conduct which prolongs unnecessary litigation" (para.54).

Key Principle: **If the residential parent's refusal to allow contact is causing harm to the child, it may be appropriate to transfer residence to the other parent**

V v V (Contact: Implacable Hostility) 2004
After the parents separated, the two children lived with their mother, who refused to let the father have any contact with them. He applied for a contact order, but the mother made a number of allegations against him relating to sexual and physical abuse. These allegations were not found to be substantiated. There was also evidence suggesting that the mother had been responsible for a number of false complaints about the father and his family that had been made anonymously to the police and to the NSPCC. The father applied for a residence order.

Held: The disruption that would be caused to the children by moving to live with their father was less than the emotional harm that was being caused to them by their mother's attitude.

The children had been coached to make false allegations against their father and had, at the mother's instigation, been subjected to repeated and intrusive examination by the police, social services and doctors in her attempt to provide evidence against the father. It was therefore in their best interests to live with their father.

Commentary

In this case Bracewell J. held that the mother's actions constituted emotional abuse and that her continued care of the children was "incompatible with the children enjoying and benefiting from a normal relationship with their father." (para.43). It should be noted that the children had expressed their wish to remain with their mother, but the judge held that their wishes could not determine the outcome of the case, partly because of their ages (one was eight and the other six), and partly because of her view that they had "learnt to say what they think is expected of them." (para.44). The case thus provides a reminder that what is deemed to be in the best interests of children may be at odds with their wishes (see further chapter 11).

The option of transferring residence to the parent who is being denied contact with the children has been exercised in a number of recent cases, but it will not be an appropriate solution in every case. First, the parent seeking contact might not wish to take on the task of caring for the child on a full-time basis. Secondly, even if he or she wishes to care for the child, it may not be in the best interests of the child for residence to be transferred. As Bracewell J. pointed out, "the other parent may not have the facilities or capacity to care for the child full-time, and may not even know the child." (para.10). This underlines the fact that a decision to change the child's residence should not be made to punish the parent opposing contact. The child's welfare is the paramount consideration for the court in deciding whether or not to make a residence order (in contrast with the decision whether or not to commit a parent to prison for breaching a contact order).

Key Principle:　**The welfare of the child may require the court to abandon attempts to enforce contact**

Re S (Contact: Promoting Relationship With Absent Parent) 2004

The child remained with her mother after her parents separated. She continued to have contact with her father but the parents' relationship then deteriorated in the wake of allegations of domestic violence, and contact ceased. The father applied for a contact order. The judge refused the father's application for a psychological assessment of the child, made an order for indirect contact, and debarred the father from making a further application for contact for a year.

Held: (CA) Although there might come a point at which it would be necessary to abandon attempts to enforce contact in the interests of the child, that point had not yet been reached in this case. The father had a genuine desire for contact with his daughter and it was the mother who was primarily responsible for the failure of direct contact. A psychological assessment of the child and her parents should be carried out in order to explore the problems of the mother's hostility to contact and the father's aggression, as well as how the child would react to direct contact. The restriction on further applications for a contact order would be set aside.

Commentary
The case illustrates that the courts are extremely reluctant to abandon attempts to enforce contact. The court in this case recognised the problems that direct contact might cause and that there were certain barriers to making such an order, not least the father's "aggressive approach to contact and his unrealistic and idealised concept of the prospects of good contact with [his daughter] and that he is a 'perfect father'"(para.35). Ordering a psychological assessment was seen as a means of obtaining information about the family so that a judge could make an informed decision "as to whether and in what circumstances a further attempt should be made" to restart contact. Despite these efforts, Butler-Sloss P did warn that the time might come when it would be inappropriate for the court to persevere: "[o]ne aspect of proportionality which has to be weighed in the balance is the extent to which a court should go to force contact on an unwilling child and on the apprehensive primary carer. At this point the factor of proportionality becomes all-important since there is a limit beyond which the court should not strive to promote contact and the court has the overriding obligation to put the welfare of the child at the forefront and above the rights of either parent." (para.28).

Re O (Contact: Withdrawal of Application) 2003
After the parents divorced, arrangements for the father to have contact with his son were agreed. The father subsequently

sought and obtained an order for increased contact. The terms of the order were not followed, and he sought to enforce the order. At the same time the mother and son sought to reduce the amount of contact. The evidence was that the boy was unhappy with the level of contact and would prefer less-frequent contact. Orders were made first reducing the level of contact, and then suspending it. A judge subsequently ordered that only indirect contact should take place. The father applied for leave to withdraw his application for contact.

Held: The father would be given permission to withdraw his application. Even though it was in the best interests of the son to have contact with his father, direct contact could not take place without a radical change in the father's attitude. The possibility of repairing the relationship between father and son had to be balanced against the stress of already protracted legal proceedings continuing.

Commentary
The case provides a useful reminder that contact may fail because of the conduct of the parent seeking contact rather than because of obstruction by the residential parent. The father alleged that the mother had alienated the son from him, but Wall J. rejected this argument, further noting that the term "parental alienation syndrome" was a misnomer and that the term "implacable hostility" was to be preferred. The distinction between the two terms is that the latter does not imply that the child is suffering from a recognised psychological syndrome for which a single prescribed form of intervention will be appropriate. In this case, responsibility for the breakdown of the relationship between father and son was ascribed to the father, although Wall J. did acknowledge the force of some of his criticisms of the family law system. In the wake of widespread criticism of the current options for enforcing contact orders, the Children and Adoption Act 2006 introduces a number of initiatives that may require either parent to participate in activities designed to facilitate contact.

Removal from the Jurisdiction

Key Principle: **There is no presumption in favour of the primary carer's plans in deciding whether leave to remove the child from the jurisdiction should be granted**

Payne v Payne 2001
The mother planned to return to her home country of New Zealand and take up residence there permanently. She sought

the permission of the court to take her four-year-old son with her. The application was opposed by the father.

Held: (CA) In considering applications of this kind, the welfare of the child was paramount, and there was no presumption that the court would accede to the wishes of the residential parent to relocate. However, it should be borne in mind that the welfare of the child would be dependent on the well-being of the primary carer, and that a refusal to allow the family to relocate might have a detrimental effect on both. In the circumstances, permission to remove the child would be granted.

Commentary
The importance of the case lies in the principles that were set out by Thorpe L.J., which have been extremely influential in subsequent cases. The first factor to consider is whether the primary carer's application was realistic and genuine. If a primary carer presents the court with an ill-conceived and impracticable plan, it would fail at the first hurdle. In this case the mother was returning home, to a support network, so this requirement was satisfied. The second factor to be considered is whether the other parent's opposition is based on genuine concern for the child, or is driven by ulterior motives. The court should examine what the detriment to that parent would be if the move was allowed, as well as how the move would affect the relationship with the child. Thirdly, the court should ask what impact a refusal would have on the residential parent. The court then decides what course would be in the best interests of the child in the light of the answers to the second and third questions.

Change of Surname

As noted in the introduction, specific restrictions on changing a child's name apply if a residence order is in force. If a residence order is not in force, a parent may apply for a specific issue order or prohibited steps order to require or to block a change of name.

Key Principle: **A change of name should not be ordered unless this would be to the child's benefit**

Dawson v Wearmouth 1999
The mother had two children from a previous marriage. She separated from the father of her third child when the child was

only one month old, and registered the child with the surname
of her former husband, which she and her other children had
continued to use. The father sought a specific issue order to
change the child's surname. At first instance the order was
granted but the Court of Appeal allowed the mother's appeal.

Held: (HL) An order changing the surname of a child should
not be made unless there was evidence that this would benefit
the child. In this case the benefit of the child sharing a surname
with his mother and half-siblings was greater than the benefit of
sharing a name with his father. The appeal would be dismissed.

Commentary

The case demonstrates the reluctance of the courts to authorise a
change of surname. In many cases it will be difficult to show that
the change will lead to a positive improvement in the child's
welfare. This means that the parent who initially registers the
name of the child has an advantage over the other parent in
deciding what the name of the child should be. If the parents are
unmarried, the mother is entitled to register the birth either alone
or with the father, but the father has no right to register the birth
unilaterally. Of course, in many ongoing relationships the child
may be registered with the name of the father, which means that
the onus will be on the mother to find reasons to justify a change if
the relationship later comes to an end.

Key Principle: **The burden lies on the parent seeking to
change the child's surname to justify such a course of action**

Re R (Surname: Using Both Parents') 2001

At birth, the child was registered with his father's surname, but
after his parents separated his mother began to use the surname
of her own step-father. The father opposed the change of
surname. The judge allowed the change on the basis that it
would be in the best interests of the child to have the same
surname as his mother and the wider family with whom it was
proposed he should live in Spain.

Held: (CA) The burden lay on the parent seeking to change
the child's surname to justify such change. In this case the
mother had adopted a new surname for the child without

consulting the father. The advantages of the child bearing the same surname as those around him had to be balanced against the desirability of ensuring that he remained aware of his link to his father.

Commentary

The move to Spain suggested a solution to the court, namely the Spanish practice of using the surnames of both parents. It was felt that this would be appropriate as it offered a means of recognising the importance of both parents, although it was left to the parents to decide for themselves whether to adopt this practice. Hale L.J. did, however, note that the relationship between parent and child did not depend on a shared surname, suggesting that "[i]t is a poor sort of parent whose interest in and commitment to his child depends upon that child bearing his name." (para.18).

9. STATE INTERVENTION

So far the focus has been on the power of the courts to adjudicate on disputes between various family members. This chapter considers the way in which the state may play a more direct role in family life, by providing services for children or by intervening to protect a child who is at risk of harm.

Local Authorities' Powers and Duties

Part III of the Children Act 1989 sets out the duties of local authorities towards children in their area. Given the breadth of these duties this section will focus on just two issues: the nature of the duties owed to children generally, and the relationship between Parts III and IV of the 1989 Act.

Key Principle: **Section 17 imposes only a general duty on local authorities and does not require the needs of individual children to be met**

R (G) v Barnet London Borough Council; R (W) v Lambeth London Borough Council; R (A) v Lambeth London Borough Council 2003
The conjoined appeals before the House of Lords all concerned children who had been assessed by their local authority as "a child in need." In each case the need related to accommodation: in one case because the mother of the child was a recent immigrant who did not satisfy the "habitual residence" test for assistance with housing; in the second because the children had learning difficulties and the accommodation provided for them was unsuitable; and in the third because the mother had become intentionally homeless. In each case the mother argued that under s.17 the local authority had a duty to meet the needs of a child identified as being "in need."

Held: (HL) Section 17 set out the general duties of a local authority towards the children in its area. The local authority had the power to provide accommodation for the children whom it had assessed as being in need of such accommodation. However, it was under no duty to do so.

Commentary

The case was one in which broad issues of social policy played an important role. It is true that the terms of s.17 did not offer much scope for the mothers' argument that the local authority had a duty to meet their children's needs: it refers to the "general duty" of local authorities "to safeguard and promote the welfare of children within their area who are in need" and provides, in subsection (6), that the services provided by the local authority "may" include the provision of accommodation. However, even more important was the issue of resources and housing policy. First, the House of Lords were understandably unwilling to impose on local authorities a duty to meet all the needs of every child in their area. Even Lords Nicholls and Steyn, who dissented from the majority, did not suggest that this was the effect of s.17, arguing that although a local authority was under a duty to take reasonable steps to assess the needs of children in its area and to provide a range and level of services appropriate to those needs, a local authority would enjoy a degree of latitude in deciding how it should carry out this duty. Secondly, the majority of their Lordships was keen to maintain a clear distinction between the local authority's duties under the Children Act and its responsibilities under the housing legislation. Under s.17 a local authority *may* provide a child with accommodation, while under s.20 it *must* provide accommodation for a child who needs it either because there is no person available to care for the child (for example if the child has been abandoned) or because the child's carers are unable to provide suitable accommodation. Similarly, under s.23 it *must* provide accommodation for a child it is looking after. But the mandatory duties of the local authority under s.20 and s.23 are owed to the child alone, and, as Lord Scott of Foscoe pointed out, "nowhere in the Children Act 1989 is it expressly stated that if a child's assessed needs include the provision of proper accommodation, and that he should continue to live with his parent (or parents), the local authority must, regardless of cost, provide the parent (or parents) with the requisite accommodation." (p.489). Nor was such a duty to be inferred from the Act. This means, of course, that the local authority's duty to provide accommodation for a child who would otherwise be homeless may necessitate the separation of that child from a parent who is actually homeless. This is unlikely to be beneficial to the child and is likely to prove more expensive than providing accommodation for the child and parent together. Despite this, the House of Lords endorsed a strict demarcation between the housing legislation and the Children Act, allowing local authorities to adopt a policy that "will not permit the parents to use the children as stepping stones by means of which to obtain a greater priority to be rehoused than that to which they would otherwise be entitled." (p.492).

Key Principle: **The parents of a child who is voluntarily accommodated by the local authority under s.20 of the Children Act 1989 retain the right to determine how the child should be brought up**

R v Tameside MBC ex parte J 2000

The parents of a severely disabled girl were unable to cope with her needs and she was accordingly accommodated by the local authority in a residential home for disabled children. After three years the local authority decided that it would be in the girl's best interests to be moved to foster parents. The parents opposed this but the local authority decided to go ahead with the move anyway. The parents sought judicial review of this decision.

Held: Judicial review would be granted. While the local authority was able to exercise day-to-day powers of management in relation to the girl, it did not have the power to override the wishes of those with parental responsibility for her.

Commentary

The case illustrates that although parents do not have a power to dictate what action the local authority takes under Part III, they do have a right to veto a course of action of which they disapprove. The judge expressed the hope that "the parties will now be able to continue their discussions with regard to the future of J on what may perhaps be considered to be a rather more level playing field than the local authority has appreciated in the past." (p.952). Yet despite the fact that the parents of a child who is voluntarily accommodated under s.20 retain parental responsibility, and despite the principle of partnership between state and parent that underpins the 1989 Act, the balance of power between the local authority and the parent remains unequal. As the judge also noted, the local authority had the power to apply for a care order if it felt that there was a risk of significant harm to the child if its view did not prevail. If the court were to grant a care order, the local authority would acquire parental responsibility and would be able to override the parents' wishes. The fear that a local authority might resort to such coercive measures undoubtedly leads many parents to agree to "voluntary" arrangements that they do not consider ideal.

The Relationship between the Court and the Local Authority

Part IV of the Children Act 1989 sets out a number of orders that the court can make: a child assessment order; an emergency protection order; a supervision order (interim or full); and a care order (interim or full). However, there are certain constraints on the powers of the court to make such orders. One key consideration is the relationship between the court and the local authority applying for an order.

Key Principle: **The court cannot make a care or supervision order of its own motion**

Nottingham CC v P 1993
An investigation had found that the father had sexually abused his eldest daughter and that the two younger daughters were also at risk of abuse. The local authority applied for a prohibited steps order to exclude him from the family home.

Held: (CA) The court did not have the power to make a prohibited steps order to achieve this particular end: s.9(5) of the 1989 Act barred a court from exercising its powers to make either an specific issue order or a prohibited steps order with a view to achieving a result that could be achieved by making a residence or contact order, and the order sought in this case was one that fell within the ambit of a contact order (see further chapter 8). Moreover, a prohibited steps order would be an inappropriate means of protecting the children, since it would not confer any authority on the local authority as to how it might deal with the children. The appropriate course was for the local authority to apply for a care order or supervision order. However, the court had no power to order the local authority to take steps to protect the children and could not make a care or supervision order of its own motion. Thus there were no orders in place to protect the children.

Commentary

The case illustrates the way in which the Children Act 1989 clearly demarcates the respective roles of the court and the local authority, as well as the ambit of the different orders available. The court has a broad discretion to make any of a range of orders, but in the context of care and supervision order it is powerless to act without an application by the local authority. As Sir Stephen Brown P noted with evident disapproval, "if a local authority doggedly resists taking the steps which are appropriate to the case of children at risk of suffering significant harm it appears that the court is powerless." (p.148). The failure of the local authority to apply for at least a supervision order appears particularly foolish in the light of the fact that all of the parties would have been willing to accept such an order.

Key Principle: **Once a care order has been made, its implementation is a matter for the local authority**

Re S (Minors)(Care Order: Implementation of Care Plan); Re W (Minors)(Care Order: Adequacy of Care Plan) 2002

In both cases, care orders had been made: in the first case, however, the care plan had not been implemented and in the second the judge had described the care plan as "inchoate" but had felt constrained by precedent to make a full care order. The Court of Appeal allowed the appeal in the second case and also proposed a system of "starred milestones" whereby a failure to achieve a certain aim within a reasonable time would enable the case to be brought back before the court. It also suggested that the courts should have wider powers to make interim rather than final care orders.

Held: (HL) The innovations suggested by the Court of Appeal were ones that the court did not have the power to make. It was a cardinal principle of the 1989 Act that once a care order had been made, responsibility for its implementation lay with the local authority and the court retained no supervisory role. Thus a court is not entitled to make successive interim orders with the aim of exercising a supervisory role, and the proposed system of "starred milestones" was an innovation that could only be introduced by Parliament.

Commentary

The case includes a detailed discussion of the impact of the Human Rights Act 1998 and the extent to which innovations can be "read into" legislation to ensure that it complies with the European Convention on Human Rights. The House of Lords disapproved of the Court of Appeal's creative interpretation of the 1989 Act and declared that the Children Act was in any case compliant with the ECHR. The key interest of the case for current purposes lies in the clear statement that the court's role is over once it has decided that it is appropriate to make a care order. This was expressed in unambiguous terms by Lord Nicholls: "[t]he Children Act 1989 delineated the boundary of responsibility with complete clarity. Where a care order is made the responsibility for the child's care is with the authority rather than the court." (para.25). The subsequent reforms enacted in the Adoption and Children Act 2002 reflected the division of responsibility established by the 1989 Act while introducing some of the advantages that "starred milestones" would have brought: a local authority is now required to appoint an Independent Reviewing Officer to review each case and monitor compliance with the care plan. These officers have the power to refer the case to CAFCASS to take legal action as a last resort.

As the second case in this appeal illustrates, one problem for the court in deciding what order is appropriate may be a lack of information. The following cases illustrate how the court may seek further information about the families involved.

Key Principle: **Section 38(6) of the Children Act 1989 allows the court to order an assessment of the parents' ability to care for their child**

Re C (Interim Care Order: Residential Assessment) 1997

A baby suffered severe and unexplained injuries that were thought to be non-accidental. The local authority obtained an emergency protection order, and subsequently an interim care order, placing the baby with foster parents. The baby's teenage parents had poor parenting skills but made some progress while the local authority's investigation was underway. The social workers investigating the case concluded that the possibility of rehabilitation could only be determined by means of a residential assessment of the parents' ability to cope with the baby. The local authority refused to agree to, or pay for, such an assessment, which would be costly and might pose risks to the baby.

Held: (HL) Section 38(6) should be construed purposively in order to give effect to the intention of Parliament that the court should have sufficient information available to it properly to exercise its discretion whether or not to make a care order. Thus the court had the power to direct an assessment of the capability of the parent(s) to care for the child.

Commentary

The issue in this case was once again the demarcation of responsibilities between the court and the local authority. As Lord Browne-Wilkinson noted, the fact that the baby was in the care of the local authority under an interim care order meant that responsibility for the baby was vested in the local authority rather than the court. Yet to allow the local authority to block the assessment of the child would mean that the evidence before the court when making its final decision would be limited: "[t]o allow the local authority to decide what evidence is to go before the court at the final hearing would be in many cases, including the present, to allow the local authority by administrative decision to pre-empt the court's judicial decision." (pp.7–8). Thus the court had the power to order an assessment under s.38(6), even against the wishes of the local authority, in order to ensure that it had the information necessary to make a final decision. The case illustrates that although the courts will not trespass on those areas that the 1989 Act allocated to local authorities, they are equally keen to ensure that their decision-making power is not constrained by the actions of the local authority.

As the next case shows, there are limitations on what s.38(6) authorises the court to order.

Key Principle: **Section 38(6) does not authorise the court to order the provision of services for the family**

Re G (Interim Care Order: Residential Assessment) 2005

The mother's second child had died from non-accidental injuries. As a result, her eldest child was placed with his father and care proceedings were initiated in relation to the third, whose father was the mother's current partner. The court ordered that the child and her parents should participate in a residential assessment at a specialist hospital for six to eight weeks. Since this was not sufficient time to address all the issues, a second order for a further six-week period of assessment was made. The hospital then recommended that the family remain there for a further four months, to enable the mother to undergo psychotherapy. The question for the court was whether s.38(6) of the Children Act authorised the court to make such an order.

Held: (HL) Section 38(6) did not authorise the court to order treatment of the family, since its purpose was the obtaining of information about the family, not the provision of services for the family.

Commentary
Once again, the demarcation of roles between the court and the local authority was central to the case. As Baroness Hale of Richmond pointed out, the modern emphasis "upon careful scrutiny of the care plan, formulated in the light of a comprehensive assessment of the child and her family, has inevitably put back the point at which the court is ready to make a final order and thus to relinquish control to the local authority." (para.55). Yet the power of the court to obtain information by ordering an assessment under s.38(6) did not include a power to order that services be provided for the family in question: to imply such a power "would be quite contrary to the division of responsibility which was the 'cardinal principle' of the 1989 Act." (para.67). One justification for this interpretation of the section was the fact that interim orders were intended to be temporary measures and any assessment should be capable of being completed within a relatively short time-frame. It might well be the case that treatment of the kind provided in this case would bring about a change in the parents' ability to care for their child, but it was not the role of the court to seek to bring about such change by ordering particular forms of treatment.

It is worth noting that the outcome for this particular family was a happy one. As a result of the services provided at the hospital, and the support for the family once back in the community, the court deemed that no care order was necessary. The cost of the family's stay in the hospital—more than £200,000—may appear high, but must be weighed against the costs that would have resulted had the child been taken into care. The outcome for similarly-placed families in the future is, however, less hopeful as a result of the decision in this case that the court cannot order the local authority to pay for such treatment. Of course, a local authority may decide that such treatment is in the best interests of the family, but that it is a decision for it, rather than the court, to make.

The Threshold Criteria

Before the court can make a care or supervision order, it must be satisfied that the threshold criteria in s.31(2) are satisfied, namely:

(a) that the child concerned is suffering, or is likely to suffer, significant harm; and

(b) that the harm, or likelihood of harm, is attributable to—

(i) the care given to the child, or likely to be given to him if the order were not made, not being what it would be reasonable to expect a parent to give to him; or

(ii) the child's being beyond parental control.

Given the seriousness of the issues at stake—the power of the state to intervene in family life, perhaps even separating family members against their wishes; or, from another perspective, the ability of the state to protect vulnerable family members from serious injury and even death at the hands of other family members—it is unsurprising that a number of cases have been fought all the way to the House of Lords over the meanings of the words and phrases used in s.31(2), as the following cases illustrate.

Key Principle: **In deciding whether a child has suffered significant harm, the court must take into account emotional harm as well as physical abuse**

Haringey London Borough Council v C, E and Another Intervening 2004
The parents had tried unsuccessfully to have a child of their own, and joined a religious group which claimed that divine intervention could facilitate "miracle births." The wife travelled to Kenya and was led to believe that she had given birth to three miracle children as a result of prayer. One of the children died

and one remained in Kenya, but the third travelled back to the UK with the wife. The local authority obtained an emergency protection order in relation to this child and sought a care order. DNA evidence established that the child was not biologically related to either the husband or the wife.

Held: Although the husband and wife were good and loving carers, and there was no dispute as to their ability to provide for the child's physical needs, they were unable to accept that he was not in fact their child. If the child's future care was founded on a lie he would be likely to suffer profound harm (including the potential for disruption if the truth became known, feelings of grief and loss, and the lack of any family medical history). The threshold criteria were therefore satisfied.

Commentary
This unusual case illustrates the broad concept of "significant harm", which forms the basis of the threshold criteria (and which is defined further in s.31(9)). The modern importance attached to ascertaining the truth (see further chapter 7) underpinned the court's decision that this child would be likely to suffer significant harm if he remained with a couple who continued to maintain that his birth was the product of faith rather than fraud.

Key Principle: **Allegations that a child has suffered harm must be proved on the balance of probabilities**

Re U (Serious Injury: Standard of Proof); Re B 2004
Each of the two appeals concerned a child who had experienced a number of health problems. In each case there was suspicion that the mother was responsible for those health problems (for example by deliberately obstructing the child's airway or interfering with the tube that had been inserted into the child while in hospital). The key question for the court was the standard of proof to be applied in deciding whether the mother had harmed the child.

Held: (CA) The standard of proof to be applied in Children Act cases was the balance of probabilities (as distinct from the requirement in criminal cases that allegations be proved beyond all reasonable doubt).

Commentary

There had been suggestions in a number of cases that in the context of an application for a care order the distinction between the civil and criminal standards of proof was "largely illusory". It was thus necessary for the Court of Appeal to reiterate the basic principle that the test to be applied in such cases was to ask whether it was more likely than not that the allegations were true, in line with the approach established in *Re H and R (Child Sexual Abuse: Standards of Proof)* [1996] 1 F.L.R. 80 (considered below). The weight to be given to particular types of evidence in answering this question was also considered. The then President of the Family Division, Butler-Sloss P, took the opportunity to note the impact of a number of criminal cases in which mothers had been found to have been wrongly convicted of murdering their children (see e.g. *R v Cannings* [2004] EWCA Crim 1). While acknowledging that the decision "provided a useful warning to judges in care proceedings against ill-considered conclusions or conclusions resting on insufficient practice", she "robustly reject[ed] [the] submission that the local authority should refrain from proceedings or discontinue proceedings in any case where there is a substantial disagreement amongst the medical experts." (p.273).

Of course, the mere fact that a child has suffered harm at the hands of a parent in the past does not automatically mean that the threshold criteria are satisfied, since the court must be satisfied that the child is currently suffering significant harm or is likely to suffer such harm in the future.

Key Principle: **In deciding whether a child 'is suffering' harm, the court may look back to the time at which measures were first taken, as long as these protective measures have continued until the date of the hearing**

Re M (A Minor)(Care Order: Threshold Conditions) 1994

M's father had murdered M's mother in the presence of M and his three older half-siblings. As a consequence, emergency measures were taken and the three eldest children went to live with a cousin of their mother, while M was placed in short-term foster care. Residence orders were made in favour of the cousin in respect of the three eldest children, and a care order was made in relation to M with a view to him being adopted. The Court of Appeal allowed the appeal on the basis that there was no jurisdiction to make a care order as the child was not suffering harm at the time of the hearing. It therefore substituted a residence order in favour of the mother's cousin, with whom M accordingly went to live.

Held: (HL) The court did have jurisdiction to make a care order. While the child was not suffering harm at the time of the hearing, the court may look back to the point in time at which protective measures were initially taken by the local authority in determining whether the child "is suffering" harm, as long as such measures have continued up to the date of the hearing. In the circumstances, it would be wrong to disturb the current arrangements for the time being, since M was thriving with his mother's cousin, but it would be appropriate to restore the care order to enable the local authority to take action if the difficulties foreseen by the trial judge did materialise.

Commentary
It was a deliberate policy in the 1989 Act that it should not be possible to remove a child simply because that child had at some point suffered harm: to satisfy the threshold criteria either *present* harm or the likelihood of *future* harm had to be established. The problem with the formulation was that a child who had been removed from his parents because he was suffering harm—for example under an emergency protection order or interim care order—would presumably no longer be suffering harm by the time that the application for a care order actually came to court, but might well suffer harm if no care order were made and he was returned to his parents. The decision of the House of Lords in *Re M* struck a sensible balance between the policy of the legislation and the need to ensure that care orders could be made where appropriate.

Key Principle: **In ascertaining whether a child is "likely" to suffer significant harm, the court must ask whether there is a "real possibility" of such harm occurring**

Re H and R (Child Sexual Abuse: Standard of Proof) 1996
A teenage girl accused her step-father of rape and other forms of sexual abuse and was placed with foster parents. The step-father was acquitted of the rape charge. The local authority

applied for care orders in relation to the girl's younger sister and two half-sisters. The trial judge held that he could not be sure on the balance of probabilities that the girl's allegations were true and that therefore the threshold criteria were not fulfilled. The Court of Appeal dismissed the local authority's appeal.

Held: (HL) The appeal would be dismissed. Since the allegations of abuse had not been proved, there was no basis on which the court could find that the three younger girls were likely to suffer significant harm. Any facts alleged must be proved on the balance of probabilities. The court was not entitled to take into account the suspicion that the step-father might have perpetrated the abuse in question in considering the likelihood of the other children suffering harm. In deciding whether or not a child is likely to suffer significant harm, the test is whether there is a "real possibility" of such harm occurring.

Commentary

The case illustrates the different questions that must be asked by the court in determining whether a child has suffered harm in the past or is likely to suffer significant harm in the future. Whether or not harm has occurred in the past is a question of fact, and accordingly any allegations of harm must be proved on the balance of probabilities (i.e. by showing that it is more likely than not that the harm took place). By contrast, in predicting whether a child is likely to suffer harm in the future, the court does not need to be satisfied that it is more likely than not that such harm will occur. It is sufficient if there is a "real possibility" of such harm occurring. However, the court is not entitled to take into account unproved allegations of harm in deciding whether there is a real possibility of harm occurring in the future.

This interpretation of the legislation has not gone uncriticised: indeed, two members of the House of Lords dissented, being of the opinion that the girl's evidence remained evidence that could be taken into account by the court in deciding whether or not there was a risk. Lord Nicholls himself suggested that a court might well be satisfied that there was a real possibility of a child suffering significant harm if there were what he termed "a combination of profoundly worrying features affecting the care of the child within the family" (p.591), even if allegations of mistreatment had not been substantiated.

One further suggestion by Lord Nicholls in this case has also proved controversial. He noted that "the more serious the allegation the less likely it is that the event occurred and, hence, the stronger should be the evidence before the court concludes that the allegation is established on the balance of probability." (at p.586). While it is true that minor injuries are more common than serious injuries—whether deliberately inflicted or not—does it necessarily follow that *allegations* of serious injuries are less likely to be true? In the wake of *Re H and R* it was suggested in a number of cases that a higher standard of proof applied in relation to more serious allegations. However, it has recently been confirmed that the standard of proof remains the same, namely that of the balance of probabilities (see *Re U (Serious Injury: Standard of Proof); Re B* [2004] EWCA Civ 567 above).

Rather different questions arise if it is obvious that someone has deliberately harmed the child but it cannot be ascertained which of the carers is responsible for the injuries, as the next case shows.

Key Principle: **The threshold criteria are met if the court is satisfied that the harm suffered by the child is attributable to the care (or absence of care) provided by any of the primary carers**

Lancashire CC v B 2000

A seven-month-old baby sustained serious non-accidental head injuries. The medical evidence was that she had suffered at least two episodes of violent shaking. It was not possible to identify which of the baby's three carers—her parents and a paid child-minder—were responsible for these injuries. The local authority applied for a care order in relation to the baby and in respect of the childminder's own son. The judge dismissed both applications, but the Court of Appeal allowed the local authority's appeal in relation to the baby.

Held: (HL) The parents' appeal would be dismissed. Section 31(2)(b)(i) provided that the harm must be attributable to the "care given to the child." While in most cases this would refer to the care given to the child by the parents or other primary carers, it could also include the care given by other carers where the parents shared the care of the child with those other carers. Thus in this case the threshold conditions were satisfied as the child had suffered harm that was attributable to the actions of at least one of her three carers.

Commentary

As Lord Nicholls pointed out, this interpretation of the legislation was necessary in order to protect children who had suffered harm: to return a child who had suffered serious non-accidental injuries to the parents simply because it might have been the non-parental carer who committed the acts in question "could be dangerously irresponsible." (p.588). Of course, such an interpretation does mean, as he acknowledged, that "the attributable condition may be satisfied when there is no more than a possibility that the parents were responsible for inflicting the injuries which the child has undoubtedly suffered." (p.589). However, a number of factors limit the impact of this. First, the threshold criteria will not be satisfied if the harm to the child was caused by the actions of an unconnected third party, unless the parents had the chance to prevent such harm occurring and failed to do so: the principle established in *Lancashire CC v B* only applies if the care of the child is shared between a number of persons. Secondly, the fact that the threshold criteria are satisfied does not mean that a care order must be made: the court has a discretion whether or not to make such an order, and the risk posed by the parents can be evaluated at this stage. Thus, as Lord Clyde argued, "it is reasonable to allow a degree of latitude in the scope of the jurisdictional provision, leaving the critical question of whether the circumstances require the making of an order to a detailed assessment of the welfare of the child." (p.593). Of course, the fact that the court does not need to ascertain the perpetrator of the injuries at the threshold stage does pose certain problems at the next stage, as the cases of *Re O and N; Re B* [2003] UKHL 18— discussed below—illustrate. The way in which the court may eliminate certain possible perpetrators at the threshold stage was considered in the next case.

Key Principle: **The court should ask itself whether there is a likelihood or real possibility that any given individual is the perpetrator, or a perpetrator, of the child's injuries**

North Yorkshire CC v SA 2003

The medical evidence was that the child had suffered serious non-accidental injuries on at least two occasions. The possible perpetrators of the second incident, which had occurred only a few hours before the child was taken to hospital, included the parents, the maternal grandmother, and the night nanny. The judge took the view that he could not say that there was no possibility that any one of them was not a perpetrator and that each had therefore to be regarded as a potential perpetrator.

Held: (CA) The test applied by the judge was too wide. The appropriate approach was to ask "[i]s there a likelihood or real possibility that A or B or C was the perpetrator or a perpetrator of the inflicted injuries?" (para.26). On the evidence it was unlikely that either the maternal grandmother or the night nanny was responsible for the child's injuries: the night nanny could be positively excluded from responsibility for the first injury and all of the parties had asked that the grandmother be excluded as a possible perpetrator.

Commentary
The test formulated by Butler-Sloss P in this case applies the test for deciding whether a child is likely to suffer harm (as set out in *Re H and R*, above) to the "uncertain perpetrator" case of the type considered in *Lancashire CC v B*. This is of course a less exacting test than that which must be satisfied in deciding whether an event has actually occurred, but to require the local authority to establish who was responsible for the child's injuries on the balance of probabilities would effectively reverse the decision in *Lancashire CC v B* and put children at risk in cases in which the perpetrator could not be ascertained. The test formulated in *North Yorkshire CC v SA* strikes a balance between setting the threshold too high and, on the other hand, casting the net of potential perpetrators too widely.

Key Principle: **A concession that the threshold criteria are satisfied does not preclude investigation of other allegations**

Re M (Threshold Criteria: Parental Concessions) 1999
Allegations of sexual abuse were made by three children against their adoptive father. He was subsequently acquitted, but the relationship between the adoptive parents and the children had broken down and neither wanted the children to return to their care. They conceded that they had caused the children significant harm as a result of their rejection of the children following the allegations, the use of inappropriate forms of punishment

and their failure to pay sufficient attention to the children's emotional needs, and that as a result the threshold criteria were satisfied. They therefore argued that the allegations of sexual abuse should not be investigated.

Held: (CA) Whether or not further investigations were necessary following concessions would depend on the circumstances of each individual case. Here the concessions made by the adoptive parents were different in nature and significance from the allegations made against the adoptive father. It was therefore appropriate for the local authority to provide evidence of the allegations and for the court to make findings in relation to those allegations.

Commentary
The court in this case acknowledged the importance of avoiding unnecessary litigation but held that a finding on the truth of the allegations of sexual abuse was important, since it would be relevant to the question as to whether there should be contact between the children and their adoptive parents, as well as to the therapy with which the children would be provided. It would also make the children feel that the court had listened to them. The case illustrates the inquisitorial role played by the court in care proceedings and the importance of the court being in full possession of the facts, so far as they can be ascertained.

Should the Court make an Order?

Once the threshold criteria have been satisfied, the court has the power to make a care or supervision order (or indeed any of the s.8 orders) but is not obliged to do so. In deciding what order it should make, the court must apply the principle that the child's welfare is paramount (see further chapter 11). This second stage of the process is therefore sometimes referred to as the "welfare" stage (as opposed to the 'threshold' stage, which focuses on whether the threshold criteria are satisfied).

Key Principle: **If the court has been unable to identify which parent or carer was responsible for inflicting non-accidental injuries on the child, it must proceed on the basis that each parent or carer was a possible perpetrator**

Re O and N; Re B 2002

The conjoined appeals before the House of Lords were both cases in which children had suffered serious non-accidental injury but in which it was not possible to ascertain which parent was responsible for inflicting those injuries. In each case the threshold criteria were satisfied (according to the principle established in *Lancashire CC v B* [2000] 2 A.C. 147, discussed above), and the issue for the court was how to dispose of the case at the "welfare" stage. The question as to which parent was responsible for the injuries was particularly relevant to the disposal of the case as in each case the parents had separated. Two differently constituted Courts of Appeal had taken different approaches: one holding that both parents must be regarded as potential perpetrators, the other deciding that the welfare stage should proceed on the basis that the mother did not pose a risk to the child.

Held: (HL) If it was not possible to identify the parent who was responsible for the injuries the case had to proceed on the basis that either was potentially the perpetrator.

Commentary

The issue in this case was essentially this: if it is not possible to identify the parent who was responsible for the injuries, should the case proceed on the basis that neither was responsible, or on the basis that both were responsible, or on the basis that it is more likely that one of them was responsible? The first was not a realistic option. As Lord Nicholls pointed out, it would defeat the purpose of the legislation if the first course was adopted: "it would be grotesque if such a case had to proceed at the welfare stage on the footing that, because neither parent, considered individually, has been proved to be the perpetrator, therefore the child is not at risk from either of them." (p.1177). Such an interpretation would obviously create the risk of the child being returned to the perpetrator. The third option was desirable if supported by sufficient evidence: Lord Nicholls encouraged trial judges "to express such views as they can at the preliminary hearing" and noted that "the judge at the disposal hearing will take into account any views expressed by the judge at the preliminary hearing on the likelihood that one carer was or was not the perpetrator, or a perpetrator, of the inflicted injuries." (p.1178). In the instant case, however, the Court of Appeal should not have proceeded on the basis that the mother did not pose a risk to the child, as this went against the findings of the trial judge, who had been unable to exonerate either parent. In this type of case, where there is simply insufficient evidence to identify the parent responsible, the only possible option is to proceed on the basis that either is potentially the perpetrator.

Key Principle: **The order made by the court must be necessary and proportionate**

Re B (Care: Interference with Family Life) 2003

In the course of discussions with a psychiatrist, a young woman reported that she and some of her sisters had had some sexual involvement with their grandfather. This led to an intervention by the local authority in relation to those of her siblings who were still minors. Interim care orders were made, the terms of which required the local authority to give the parents 48 hours' notice if it was decided to remove the children, in order to allow the parents time to apply to the court for such removal to be vetoed.

Held:　(CA) While there was sufficient evidence for the judge to conclude that the threshold criteria had been satisfied in this case, this did not mean that a care order was necessarily the appropriate order. A judge had to consider Art. 8 of the ECHR and "must not sanction such an interference with family life unless he is satisfied that that is both necessary and proportionate and that no other less radical form of order would achieve the essential aim of promoting the welfare of the children." (para.34). In the circumstances, it would be more appropriate to adjourn the local authority's application for an interim care order with liberty to apply on short notice, rather than placing the onus on the parents to apply to prevent removal.

Commentary

This relatively short and straightforward case illustrates the increased prominence given to the issue of proportionality at the "welfare" stage of care proceedings. The next case underlines the importance of ensuring that orders made by the court do not go further than is required for the protection of the child.

Key Principle: **An intervention that is not necessary or proportionate will breach Art. 8 of the ECHR**

P, C and S v UK 2002
The mother, whose eldest child was already in care, was suspected of suffering from Munchausen's syndrome by proxy. The local authority decided that an emergency protection order should be taken out as soon as her second child was born, in part because she and her new partner had failed to comply with the local authority's risk assessment. Accordingly, the baby was taken from the mother while the latter was still in hospital, and was subsequently adopted.

Held: (ECHR) In the circumstances, the decision to seek an emergency protection order was justifiable. However, the implementation of the order breached art.8: it was neither necessary nor proportionate to remove the child immediately, as her safety could be ensured while she and her mother remained in the hospital.

Commentary
As the European Court of Human Rights pointed out, the mother's opportunity and ability to harm her baby immediately after the birth was somewhat limited in the light of the fact that she had undergone a caesarean section and was confined to bed due to the after-effects of blood loss and high blood pressure. The case illustrates that the manner in which protective measures are implemented may be deemed to violate the rights of those concerned, even if the court agrees that protection was necessary on the facts of the case.

If a care order is made, the court may also need to consider whether the parents should continue to have contact with the child. Under s.34 of the Children Act 1989, a local authority may apply for an order authorising it to refuse such contact.

Key Principle: **There is a presumption of continuing contact between parent and child**

Re E (A Minor)(Care Order: Contact) 1994
Care orders were made in respect of two young boys whose parents were unable to care for them. The local authority made

an application to refuse contact between the parents and their children on the basis that there was no possibility of rehabilitation and continued contact might interfere with the care plan, which was for closed adoption. The order was made.

Held: (CA) The appeal should be allowed, as in the circumstances it was premature to terminate contact between the parents and their children. Section 34 of the 1989 Act began with the provision that a local authority should allow children in care reasonable contact with their parents and the onus was therefore on the local authority to provide justifications for a care plan that excluded such contact. If the benefits of continuing contact outweighed the disadvantages of disrupting the local authority's care plan, then the court should refuse the local authority's application that contact be terminated.

Commentary
Once again, the balance of power between the local authority and the court was central to the decision in this case. Simon Brown L.J. emphasised that the role of the court was not to monitor the local authority's plan, but rather to exercise the duty laid down by Parliament to decide whether contact should continue. It should however be noted that the approach adopted in this case—following the Court of Appeal decision in *Re B (Minors) (Care: Contact: Local Authority's Plans)* [1993] 1 F.L.R. 543—showed considerably less deference to the plans of the local authority than that adopted in previous cases. Moreover, the case contains a strong statement of the benefits of contact: according to Simon Brown L.J., "even when the s.31 criteria are satisfied, contact may well be of singular importance to the long-term welfare of the child: first, in giving the child the security of knowing that his parents love him and are interested in his welfare; secondly, by avoiding any damaging sense of loss to the child in seeing himself abandoned by his parents; thirdly, by enabling the child to commit himself to the substitute family with the seal of approval of the natural parents; and, fourthly, by giving the child the necessary sense of family and personal identity." (pp.154–55). Such a strong judicial endorsement of the benefits of contact renders it more likely that the balance will tip in favour of refusing the application of the local authority to refuse contact.

Key Principle: **Contact is only to be terminated if rehabilitation is not an option and post-adoption contact would not be beneficial**

Re H (Termination of Contact) 2005

The local authority's care plan provided for the adoption of the two children. It sought an order to suspend contact temporarily in order to facilitate the move from foster care to a placement with prospective adopters (who had not yet been identified). The order was refused.

Held: (CA) The judge had been correct to refuse to make such a powerful order for an uncertain and limited future use.

Commentary

The case confirms that the role of the judge is to grant orders under s.34(4) "restrictively and stringently". In this case, even though there was no prospect of the children being rehabilitated with their parents, it was intended that contact between the parents and their children should continue even after they had been adopted. All that the local authority was seeking was a suspension of contact; the problem was that it wanted the order to deal with a future transfer of the children to as-yet-unidentified adopters. It was argued by the local authority that the refusal of the order would simply mean that it would need to return to court once adopters had been identified to seek such an order all over again, and it was accepted by the judge at first instance that it might be easier for the local authority to find potential adopters if a s.34(4) order were in place. Nevertheless, it was not felt appropriate to give the local authority the right to refuse contact at this stage.

The stringent approach of the courts in this context receives further support from the jurisprudence of the European Court of Human Rights (see further *Johansen v Norway* (1997) 23 EHRR 33, discussed in chapter 11, and *K and T v Finland* [2001] 2 F.L.R. 707).

Challenging the Actions of the Local Authority

There are a number of ways in which persons aggrieved by the action (or indeed inaction) of a local authority may seek to challenge the course adopted.

Key Principle: **A local authority is not bound to follow the recommendations of its complaints review panel**

Re T (Accommodation by Local Authority) 1995

An application was made for a 17-year-old girl to be accommodated by the local authority. The application was refused. The girl's complaint was subsequently upheld by the complaints review panel, which recommended that the girl be provided with accommodation. This recommendation was not followed.

Held: The decision was one for the local authority to take and the court should only intervene if there had been a mistake as to the applicable law or the decision was *Wednesbury* unreasonable. (In this case, however, the local authority had erred in not taking all the relevant factors into account and the application for judicial review would be granted.)

Commentary

Whether or not a complaint is upheld or an application for judicial review granted, the power of the court to dictate what course of action the local authority should adopt remains limited, as the next case further illustrates.

Key Principle: **In judicial review proceedings, the court may quash a decision that is irrational and/or *Wednesbury* unreasonable but cannot dictate what alternative course of action the local authority should take**

Re T (Judicial Review: Local Authority: Decisions Concerning Child in Need) 2003

A risk-assessment report recommended that a 14-year-old boy with a history of sexual offending should attend a specialist residential placement. The local authority rejected this recommendation, deciding that his needs could be met through an educational programme at the children's home where he was living. The boy sought an order challenging the decision.

Held: The decision of the local authority would be quashed as it was irrational and/or *Wednesbury* unreasonable. The local authority was ordered to reconsider what services it should provide for the boy, who was a "child in need" under s.17 of the 1989 Act. However, the court had no power to direct the local authority to provide any specific form of provision for the boy.

Commentary
The case illustrates the limitations of judicial review as a means of challenging a decision by a local authority. Judicial review is simply a means by which the court may decide upon the lawfulness of a particular decision or course of action, rather than the merits of the case. Thus a judge may quash a decision on the basis that it was illegal (based on an error of law), procedurally improper, or irrational, but not on the basis that he or she would have reached a different decision on the facts.

Key Principle: **A local authority may be liable in negligence for its actions towards a child in its care**

Barrett v Enfield London Borough Council 1999
A care order was made in respect of the plaintiff when he was 10 months old, and he remained in the care of the local authority until he reached adulthood. He subsequently claimed that he had suffered various psychiatric problems as a result of the local authority's failure to make proper arrangements for him and that the defendant had breached its duty of care towards him. The local authority's application to strike out the claim was refused by the district judge but allowed by the High Court judge. The Court of Appeal dismissed the appeal.

Held: (HL) The application should not have been struck out, and the case should proceed to trial.

Commentary
In this case the House of Lords distinguished its earlier decision in *X (Minors) v Bedfordshire CC* [1995] 2 A.C. 633. Since that decision, the European Court of Human Rights had expressed disapproval of the practice of striking out applications. Moreover, a distinction could be drawn between the local authority's decision whether or not to take a child into care (the issue in the *Bedfordshire* case) and the local authority's actions in relation to a child already in its care. However, it should be noted that the case did not decide that a duty of care *did* lie in this situation, merely

that this was an issue that should be tried. Successful claims have since been brought by individuals who suffered harm as a result of the local authority's negligence (see e.g. *C v Flintshire CC* [2001] 2 F.L.R. 33).

Key Principle: **A local authority investigating allegations of child abuse owes no duty of care to the parents of the child**

D v East Berkshire Community Health NHS Trust; MAK v Dewsbury Healthcare NHS Trust; RK v Oldham NHS Trust 2005
In each of the three cases, doctors had suspected that a child had been injured by a parent or that a parent had fabricated the child's medical condition, but upon further investigation each of the parents was cleared. The parents then alleged that they had suffered psychiatric injury and disruption to their family life as a result of a negligent misdiagnosis. The claim for damages was struck out, and the parents' appeal was dismissed by the Court of Appeal.

Held: (HL) Investigations into suspected child abuse should be conducted in good faith, but the professionals involved owed no duty of care to the parents not to make negligent allegations of child abuse. The parents' appeal would therefore be dismissed.

Commentary
As Lord Nicholls pointed out, the law has to strike a balance between protecting children suspected to be at risk and intruding unnecessarily into family life. In a case of this kind, it was necessary that those investigating suspected abuse should be free from any conflict of interest: "a doctor must be able to act single-mindedly in the interests of the child." (p.312). It was accepted, however, that a duty of care was owed to the children in this situation, marking a further retreat from the decision in the *Bedfordshire* case.

As the following case shows, the children in the *Bedfordshire* case were not left without any remedy.

Key Principle: **The failure of a local authority to take steps to protect children known to be at risk may constitute a violation of Art.3 of the ECHR**

Z v UK 2001

Concerns about the four children were first voiced in 1987, and various meetings to discuss the case took place, but it was not until 1992 that they were placed with foster-carers. A child psychiatrist described it as the worst case of neglect and emotional abuse that she had seen in her professional career. Proceedings against the local authority were struck out as disclosing no cause of action (*X (Minors) v Bedfordshire CC* [1995] 2 A.C. 633). Before the European Court of Human Rights the children argued that there had been a breach of their human rights.

Held: (ECHR) The UK was under an obligation to take measures designed to ensure that individuals within its jurisdiction were not subjected to torture or inhuman or degrading treatment, including ill-treatment administered by private individuals. The neglect and abuse suffered by the children in this case reached the threshold of inhuman and degrading treatment. The treatment had been brought to the attention of the local authority and there was no doubt that the system had failed to protect them. Accordingly, there had been a violation of art.3.

Commentary

As the court acknowledged, a local authority does have the difficult task of balancing the need to protect children at risk with the need to respect the rights of the family to private and family life (and art.8 may be breached if the actions of the local authority are not proportionate to the risk, as in *P, C and S v UK* [2002] 2 F.L.R. 631). The failings of the local authority in this particular case were all too obvious. By contrast, no violation of Art.3 will occur if the local authority is not aware of the abuse being suffered by the children.

Since the passage of the Human Rights Act 1998, claims of this kind may be brought in the domestic courts, and the next case explains the procedure to be adopted.

Key Principle: **Claims raising human rights issues should be dealt with in the context of care proceedings rather than as a separate issue**

Re L (Care Proceedings: Human Rights Claims) 2003

In the course of care proceedings, the mother sought the transfer of the case to the High Court, seeking to challenge the local authority's care plan under the Human Rights Act 1998.

Held: The matter should not have been transferred to the High Court. Save in exceptional cases, human rights arguments should be dealt with in the context of the care proceedings.

Commentary

In this case the mother wanted the court to compel the local authority to change its care plan; but, as Munby J. pointed out, this lay beyond the powers of the court, which could not dictate the terms of the care plan. The main interest of the case, however, lies in the careful discussion of the procedure to be adopted in cases involving human rights claims. Although the Human Rights Act 1998 allows a freestanding application to be brought, such an application is only appropriate once the care proceedings have come to an end. While such proceedings are pending, any human rights arguments should be dealt with in the context of those proceedings. Munby J. expressed his confidence in the ability of the lower courts to deal with such arguments, although he acknowledged that there might occasionally be a novel or particularly complex point that should be heard in the High Court.

10. WARDSHIP AND THE INHERENT JURISDICTION

The High Court may exercise its inherent jurisdiction to make a child a ward of court or to sanction (or prohibit) specific decisions or steps. The inherent jurisdiction is both broad in scope and narrow in application: if it is appropriate for the court to exercise its inherent jurisdiction, its powers are theoretically limitless, but it will only be appropriate for it to do so in certain circumstances, for example in situations that are not already the subject of statutory regulation. This chapter first sketches out the powers of the court and then the limitations on the exercise of the jurisdiction.

Key Principle: **The powers of the court under its inherent jurisdiction are more extensive than the powers of a parent**

Re R (A Minor) (Wardship: Medical Treatment) 1992
A 15-year-old girl with mental health problems refused the medication deemed necessary to control her psychotic behaviour and suicidal tendencies. The issue for the court was whether this refusal could be overridden. At first instance it was decided that the girl was not *Gillick*-competent and therefore not able to refuse treatment.

Held: (CA) The court has the power, in the exercise of its wardship jurisdiction, to override the refusal of even a competent adolescent. Leave to administer treatment to the girl would be given.

Commentary
The cases in which the courts have overridden the wishes of a *Gillick*-competent minor were considered in chapter 7. Our interest here lies in the scope of the wardship jurisdiction, as spelt out by Lord Donaldson of Lymington M.R. He opined that the judgment of the House of Lords in *Gillick* was of limited relevance to this particular case, as the powers of the court were more extensive than those of a parent. The wardship jurisdiction of the court "is not derived from the parents' rights and responsibilities,

but . . . is the delegated performance of the duties of the Crown to protect its subjects." (p.199).

Key Principle: **No important decision or step relating to a ward may be taken without the prior consent of the court**

Kelly v BBC 2000

A 16-year-old boy who had left home to join a religious group was made a ward of court. An order was made to allow the Official Solicitor to publicise the issue for the purpose of tracing the boy. The BBC subsequently traced him and interviewed him by telephone. An injunction was obtained to prevent the broadcast of this interview.

Held: The injunction would be lifted. It was not a contempt of court to publish information about a ward of court, and a media interview was not a step that required the prior consent of the court.

Commentary

The key interest of this case for current purposes lies not in the reasons that led the judge to discharge the injunction, but in the discussion of the status of a ward of court. Munby J.'s characteristically thorough judgment helpfully set out the types of decisions or steps that previous courts had decided *did* require the prior consent of the court: marriage with a ward; removing the ward from the jurisdiction; materially changing the ward's education or residence; changing the ward's name; instituting adoption proceedings; and significant forms of medical treatment. He also noted that certain types of interviews had been held to require the consent of the court, including "a psychiatric examination for forensic purposes; interviews by an independent social worker; police interviews; and interviews on behalf of a defendant in criminal proceedings." (p.218). Interviews of this kind—involving specific proceedings in which the child was or might be involved—were not, however, thought to be analogous to a media interview. As the judge pointed out, "one would not in this age of media saturation usually consider an interview by the media an 'important' or 'major' step in a child's life, however interesting or exciting it may be for the child." (p.219).

Key Principle: **The court will not exercise its jurisdiction to interfere with an exercise of discretion under a statutory code**

A v Liverpool CC 1981

The local authority obtained a care order in respect of a child and decided that contact with his mother would be restricted. The mother sought to challenge this decision through wardship proceedings. It was held that the court had no jurisdiction in the circumstances.

Held: (HL) As Parliament had entrusted the decision regarding contact to the local authority in cases of this kind, the court should not interfere.

Commentary

In this case the House of Lords confirmed a rule that was already well-established in the lower courts, namely that 'the courts must not, in purported exercise of wardship jurisdiction, interfere with those matters which Parliament has decided are within the province of a local authority to whom the care and control of a child has been entrusted pursuant to statutory provisions." (*per* Lord Roskill at p.379). This did not mean that the inherent jurisdiction of the court was ousted in such cases: as Lord Wilberforce pointed out, it could still be invoked if the issue fell outside the statute: "[t]he court's general inherent power is always available to fill gaps or to supplement the powers of the local authority" (p.373). Furthermore, the local authority's decision would be amenable to judicial review (see further chapter 9).

As the next case illustrates, the passage of the Children Act 1989 reduced the scope of the wardship jurisdiction still further.

Key Principle: **The wardship jurisdiction should only be invoked if the issue cannot be dealt with under the Children Act 1989 or other statutory scheme**

Re CT (A Minor) (Wardship: Representation) 1993

An adopted child wished to return to her biological family. Having satisfied a solicitor that she was capable of giving instructions, she applied for and was granted leave to apply for a residence order in favour of her paternal aunt. Her adoptive parents successfully applied for leave to institute wardship proceedings, and obtained an order consolidating the two sets of proceedings. As a result, the Official Solicitor was appointed as the girl's guardian *ad litem*.

Held: (CA) The wardship proceedings would be discontinued and the application for a residence order would proceed. Under the current family proceedings rules, the girl was entitled to bring proceedings without a guardian *ad litem*, and the wardship jurisdiction should not be used for the purpose of imposing a guardian.

Commentary

The narrow point established by this case related to the circumstances in which a minor may bring or defend proceedings without a guardian *ad litem* (whose role was to act in the child's best interests, rather than simply to represent the child's views). The wider point related to the relationship between the then newly-implemented Children Act 1989 and the court's wardship jurisdiction. As Waite L.J. noted, "[t]he courts" undoubted discretion to allow wardship proceedings to go forward in a suitable case is subject to their clear duty, in loyalty to the scheme and purpose of the Children Act legislation, to permit recourse to wardship only when it becomes apparent to the judge in any particular case that the question which the court is determining in regard to the minor's upbringing or property cannot be resolved under the statutory procedures under Part II of the Act in a way which secures the best interests of the child; or where the minor's person is in a state of jeopardy from which he can only be protected by giving him the status of a ward of court; or where the court's functions need to be secured from the effects, potentially injurious to the child, of external influences . . . and it is decided that conferring on the child the status of a ward will prove a more effective deterrent than the ordinary sanctions of contempt of court." (p.282). The restraint now exercised by the courts in exercising their wardship jurisdiction is reflected by the fact that the number of applications have fallen from 4,961 in 1991 to a few hundred per year.

11. THE WELFARE PRINCIPLE

Section 1(1) of the Children Act 1989 declares that: "When a court determines any question with respect to—(a) the upbringing of a child; or (b) the administration of a child's property or the application of any income arising from it, the child's welfare shall be the court's paramount consideration."

General Principles

Key Principle: **To say that the child's welfare is 'paramount' means that it is the only consideration**

J v C 1970
The child at the centre of the dispute was born in England to Spanish parents in 1957. As his mother was suffering from tuberculosis at the time of his birth, the child was placed with foster parents when only four days old. He remained with them for almost a year, and was then reunited with his parents, who subsequently returned to Spain. However, when he became unwell in 1961 his mother asked the former foster parents if they would be able to look after him again. This was not intended to be a permanent arrangement, but the child thrived in England. In 1963, however, following a rather tactless letter from the foster mother, the parents asked that their child be returned to them. The child was made a ward of court and in 1965 it was ordered that his care and control should be committed to the foster parents. The Court of Appeal subsequently dismissed the parents' appeal.

Held: (HL) The relevant legislation, the Guardianship of Infants Act 1925, stated that in reaching decisions about a child's upbringing the court was to "regard the welfare of the infant as the first and paramount consideration . . ." (s.1). In the circumstances, the welfare of the child dictated that he should remain with the foster-parents. The welfare principle was applicable whether the court was required to decide which of two parents the child should live with, or whether the choice lay between the parents and persons to whom the child was unrelated by blood. Even if the parents were unimpeachable, their wishes and rights would not prevail against the welfare of the child.

Commentary

The key point established by the case is that in circumstances where the child's welfare is paramount, that child's welfare is the only consideration for the court. As Lord MacDermott stated, the principle that the child's welfare is paramount means ". . . more than that the child's welfare is to be treated as the top item in a list of items relevant to the matter in question. [The words] connote a process whereby, when all of the relevant facts, relationships, claims and wishes of parents, risks, choices and other circumstances are taken into account and weighed, the course to be followed will be that which is most in the interests of the child's welfare as that term is now to be understood. That is the first consideration because it is of first importance and the paramount consideration because it rules upon or determines the course to be followed." (pp.710–11).

This approach was subsequently endorsed by the Law Commission in its report *Family Law: Review of Child Law, Guardianship and Custody* (1988) Law Com No. 172. The Commission noted that "the word 'first' had caused confusion in that it had in the past led some courts to balance other considerations *against* the child's welfare rather than to consider what light they shed upon it. Since *J v C* that view has been decisively rejected in the courts and a modern formulation should reflect this" (para.3.13). The 1989 Act accordingly refers simply to the welfare of the child being the "paramount" consideration.

Of course, as Lord MacDermott acknowledged, the relationship between parent and child was a special one and this factor would in itself be relevant in assessing what course would best promote the welfare of the child. The precise weight to be attached to the importance of the child's relationship with his or her biological parent not only varies according to the particular circumstances of the case (see e.g. *Re M (Child's Upbringing)* [1996] 2 F.L.R. 441; *Re G (Children)* [2006] UKHL 43), but may also change over time, illustrating that what is deemed to be in a child's best interests may change in the light of changing social attitudes and the emergence of new evidence about child development.

The language of "parental rights" has enjoyed something of a revival in recent years, as a result of the passage of the Human Rights Act 1998 and the increased awareness of individual's rights under the European Convention on Human Rights. The extent to which the welfare principle is compatible with the Convention is considered further at the end of the chapter.

No Delay

Section 1(2) of the Children Act 1989 states that: "In any proceedings in which any question with respect to the upbringing of a child arises, the court shall have regard to the general principle that any delay in determining the question is likely to prejudice the welfare of the child." It is of course implicit in this that there may be exceptions to this general principle, as the following case shows.

Key Principle: **Planned and purposeful delay may be in the best interests of the child**

C v Solihull MBC 1993

The parents had two children. There had been an incident when the first child—then aged 12 months—had been slapped across the face by the father with sufficient force to leave a mark. When the younger child was only a few months old, she sustained a fracture, which according to the medical evidence was non-accidentally inflicted. Neither parent could give any satisfactory explanation for the injury, and upon discharge from hospital the child was placed with foster parents. After a number of hearings the justices decided to return the child to her parents subject to a supervision order. The guardian *ad litem*, supported by the local authority, appealed.

Held: The appeal would be allowed. It was consistent with the welfare of the child for there to be a short delay in the final disposition of the case in order to allow a proper programme of assessment to be undertaken. The appropriate arrangement would be to make interim orders, including a residence order that was conditional upon the parents undertaking a programme of assessment and co-operating with all reasonable requests by the local authority to participate in that programme, together with a supervision order which required the parents to submit the child for medical examinations and take her to the health visitor as directed.

Commentary

As the judge pointed out, the court simply lacked sufficient information to make a final order at that time. The order made by the justices abdicated the responsibility of caring for the child to the parents "at a time when the matters are still too uncertain to be confident of their ability properly to exercise that care." (p.301); by contrast, a care order would relinquish responsibility to the local authority. The solution was to put in place a combination of orders that would allow the parents' ability to care for their child to be assessed. Even though this would create a delay before the final disposition of the case, the judge emphasized that "delay is ordinarily inimicable to the welfare of the child, but . . . planned and purposeful delay may well be beneficial. A delay of a final decision for the purpose of ascertaining the result of an assessment is proper delay and is to be encouraged." (p.304).

Key Principle: **Further delay in resolving a case may be required in the interests of justice**

Re K (Non-accidental Injuries: Perpetrator: New Evidence) 2004

An arranged marriage took place and the couple subsequently lived with the husband's parents. Their first child was taken to hospital twice in the two months following her birth, with what were identified as serious non-accidental injuries. An interim care order was made in relation to the child. The judge hearing the application for a full care order was unable to decide who was responsible for the child's injuries, on account of what he described as a conspiracy of silence between the child's main carers—the parents and the paternal grandmother. Full care orders (and orders freeing them for adoption) were subsequently made in relation to both the first child and a second child who had been born after proceedings started. The mother then retracted her previous evidence, accused both paternal grandparents of mishandling the first child, revealed that an attempt to kidnap her had been made by her husband, and appealed against both orders.

Held: (CA) In the circumstances of the case, "justice require[d] the question of perpetration to be revisited." (para.61). While the court had to take account of the principle in s.1(2) that delay is likely to be prejudicial to the children's welfare, this consideration was outweighed by the issues of justice and the public interest in identifying the person who had perpetrated the injuries. In addition, there was a possibility that the children might be reunited with their mother if it were to be decided that she had not inflicted the injuries. The appeal would therefore be allowed and the final care orders and freeing orders set aside. Interim care orders would be substituted while the substantive issue as to who was responsible for the child's injuries was remitted to a first instance judge.

Commentary
It would have been possible for Wall L.J. to have argued that delay would in this case be beneficial on account of the possibility that the children might be reunited with their mother at the end of the process. However, he placed more weight on the considerations of justice and the public interest, holding that these might, as here, outweigh the principle enshrined in s.1(2). There is, after all, no absolute rule that the courts must avoid delay, since s.1(2) merely requires the court to 'have regard' to the general principle that delay is best avoided.

Orders not to be Made Unnecessarily

Section 1(5) of the 1989 Act provides that "Where a court is considering whether or not to make one or more orders under this Act with respect to a child, it shall not make the order . . . unless it considers that doing so would be better for the child than making no order at all."

Key Principle: **Before making an order, the court must ask "will it be better for the child to make the order than to make no order at all?"**

Re G (Children) 2005
The unmarried parents separated and, after much discussion, agreed that the father should have parental responsibility and that a residence order should be made in favour of the mother. The judge refused to make the residence order on the basis that it was unnecessary in the light of the agreement between the parties.

Held: (CA) A residence order should be made. Section 1(5) of the Children Act did not create a presumption against making an order in cases concerning children, but merely required the court to ask itself whether the making of an order would be better for the child than making no order at all.

Commentary

Although Ward L.J. formulated the question for the court as being "will it be better for *the child* to make the order than making no order at all?" (para.10, emphasis added), the reasons that he gave for making the residence order in this case focused largely on the advantages to the *parents* of making such an order, although the knock-on benefits to the children were also noted. Thus he noted that it gave the mother security, and added to her peace of mind, which was "an integral and important factor in producing stability in the lives of the children in care of the parent." (para.11); that the agreement between the parents had dissipated their earlier mistrust and "where parents can agree future dealings with regard to the children, that is better for the children than having bitterly contested court proceedings" (para.12); and, finally, what was for him the critical factor, that "the court should not be astute to go behind agreements carefully negotiated in difficult questions of this sort" (para.13). His view was that the court should respect the view of the parents that an order would be beneficial to the management of their children's lives. The court thus both deferred to the fact that both parents wished for an order at this time and recognised the importance that a court order might have in the future should either party change their mind.

The statistics on the disposal of applications under s.8 of the Children Act would suggest that the approach endorsed by the Court of Appeal in this case reflects what is happening in practice: across all categories the numbers of orders made far outnumbers those withdrawn, refused, or made as orders of "no order". In the circumstances, though, it can be argued that the Court of Appeal was right to make the order in this case. Although the Law Commission had initially suggested that an order might be unnecessary where the parents were co-operating, the long history of disagreement between the parties in this case meant that it was preferable to enshrine the agreement they had reached in a court order rather than have to resolve the issues if the agreement subsequently broke down.

B v B (A Minor) (Residence order) 1992

A grandmother made an application for a residence order in relation to her granddaughter, then aged 11. The girl had lived with her grandmother for all but the first six weeks of her life.

Until a short time earlier the girl's mother had also lived there, but she had since left home. She supported her mother's application for a residence order. The justices refused to make the order on the basis that in the light of the mother's agreement there was no risk of the girl being taken away from her current home.

Held: It would be to the advantage of the girl if the order were made in favour of her grandmother. Making a residence order would confer parental responsibility upon the grandmother, and thereby make it easier for her to deal with the education authorities (who had been reluctant to accept her authority in matters relating to the girl's schooling and had insisted on having the mother's written authority) and with medical professionals (should consent to medical treatment be required). In addition, given that the mother was of an impulsive nature, her wishes might change in the future, and the girl herself wanted the stability that a residence order would bring.

Commentary
The case further illustrates that there may be practical reasons for making an order even if there is consensus between the parties at the time of the application. Once again, the court displayed an awareness that a consensus might not last.

The Applicability of the Welfare Principle

When does the Welfare Principle Apply?

It should be borne in mind that although s.1(1) of the 1989 Act would appear to be couched in very wide terms, not every issue that affects a child has to be resolved in a way that best promotes the welfare of that child. In addition, different statutes may use different formulations that displace the application of the welfare principle in particular contexts (see e.g. *Suter v Suter* and *J v C (Child: Financial Provision)* [1999] 1 F.L.R. 152).

Key Principle: **The welfare principle only applies if the upbringing of the child is directly in issue**

R ota P v Secretary of State for the Home Department; R ota Q v Secretary of State for the Home Department 2001
The appeal concerned two mothers, each of whom had been sentenced to a term of imprisonment for drug offences. They challenged the policy of the Prison Service that babies could not remain with their mothers in prison beyond the age of 18 months, invoking, *inter alia*, section 1(1) of the 1989 Act.

Held: The Children Act 1989 had no direct application to the Secretary of State or the Prison Service in the context of this case, and therefore the best interests of the children of these mothers were not the paramount consideration.

Commentary
While the upbringing of the children of these mothers would clearly be affected by the policy adopted by the Prison Service, it was not directly in issue in the case and so the welfare principle was not applicable. There will be many similar cases involving broad issues of social policy and resource allocation that are similarly deemed to have only an indirect effect on the children affected.

To Whom does the Welfare Principle Apply?

In most cases the answer to this will be straightforward, since there will only be one child involved in the case. But what if the applicant is also a child? Or if the application relates to more than one child?

Key Principle: **The welfare of the child who is the subject of the proceedings is the paramount consideration, even if the applicant is also a child**

Birmingham CC v H (No.3) 1994
A girl aged fourteen gave birth to a baby. She initially cared for him satisfactorily but it was then discovered that she was handling him roughly, in a manner that could cause him

physical injury. The girl's violence led to the baby being placed with foster parents (and to the girl being placed in secure accommodation). Care orders were made in relation to both the girl—on the basis that she was beyond parental control—and her baby). The girl continued to have contact with her baby but continued to handle him roughly. The local authority planned to place the baby for adoption and sought to prevent contact between the girl and the baby under s.34 of the Children Act 1989. At first instance an order allowing the local authority to refuse contact was made, but the Court of Appeal allowed the appeal on the basis that the welfare of both girl and baby should be taken into account and that contact might be beneficial to the girl and would not necessarily harm the baby.

Held: (HL) The appeal by the local authority would be allowed and the order of the judge at first instance restored. The child whose welfare was relevant was the child in care to whom the application related. It was the upbringing of this child that was in question. The fact that the parent of the child was also a child did not make the parent's welfare a relevant consideration as the court was not considering any issue relating to the parent's upbringing. There was thus no need to balance the welfare of the baby in this case against the welfare of the girl.

Commentary
While the judgment of Lord Slynn of Hadley was based on the particular terms of s.34, rather than the 1989 Act as a whole, it has been accepted that the same principle is applicable to other Children Act proceedings.

Key Principle: **If two or more children are the subject of the same proceedings, the task of the court is to balance the interests of both**

Re A (Conjoined Twins: Medical Treatment) 2001
Conjoined twins were born. The medical evidence was that if an operation was not carried out to separate them both would eventually die. If such an operation were to be carried out, Mary, the weaker twin, would die almost immediately but Jodie, the stronger twin, had a good chance of survival.

Held: (CA) While it would be in the best interests of Jodie for the operation to be carried out, it would not be in the best interests of Mary for the operation to be carried out. As a decision had to be made, it was the role of the court to find the least detrimental alternative. In the circumstances, that was for the operation to go ahead, since this would give the chance of life to at least one of the twins and without it both would die. (See also chapter 7 on the weight to be given to the wishes of the parents, who opposed the operation).

Commentary
It should be noted that the approach adopted in this case—balancing the best interests of one child against the best interests of the other—is in accord with the original recommendations of the Law Commission in relation to the application of the welfare principle more generally. The Commission had argued that "the interests of the child whose future happens to be in issue in the proceedings before the court should not in principle prevail over those of other children likely to be affected by the decision. Hence their welfare should also be taken into consideration." (para.3.13). In practice, however, as the case of *Birmingham CC v H (No.3)* illustrates, the courts have adopted a narrower approach, focusing on the welfare of the child who is the subject of the application.

The Welfare Checklist

Section 1(3) of the Children Act 1989 sets out a checklist of factors to which the court is to have regard in deciding whether to make, vary or revoke a contested s.8 order, a special guardianship order, or an order under Part IV of the Act. The specified factors are:

(a) the ascertainable wishes and feelings of the child concerned (considered in the light of his age and understanding);

(b) his physical, emotional and educational needs;

(c) the likely effect on him of any change in his circumstances;

(d) his age, sex, background and any characteristics of his which the court considers relevant;

(e) any harm which he has suffered or is at risk of suffering;

(f) how capable each of his parents, and any other person in relation to whom the court considers the question to be relevant, is of meeting his needs;

(g) the range of powers available to the court under this Act in the proceedings in questions.

It is difficult to distil key principles from the abundant case-law, since each case turns on its own facts, and an element that was decisive in one case may be outweighed by another factor in a different case. The only constant is that the welfare of the child is the paramount consideration, but perceptions of what is in the best interests of a child may vary significantly over time. The principles discussed below should be viewed merely as illustrations of the way in which the courts have decided what is in the best interests of a child at any given time.

***

Key Principle: **There is no presumption in favour of either parent, but the natural ability of a mother to care for a very young child should not be ignored**

Brixey v Lynas 1996

A child was born in Scotland to a middle-class father and a mother who had not had the same educational and social advantages. The parents separated when their child was only a few months old; thereafter the child lived mostly with her mother. The father was subsequently awarded custody, largely on the basis that he could provide his daughter with more material advantages and stability. The mother's appeal was allowed on the basis that the sheriff had failed to take into account the advantages of retaining the status quo and of maternal care.

Held: (HL) There was no legal presumption in favour of either parent in deciding with whom a child should live. However, the advantage to a very young child of being with his or her mother should be taken into account in deciding on that child's best interests. The father's appeal would be dismissed.

Commentary

The case illustrates a number of themes within the welfare checklist: the importance of maintaining the status quo (assuming that the current arrangements are satisfactory); the fact that relatively little weight is attached to the fact that one parent may be able to offer the child a better standard of living in material terms; and the way in which the welfare principle is interpreted according to prevailing social attitudes. Lord Jauncey robustly rejected the suggestion that the current law was discriminatory in attaching weight to a mother's care, asserting that 'mothers are generally better fitted than fathers to provide for the needs of very young children' (p.504). He did however acknowledge that other factors might, in a suitably compelling case, tip the balance in favour of a father (for example if the mother was unable to care for the child or the father had been caring for the child).

Key Principle: **There is a strong supposition that the biological parents are the best persons to bring up their child**

Re M (Child's Upbringing) 1996

The boy at the centre of the dispute was born in South Africa to Zulu parents. His mother was employed by a white woman, who became attached to the boy. When she returned to England the boy's parents agreed that she could take him with her, although the parties gave different accounts of the intended duration of this arrangement. She then decided that she would like to adopt him, a decision that was opposed by his parents. At first instance a plan for the boy's return to South Africa was drawn up, which involved him visiting his parents to be reintroduced to them and to the country. There were difficulties in implementing the plan and both sides appealed, the parents seeking the boy's immediate return and the other woman a review of the earlier decision.

Held: (CA) It was in the boy's best interests to be returned to South Africa immediately. There was a strong supposition that the biological parents were the best persons to bring up their child. Moreover, if he remained in England he would be deprived of his Zulu heritage.

Commentary

There are strong similarities between this case and that of *J v C*: both cases involved a ten-year-old boy from another culture who was being brought up in England as part of a family to which he was not related by blood. Yet the results of the two cases were different, reflecting the greater importance attached to biological parentage and cultural heritage in *Re M*. This outweighed both the importance of the status quo and the material advantages of remaining in England. The recent decision of the House of Lords in *Re G (children)* [2006] UKHL 43 (discussed in chapter 8) suggests that the approach in *Re M* is likely to be preferred to that in *J v C* (although it is worth noting that the child in this case subsequently returned to England as the arrangement did not work out).

Key Principle: **The court is required to consider, but not necessarily to give effect to, the wishes and feelings of the child**

In re M (Children) (Contact: Long-term Best Interests) 2005

The two children of the marriage lived with their father after their parents had divorced. Although they had initially had contact with their mother, this had ceased after an argument between the mother and the children's new stepmother that had resulted in a physical tug-of-war involving one of the children. This incident was referred to in the father's household as an "abduction", although the judge described this as a "flagrant mischaracterization". Eight years had elapsed between that incident and the current hearing, and the children, aged 15 and 13, were clearly hostile to the idea of any form of contact with their mother.

Held: (CA) While the wishes of teenage children would ordinarily be accorded considerable weight, the court was directed to bear in mind not only the age, but also the understanding, of the children. In this case the understanding of the children had been affected by the negative view of their mother that had been forced upon them, and their refusal of contact should not be viewed as decisive.

Commentary

The case illustrates the discretion that the court possesses to disregard the expressed wishes of children if those wishes do not fit with what the court regards as the children's best interests. It should be noted that the judge in this case did not actually order contact, merely that steps should be taken by an expert to review the advisability and possibility of future contact. As discussed in chapter 8, it is generally viewed as being in the best interests of a child to maintain contact with both parents after separation.

Given the differing views that may be taken by different individuals as to the best interests of a child, an appellate court is expected to exercise restraint in substituting its own decision.

Key Principle: **An appellate court should only interfere if the lower court has exceeded the generous ambit within which reasonable disagreement is possible and has reached a decision which is plainly wrong**

G v G (Minors: Custody Appeal) 1985

In a dispute between divorcing parents, custody was awarded to the father. The Court of Appeal held that there were no grounds on which it could interfere.

Held: (HL) The mother's appeal would be dismissed. No special rules applied to appeals in cases concerning children, and the mere fact that the appellate court would have preferred a different solution did not justify a different order.

Commentary

As the House of Lords recognised, in most cases involving the upbringing of children there is no objectively "right" answer: according to Lord Fraser, "the best that can be done is to find an answer that it reasonably satisfactory." (p.898). This means that the appellate court "should only interfere when it considers that the judge of first instance has not merely preferred an imperfect solution which is different from an alternative imperfect solution which the Court of Appeal might or would have adopted, but has exceeded the generous ambit within which a reasonable disagreement is possible." (per Lord Fraser at p.899).

The Welfare Principle and Human Rights

Key Principle: **The welfare principle is compatible with the European Convention on Human Rights**

Re KD (A Minor)(Ward: Termination of Access) 1988

The child of a teenage mother was placed with foster-parents. The mother initially had weekly contact with her child, but the local authority subsequently sought to terminate such contact on the basis that there was no reasonable possibility of rehabilitation and the child was distressed by his mother's visits. The order was made, and confirmed by the Court of Appeal. The mother appealed on the basis that in the light of the jurisprudence of the European Convention on Human Rights she had a right of access to her child.

Held: (HL) Even if parents did have a right of access to their child, such a right would be subject to the best interests of the child. In this case it was not in the best interests of the child for contact with his mother to continue, and the appeal would be dismissed.

Commentary
The terminology of 'access' immediately dates this case, which occurred before the passage of the Children Act 1989. In recent years the domestic courts have been wary of describing a parent as having a 'right' to contact (see further chapter 8), although the jurisprudence of the ECtHR offers stronger support for the existence of such a right. Of wider relevance is the suggestion by Lord Oliver of Aylmerton that there is no difference in substance between the pronouncements of the ECtHR on contact and the welfare principle as enunciated in *J v C*: "[s]uch conflict as exists is, I think, semantic only, and lies only in differing ways of giving expression to the single common concept that the natural bond and relationship between parent and child gives rise to universally recognised norms which ought not to be gratuitously interfered with and which, if interfered with at all, ought to be so only if the welfare of the child dictates it." (p.153).

Key Principle: **The welfare of the child may justify an interference with parental rights**

Johansen v Norway 1997
A teenage mother and her son were dependent on assistance from the social welfare authorities. When the son was 11 he began to receive treatment at the child psychiatric department of a hospital and a year later he was taken into care and placed in a children's home. The mother's second child was taken into care shortly after her birth, and contact was refused. Her son subsequently ran away from the children's home and it was decided that to implement the care decision would be detrimen-

tal to him. He therefore remained living with his mother. The mother then unsuccessfully appealed against the decision to take her daughter into care. Before the European Court she alleged that her rights under Art.8 had been violated.

Held: (ECHR) The decision to take the child into care was in accordance with Norwegian law, pursued the legitimate aim of protecting the health and "rights and freedoms" of the child and was necessary in a democratic society. Thus this step did not lead to a violation of Art.8. However, the termination of the mother's rights of access to her child did infringe Art.8. The actions of the public authorities in this respect did not satisfy the requirement that they be necessary in a democratic society. The measures taken were particularly far-reaching (the child having been placed with foster-parents with a view to adoption). Such measures should only be applied in exceptional circumstances and were not justified in this case: the risk of the mother disrupting the child's placement was not so grave as to relieve the authorities from their obligation to take steps with a view to reuniting her with the child if there was evidence that she would be able to provide the child with a satisfactory upbringing.

Commentary

The Court emphasised that taking a child into care should usually be regarded "as a temporary measure to be discontinued as soon as circumstances permit and that any measures of implementation of temporary care should be consistent with the ultimate aim of reuniting the natural parent and the child." (para.78). Yet it recognised that there would be cases in which the interests of the child would be best served by remaining in care, and that "a fair balance has to be struck between the interests of the child in remaining in public care and those of the parent in being reunited with the child." In balancing these competing interests, the court would "attach particular importance to the best interests of the child, which, depending on their nature and seriousness, *may* override those of the parent." (para.78, emphasis added). The crucial word "may" illustrates that the welfare of the child is not an automatic justification for interfering with parental rights.

Yousef v The Netherlands 2002

The unmarried parents separated when their daughter was a little over a year old. The father subsequently moved to the Middle East, and during the two-and-a-half years of his stay there contact was limited to the exchange of letters. Upon his return to The Netherlands the father had fortnightly contact with his daughter. He wished to "recognise" her legally (a procedure which under Dutch law would create a legally recognised tie between them and would result in her surname being changed to his). The terminally ill mother opposed this and made a will expressing her wish that her brother would look after her daughter after her death. After her death the girl went to live with her uncle. The father alleged that his rights under Art.8 of the ECHR had been violated by the refusal to allow him to recognise his daughter.

Held: (ECHR) There was no violation of Art.8 in this case. While there was 'family life' between father and daughter, the interference with the father's rights under Art.8(1) could be justified under Art.8(2) as it was in accordance with the law, pursued a legitimate aim of protecting "the rights and freedoms of others", and was necessary in a democratic society to protect the interests of the child. If the interests of the child had to be balanced against the interests of the parents, those of the child would prevail, as "the child's rights must be the paramount consideration." (para.73).

Commentary

The key interest of this otherwise unremarkable decision lies in the fact that the ECtHR described the rights of the child as "paramount." This should be contrasted with earlier cases which seemed to attach less weight to the interests of children (see e.g. *Scott v UK* [2000] 1 F.L.R. 958, which described them as being of "crucial importance."). It would thus appear to support the argument that the welfare principle is consistent with the ECHR. However, it should be noted that the court in this case was balancing the *rights* of the child, rather than the *welfare* of the child, against the rights of the adult. Moreover, the judgment of the ECtHR is somewhat sparse and it is clear that the court did not perceive itself to be announcing any change in policy. Thus it would be unwise to attach too much significance to the terminology used, particularly as subsequent cases have used a variety of terms to describe the weight to be given to the interests of children (see e.g. *Hoppe v Germany* [2003] 1 F.L.R. 384, "particular importance").

12. ADOPTION

The law relating to adoption was reformed by the Adoption and Children Act 2002, which came into force in December 2005. Thus much of the earlier case-law on the specific provisions of the previous legislation is now of limited relevance, while as yet there is little judicial guidance on the interpretation of the new legislation. This chapter therefore focuses on a few key principles that remain of relevance to the new scheme.

The Nature of Adoption

Key Principle: **An adopted child is regarded in law as the child of the adoptive parents for all purposes**

Re B (Adoption: Jurisdiction to Set Aside) 1995
The baby son of a Roman Catholic mother and a Muslim Kuwaiti father was placed with, and subsequently adopted by, a Jewish couple. They believed that the boy was Jewish and brought him up accordingly. The boy did not learn the truth about his background until he was an adult, and at the age of 36 he sought to set aside the adoption order.

Held: (CA) The court had no general power to set aside an adoption order. Such an order was final and for life as regards the child, adoptive parents, and natural parents. Once such an order had been made the adopted child became the child of the adoptive parents for all purposes.

Commentary
It was recognised by the court that the adoption order would not have been made if the true facts had been known. Despite this, the judges were agreed that the very nature of an adoption order dictated that it should be irrevocable (save in certain statutorily defined cases, such as procedural irregularity). The fact that the parties may regret the adoption, or agreed to it under a misapprehension about the child's health, ethnic origin or race, does not justify the court in setting aside the order. This reflects the fact that under English law adoption is not merely a means of providing carers for a child but in effect a "legal transplant" whereby the child ceases to be the child of the birth parents and becomes the child of the adoptive parents.

Alternatives to Adoption

There are a number of alternatives to adoption: fostering, residence orders, and special guardianship. The appropriateness of any particular order will depend on the circumstances of the individual case.

Key Principle: **The court should recognise that there is more than one way of securing legal permanence for children**

Re B (Adoption Order) 2001

The child was accommodated by the local authority at his mother's request and placed with a foster-mother, in whose favour a residence order was subsequently made. He continued to enjoy regular contact with his father. However, the local authority encouraged the foster-mother to apply for adoption, and an order was made in her favour.

Held: (CA) The adoption order would be set aside. A residence order was more suitable in the circumstances.

Commentary

As Hale L.J. noted, adoption was only one means of providing a permanent placement for the child. In this case, however, an adoption order would sever the child's legal relationship with his birth family. A contact order would be needed to reflect the factual relationship with his father, but it was recognised that the courts were generally reluctant to impose such orders. Moreover, the court doubted whether there was jurisdiction to make the order, given that the father could not be said to be withholding his consent unreasonably. By contrast, a residence order could give the child the security and stability he needed without affecting his continuing relationship with his paternal relations. While such an order would not be capable of creating the legal relationship of mother and child between the foster-mother and the boy, Hale L.J. noted "it is quite clear that no order is needed to create that relationship as a matter of fact." (para.27). The special feature of this case is perhaps the fact that both the foster-mother and the father were happy with the arrangement: if the former had felt more of a need for legal security, or if the father had threatened that security, it is likely that an adoption order would have been made.

Key Principle: **A special guardian may exercise parental responsibility without consulting others with parental responsibility**

A Local Authority v Y, Z and others 2006
The mother's three eldest children had been placed with relatives after proceedings initiated by the local authority. The relatives were seeking a special guardianship order, and the maternal grandparents were seeking contact with the children.

Held: Special guardianship orders would be made in respect of the three children, but no orders would be made regarding contact with their maternal grandparents.

Commentary
This is the first reported case to make use of the new option of a special guardianship order, introduced by the Adoption and Children Act 2002. The theme running through the judge's description of the various advantages of making such an order was the fact that it gave control to the special guardians. Thus, for example, making such an order was better than making no order, even though all the parties were currently in agreement, since making no order would leave the children vulnerable to a change of mind by the mother. A special guardianship order would also cement the relationship between the special guardians and the children in a way that merely making a residence order would not. It was to be preferred to fostering, which would entail the continued involvement of the local authority, and to adoption, which, while offering permanence, would skew the existing family relationships. Finally, the control vested in the special guardians meant that it was up to them—rather than the local authority—whether the children should have contact with their maternal grandparents.

Making an Adoption Order

No adoption is legally effective without an order of the court, and so the basis on which adoption orders are made merits particular consideration. However, it should also be borne in mind that many decisions about the child's welfare are taken without court sanction: it is the adoption agency that matches the child with possible adopters, and in certain circumstances the child may be placed with the prospective adopters without an order of the court (see s.19 of the ACA 2002). Students are advised to consult the relevant legislation and statutory instruments for a full understanding of the process.

Key Principle: **An adoption order may only be made if this is in the best interests of the child**

Re B (Adoption: Natural Parent) 2001
The parents separated while the mother was (unbeknownst to the father) pregnant. The mother wished to give up the child for adoption, but when the father learnt of the birth he expressed his desire to care for the child. The issue for the court was whether it would be appropriate to make an adoption order in his favour. At first instance it was held that it would be in the best interests of the child to make the order, but this decision was reversed by the Court of Appeal.

Held: (HL) It had been open to the trial judge to decide that an adoption order in favour of the father would promote the child's welfare, and the Court of Appeal should not have intervened.

Commentary
The need for the biological father to adopt his own child may not be immediately obvious. The reason for the father's application lay in his desire to ensure that the mother would not be able to disrupt his care of his daughter at a later stage, and the court felt that an adoption order offered greater security than a residence order. Lord Nicholls did acknowledge, however, that "the circumstances in which it will be in the best interests of a child to make an adoption order in favour of one natural parent alone . . . are likely to be exceptional." (para.27).

Key Principle: **The consent of a parent may be dispensed with if that parent cannot be found or is incapable of giving consent**

Re A (Adoption of a Russian Child) 2000

The Russian mother agreed to her child being adopted within 2 days of the birth. The child suffered from various medical problems and no Russian adopters were forthcoming. An English couple were seeking to adopt a child in Russia and chose A. They followed all the appropriate procedures relating to inter-country adoption and an adoption order was subsequently made in Russia. However, the couple were subsequently advised that the fact that the mother had consented so soon after the birth might be problematic.

Held: An adoption order would be made. The consent given by the mother did not meet the criteria required under English law for a valid consent, but the court had the power to dispense with such consent under the Adoption Act 1976. Given the difficulties in tracing the mother, the fact that she had agreed to the adoption and had taken no part in the Russian proceedings, and the problems that the process would create in Russia for the adopters, it would be appropriate to dispense with her consent in this case.

Commentary

The possibility of dispensing with the consent of a parent who cannot be found or is incapable of giving consent was retained by the Adoption and Children Act 2002. As the case illustrates, the courts have adopted a broad interpretation of the provision. Here, the problem was not so much the impracticality of tracing the mother as the difficulties to which the process might give rise for the potential adopters.

Key Principle: **The consent of a parent may be dispensed with if the welfare of the child so requires**

This principle was introduced by the Adoption and Children Act 2002 and as yet has not been the object of judicial interpretation.

Post-Contact Adoption

Key Principle: **The court may, if appropriate, include in the adoption order a provision that contact with the biological parents should be retained**

Re O (Transracial Adoption: Contact) 1995
The child was born in England to Nigerian parents and was subsequently taken into care. Different experts advanced different solutions.

Held: An adoption order would be made containing a specific provision that the child should have contact with the biological parents.

Commentary
Thorpe J. gave two reasons to justify the relatively unusual step of including a specific provision for contact in the order: first, that it would benefit the child to build a relationship with her mother, to correct her conviction that her mother had abused and abandoned her; secondly, that such contact would "buttress her Nigerian heritage and identity." (p.610). However, as the next case shows, it is more usual for the decision of whether to allow contact or not to be left to the adoptive parents.

Key Principle: **The decision as to whether an adopted child should have contact with the biological parents will usually be left to the adoptive parents**

Re T (Adoption: Contact) 1995
An adoption order was made in respect of a nine-year-old girl. Her mother had agreed to the adoption order being made but wished to retain contact with her daughter. The adoptive parents were willing to allow contact once a year, but the mother desired more frequent contact. It was ordered that there should be contact not less than once a year.

Held: (CA) The judge had been wrong to include a provision regarding contact. Such an order was unnecessary in view of the fact that the adoptive parents had agreed to contact. If the adoptive parents subsequently decided that contact was not in the best interests of their daughter, the onus should be on the biological mother to apply for leave to apply for a contact order rather than on the adoptive parents to ask for the order to be varied.

Commentary
The case underlines the fact that adoption severs the legal relationship between the child and the biological parents. Once the

adoption order had been made, the mother would no longer be automatically entitled to apply for a contact order, but would need to seek the leave of the court (as to which see chapter 8). It is the adoptive parents who are regarded as the "real" parents of the child, and who are entitled to decide with whom their child has contact. While the 2002 Act requires the court to *consider* the contact arrangements that have been made when making either a placement order or an adoption order, it does not require such arrangements to be made. The security of the new family continues to be accorded higher priority than maintaining links with the old.

INDEX

LEGAL TAXONOMY

FROM SWEET & MAXWELL

This index has been prepared using Sweet and Maxwell's Legal Taxonomy. Main index entries conform to keywords provided by the Legal Taxonomy except where references to specific documents or non-standard terms (denoted by quotation marks) have been included. These keywords provide a means of identifying similar concepts in other Sweet & Maxwell publications and online services to which keywords from the Legal Taxonomy have been applied. Readers may find some minor differences between terms used in the text and those which appear in the index. Suggestions to *taxonomy@sweetandmaxwell.co.uk*.

(all references are to page number)